21-DAY
WEIGHT LOSS
KICKSTART

21-DAY

WEIGHT LOSS

KICKSTART

BOOST METABOLISM, LOWER CHOLESTEROL, AND DRAMATICALLY IMPROVE YOUR HEALTH

Dr Neal Barnard

Menus and Recipes by Jason Wyrick

Foreword by Alicia Silverstone

headline

First published in 2011 in the United States by Grand Central Life & Style, an imprint
of Grand Central Publishing. The Grand Central Life & Style name and logo are
trademarks of Hachette Book Group, Inc. 237 Park Avenue, New York, NY 10017
www.hachettebookgroup.com

Published in Great Britain in 2011 by
by HEADLINE PUBLISHING GROUP

1

Cataloguing in Publication Data is available from the British Library

ISBN 978 0 7553 6242 4

Printed and bound in Great Britain by Clays Ltd, St Ives plc

Headline's policy is to use papers that are natural, renewable and recyclable products and
made from wood grown in sustainable forests. The logging and manufacturing processes
are expected to conform to the environmental regulations of the country of origin.

HEADLINE PUBLISHING GROUP
An Hachette UK Company
338 Euston Road
London NW1 3BH

www.headline.co.uk
www.hachette.co.uk

Contents

Part II THE THREE-WEEK PROGRAM

Part III   MENUS AND RECIPES

A Note to the Reader

As you get started, let me mention two simple, but important points:

See Your Health Care Provider. If you are taking medication, are seriously overweight, or have any health concern, let me encourage you to work with a physician or other health care provider, and to follow his or her advice about all aspects of your medical care. This is not because changing your diet is dangerous. Just the opposite; a diet change can be very powerful for health. So powerful, in fact, that your doctor may need to change your medication regimen, or perhaps discontinue medications altogether. Do not do this on your own. Work with your health care provider to reduce or discontinue your medicines if and when the time is right.

Also, sometimes a new way of eating can make you feel so good and energetic that you might feel like really ramping up your exercise routine. But be careful. If you have been sedentary, have any serious health problem, have a great deal of weight to lose, or are over forty, have your health care provider check whether you are ready for exercise, and how rapidly to begin.

Get Complete Nutrition. Anytime you alter the way you eat, you'll want to make sure you're getting all the nutrients you need. The way of eating presented in this book greatly improves your overall nutrition—more so than other diets. But even so, please read the information on complete nutrition presented in chapter 5. And be sure to take a daily multiple vitamin or other reliable source of vitamin B_{12}, such as fortified cereals or fortified soy milk. Vitamin B_{12} is essential for healthy nerves and healthy blood.

Acknowledgments

This book has been a team effort, and I am very grateful to many people who made it possible.

The many participants in our research studies who changed their eating habits, stood on the scale, rolled up their sleeves, and met with our research team week after week helped us understand not only how to make dietary transitions powerful, but also how to make them engaging and fun. I also appreciate the many people who have written to me to let me know of their successes and challenges.

Unlike many nutritional programs, the one described in this book is based on carefully conducted research, and I am grateful to my colleagues at the Washington Center for Clinical Research and George Washington University for their collaboration, at the National Institutes of Health for their support for our diabetes research, and at GEICO for allowing us to assess how foods can promote good health in the workplace.

Thank you to Alicia Silverstone for inspiring our Kickstart participants, for writing the foreword to this book, and for being a wonderful example of kindness, compassion, and good health.

Nanci Alexander has revolutionized the world of restaurant eating through Sublime, her wonderful creation in Fort Lauderdale, and is a constant source of inspiration as well as a perfect role model.

Through her own teaching, Marilu Henner has helped millions of people, and she has helped enormously with the Kickstart and with our many efforts to improve nutrition for children.

I am deeply grateful to the many other celebrities, athletes, and innovators who have jumped in with their inspiration and encouragement, lent their expertise, and/or allowed me to quote them in this book: Brendan Brazier, Kris Carr, Rip Esselstyn, Rory Freedman, Kathy Freston, Bob Harper, Scott Jurek, Victoria Moran, John Salley, Sarah Silverman, and Persia White.

Thank you also to the medical and scientific professionals who taught me so much and have allowed me to share their insights: Dana Armstrong, RD; T. Colin Campbell, PhD; Brenda Davis, RD; Hans A. Diehl, DrHSc, MPH; Caldwell Esselstyn Jr., MD; Jay Gordon, MD; Bill Harris, MD; Ruth Heidrich, PhD; David J. A. Jenkins, MD, PhD; John McDougall, MD; Baxter Montgomery, MD; Dean Ornish, MD; and Walter Willett, MD, DrPH.

Thank you to my colleagues at the Physicians Committee for Responsible Medicine for being a team that gets things done and makes so many people smarter and healthier.

Thank you to Jill Eckart, CHHC, Susan Levin, RD, and Betsy Wason, who played key roles in developing and implementing the Kickstart program and who helped keep many aspects of this book on track.

Thank you to Michael Greger, MD, and Joel Fuhrman, MD, for their advice on many aspects of the text.

And finally, thank you to Debra Goldstein, a skilled literary agent, and Diana Baroni, a wonderful editor at Grand Central, who made this book take shape, and to Jason Wyrick, whose delicious menus and recipes not only demystified the kitchen, but made food preparation wonderfully easy as well. I am grateful to Adelyn Pryor, Riva Gebel, and Alka Chandna for additional recipes, and to Amber Green, RD, for providing additional nutrient analyses.

Foreword

I wasn't an overweight kid. In fact I was quite skinny. But as so many young folks do, I became self-conscious about my body and was calorie counting by the time I was fourteen. I even went to Weight Watchers meetings for a little while.

I was eighteen when *Clueless* came out. That time in my life was a complete whirlwind. It was fun and so exciting. But it also meant that I was basically going through adolescence in public, which is, of course, not ideal in Hollywood. It was like the world was putting all my imperfections under a microscope and then slapping them on pages of tabloids. Good stuff.

When I was preparing to play Batgirl in *Batman & Robin*, I was chased through the LA airport by paparazzi yelling "Fatgirl!" The truth is, I was probably within an average weight range at the time. But the pressure I was feeling made me rebel, and I ended up just eating more and more of the wrong foods. I was definitely moving in the wrong direction.

Luckily, over time, I made huge, huge changes in the way I was eating. The effects were dramatic. My original motivation was compassion for animals, so it was super-easy for me to eliminate meats, dairy products, and eggs from my diet and replace them with whole grains, beans, all sorts of great vegetables, and fruits. My body gave me an instant "Thank you." Before then, I was on a steak and doughnut diet! No joke! Whatever extra weight I had began to melt away; all this by just eliminating the animal products and adding in more whole foods. I discovered that a plant-based diet has so many benefits: effortless weight loss, clear skin, off-the-charts energy, and smooth digestion, to name a few.

People really noticed a difference in the way I looked—and so did I. Since then, I have continued to refine my food choices, but I've never felt deprived. I've replaced things I may have missed with even better things from the plant-based world, and I swear they satisfy me on every level, not to mention the absolutely delectable desserts I get to eat. The more I learn about food, the more I have been able to take advantage of what it can do for me—and for all of us. It's our medicine, it's *so* important to our health.

I have worked with Dr. Barnard on many different projects for a long time now, helping people understand how to make very small changes that can create a turning point in their health. I'm thrilled by how many people have benefited from the information we have put out there. I'm so pleased to be a part of the Kickstart program as well. In just three weeks, you can shed your not-so-healthful habits and begin great new ones. The process is easier than you think, and the results will be dramatic.

If you struggle with weight, this way of eating is all you need to conquer it. You will have more energy and you will glow, I promise. People will see the difference in you. When you let healthful foods nourish you, you will be healthy from the inside out. This is what you need to start to tackle (or just prevent!) problems like overweight, high cholesterol, diabetes, high blood pressure, joint pain, and much more. I've seen so many people find great success using the tools Dr. Barnard gives you in this book.

Your goal may be to just drop weight. But guess what? While

following this program, you will feel better than you ever have. You will protect yourself from illness and will motivate everyone you know to follow your good example. Not too bad, huh? When I embraced this lifestyle, I was freed from the prison of dieting, and wow, who doesn't want that freedom? I got my brain, my body, and my life back. We spend all this time worrying about food: *Can I have this?* and *How many calories are in that?* With *21-Day Weight Loss Kickstart*, you don't have to do that anymore. You are getting more than a new waistline. You are getting a new reality— a whole new way of thinking about food.

Dr. Barnard's program is easy and effective. In just three weeks, you'll be amazed by how good you look and feel. Get ready to transform the way you think about food, and get ready to change your life with *21-Day Weight Loss Kickstart*!

Neal Barnard has helped me answer so many questions over the years. I trust him and appreciate the advice he gives me and others. With his passion, commitment, and brilliant mind, he has long been a hero of mine. In a very short time, you'll feel the same way.

Best of luck to you. Enjoy the journey.

Alicia Silverstone, author of *The Kind Diet*

Introduction

I'm guessing you're reading this book for one of two reasons. Maybe you've tried, like many people I've worked with, to get control of your weight and health and have not been as successful as you'd hoped, and you're looking for a proven solution. Or perhaps you've heard about the life-changing and weight loss benefits of a plant-based diet and want to give it a try, but don't know where to start. Either way, you might be asking yourself questions like: *Will it be easy? Will I get plenty to eat? Can I avoid feeling deprived?*

The good news is that the answer to all these questions is yes—we're actually going to make it *fun!*

Welcome to the 21-Day Weight Loss Kickstart! This book is based on a program I launched in August 2009 through the Physicians Committee for Responsible Medicine, which I founded in 1985 to change the way we think of medicine and research, and to help people learn how to prevent disease rather than just treat it. For 21 days, participants get to "test-drive" a diet that is as close to perfect as is humanly possible. They experience the weight loss, energy boost, and health improvements that come from truly healthful foods. The response has been overwhelming—well over one hundred thousand people have gotten on board for the Kickstart and have finally been able to break old habits and embark on a whole new way of eating that has changed not just their waistlines, but also their overall health and sense of well-being.

And now you get to jump in and take control of *your* weight loss and health, like so many others. You'll discover a whole new way of thinking about food as well as a chance to try a slimmer, healthier, rejuvenated body. And that will bring you a whole new outlook on life. In just three weeks, you'll break old habits, start new ones, and revolutionize your health.

The program is called the Kickstart because it focuses on a very short-term immersion experience that almost always inspires long-term changes. Once you finish the 21-day challenge and see how easy it is to gain control over your weight and health, you probably won't want to return to your former habits. Why? Because you'll be eating delicious meals, you'll never be hungry, and you'll look and feel great.

Clinically Proven

In a recent research study, we tested the Kickstart approach in a group of sixty-four women. All were moderately or severely overweight. They were all past menopause and really felt stuck with their weight. Most had tried many different diets, without lasting success.

We asked everyone to do two simple things: set animal products aside and keep oils to a minimum. That was the whole "diet." They were free to start their day with pancakes with syrup, veggie sausage, fresh fruit, or other foods, with no calorie limit at all. If they had lasagna or chili for lunch, it would be the meatless versions of these foods. If they stopped by a Mexican restaurant, we asked them to favor the bean burrito (hold the cheese) over the greasy meat taco. At an Italian restaurant, it might be spaghetti with an arabiatta or marinara sauce, pasta e fagioli, garlic-sautéed broccoli rabe or spinach, and roasted vegetables. And they could eat all the warm bread from the oven that they liked.

There were no calorie limits, no carbohydrate restrictions, and no exercise, because this was intended as a study of nutritional changes only. But we were serious about the changes we prescribed, and we helped our participants stick to them.

To their delight, the participants started losing weight. It was gradual at first—with some women faster and some slower. After fourteen weeks, we published the results in the *American Journal of Medicine*. Even without calorie counting, the weight peeled away at an average rate of about a pound per week, with some of the women losing much more quickly.[1]

But that was just the beginning. We followed them for the next two years, and, unlike typical weight loss diets that are soon followed by weight regain, these women were, on average, slimmer at one year than at the beginning, and slimmer at two years than at one year.[2] In other words, weight loss had become a one-way street.

So we went a step further to try to tease apart the biology of it all. We wanted to discover why it was that, even without exercise or calorie counting, participants were still able to lose weight. In chapters 2 and 3, I'll show you the secrets we found. As you'll probably guess, they relate to fundamental changes in their bodies—a new and surprising level of appetite control and calorie-burning speed.

We have tested this approach in men and women, in young people and older people, in healthy people and in those with health problems, in people with massive amounts of weight to lose and in those who only needed to trim a little weight. We have also tested it in people who were already at a healthy weight and just wanted to eat better. Many of these people had little or no time for food preparation or exercise, and yet it still worked well for them.

We have found that people not only slim down, but also see their cholesterol levels plummet and their blood pressure fall. If they have diabetes, it typically improves and sometimes even disappears. Arthritis pains and migraines often vanish, and energy comes racing back. Sluggishness vanishes, and they look and feel radiant.

Quick Changes, Permanent Results

The most exciting part of this Kickstart program is that it is not a five-year plan, a three-year plan, or even a six-month plan. This is three weeks. Now, it's certainly true that, to be effective, a change in the way you eat needs to be carried into longer-term good habits. But let me put things in a slightly different light:

Although my academic appointment is currently in the Department of Internal Medicine at the George Washington University School of Medicine, I began my medical career following a different path.

Initially, I wanted to tackle the issues of why we do the things we do, and how it is that things go off track behaviorally. So, after medical school, I completed a residency in psychiatry and took a position at St. Vincent's Hospital, a large medical center in downtown New York. I not only ran a psychiatric ward but also had a busy consulting practice, treating people with medical illnesses—diabetes, heart disease, cancer, and others—that were complicated by depression, anxiety, or other problems. In the course of this work, I became concerned that, in American medical practice, we were not very good at prevention. We did nothing to stop a heart attack until it arrived at the emergency room door. We were similarly slow to deal with diabetes, hypertension, cancer, and other serious problems until they became full blown or even life threatening. And doctors then, like doctors today, tended to overlook the power of nutrition. Barely any time in medical school was devoted to it. Even though food is central to so many health issues, we were quick with prescriptions and slow with nutritional information.

I founded the Physicians Committee for Responsible Medicine to restore the role of nutrition and disease prevention in medical practice. I wanted to also ensure that good research was conducted to improve medical practice, and that this research was done intelligently and ethically. My research team began conducting studies in diabetes, cholesterol, weight problems, and other health issues.

In the course of this work, it became clear to me that biology is only half the issue. In other words, *how* or *why* some foods satisfy the appetite or enhance the metabolism is not at all the whole story. The other half is psychological: How do we get the motivation to get started? And how do we stick with a healthful way of eating? How do we avoid temptation? How do we motivate our friends and family members and how do we get them to motivate us? It's important to have a powerful diet, but it is just as important to make it work in real life.

So we have investigated not only what are the best and most powerful foods for weight loss and health, but also how to make healthful habits stick.

It turns out that one of the most important keys is to *focus on the short term*. What I have found over and over is that, once we have made short-term changes, they tend to change our long-term habits.

So the first step is to get you out of your dietary rut, onto a better path. And by making that change really enjoyable, and by getting results along the way, you'll get the motivation you need to stay with it for the longer term. So we are going to focus on quick changes that are fun and effective, and that will make you want to continue with the plan.

If you were to kickstart a motorcycle, it would take just a second or two to make the engine ignite and roar into action. You would then roll out onto the highway and off you'd go. It is the same idea when you kickstart a change in your life. With a quick and easy program, you'll ignite powerful changes that will help you long into the future.

Here is just some of what you'll accomplish with the Kickstart program:

- **You will gain a new level of control over your appetite.** The success of this program is not based on willpower. Instead, it is based on using the power of foods to change the basic body processes that determine your size and shape. Certain foods trigger the appetite centers, causing you to overeat. Others trigger the satiety centers—the parts of your brain that tell you to stop eating—so you eat less. What this means is that if you've felt like your appetite is stronger than it should be, this very likely has a simple nutritional cause. By choosing the right foods—which you'll learn how to do—you can easily correct the issue.

- **You'll ramp up your after-meal metabolism—your calorie-burning speed.** By choosing certain foods, you will boost your cells' ability to turn more of what you eat into energy, not fat. I'll show you which foods work this magic.

- **You'll kickstart your health.** Some quick weight loss diets force you into semi-starvation; others let you "enjoy" less-than-healthy high-protein foods that can harm you over the long run. In this program, we go beyond those shortsighted ideas. Instead our goal is to have the best of all worlds—a healthy weight *and* a healthy body. By focusing on cardioprotection—choosing foods that rejuvenate your heart and blood vessels—you will carry good health deep into your tissues and have renewed energy and a strong measure of resistance to the health problems that trouble so many people.

What We Won't Do

There are three things this program does *not* do:

- **We will not count calories.** In theory, calories matter. But when we zero in on *what you eat*, rather than *how much* you eat, calories will take care of themselves.
- **We will not push you to exercise.** In this plan, exercise is totally optional. Surprised? Well, let me be clear: As a doctor, I highly recommend exercise, for many reasons. But some people can't do meaningful exercise, due to a weak heart, painful joints, tremendously excessive weight gain, or other reasons. If that includes you, it is important to be aware that our research studies have shown dramatic results *with nutrition alone.* So exercise is great, and it adds to the benefits of a nutritional change, but even if you never exercise, you can lose weight easily and gain tremendous health advantages.
- **We will not make you feel guilty about carbohydrates.** Many people have become nervous about bread, potatoes, and rice, fearing that these foods are fattening. What they have missed is that, once you know how to choose carbs the right way—and how not to ruin them in your kitchen— you can enjoy carbohydrate-containing foods and still lose weight.

  As a matter of fact, *we won't make you feel guilty about anything.* When it comes to food, for some reason, guilt and morality often rear their ugly heads. People sometimes talk about tasty foods as being "sinful" and "decadent." We are "bad" if we eat something that is less than healthy, and we are "good" if we resist temptation. If we fall ill, we tend to blame ourselves, our parents, our genes, the government, the food industry, or perhaps someone else.

Well, there are some moral issues when it comes to foods and health. But in this book, we are setting all of them aside. Guilt, blame, and moralizing will have no place here. Instead, we are jumping into a program that you will enjoy and that brings results. We will zero in using the power of foods for health. And if you ever eat something that is not the best choice, well, just dust yourself off and get back aboard the program.

How the Kickstart Works

As the program begins, your first job, surprisingly enough, is not to change your diet. Rather, we'll start by checking out the possibilities of healthful foods to see which ones you like the most and which ones work best for you. This takes just a few days. And you're not changing your diet; you're just trying new things. I think you will be very surprised to see how easy and delicious a plant-based diet can be!

If you like to cook, you'll have an abundance of recipes to choose from, created by Jason Wyrick, one of the world's most remarkable chefs. Jason's work has influenced many other cooks and chefs who are looking for a new emphasis on health, as well as delights for the palate. He demonstrates his deliciously easy approach to food to standing-room-only crowds, showing how easy it can be to make truly wonderful meals. Page through the menus and recipes in this book and you'll see what I mean.

If cooking is not your thing, we'll look at convenience foods and how to make the best choices at restaurants. If you think that restaurants or fast-food places are off limits, you'll learn that it's much easier than you think to enjoy a delicious meal while you're out on the town, without breaking your healthy stride.

I'll also share tips on how to shop, how to adapt your favorite recipes, and how to turn the volume down on temptation.

By the time you're finished with your exploration, you'll know exactly which foods will work for you and fit your tastes and your schedule.

Then, once you're ready and you know which foods you like best, we'll jump in and put them to work. For 21 days, you'll enjoy the healthy foods you've chosen, and you'll see what they'll do for you. I'll stay by your side every step of the way, with information and support. I'll check in on how you're doing and whatever challenges might be ahead of you. I'll give you new insights on health topics. And I'll keep you pumped up and motivated.

You'll also have friends pulling for you day by day. Best-selling author Alicia Silverstone will tell you her secrets for youthful beauty. NBA champion John Salley and ultramarathon athlete Scott Jurek will share their tips for explosive energy. Bob Harper from *The Biggest Loser* will help you develop the right attitude and mind-set. Marilu Henner, Rory Freedman, Kathy Freston, Kris Carr, and many others will share their insights as experts—and as people who have made the life-changing transition you are about to make.

The book is divided into three parts. In part 1, I'll share with you the easy ABCs of the program:

A for Appetite Control
B for Burn Enhancement
C for Cardioprotection

You'll learn how foods affect your body—which ones ramp up your appetite control, help your metabolism, and keep you healthy.

Part 2 is the Kickstart program itself. I'll give you everything you need to get ready. And then I'll have a short reading for you each day for 21 days.

Part 3 has the tools to keep you healthy for life, with menus, recipes, cooking tips, and more inspiration to keep exploring your healthy new body and the foods you can enjoy.

So let's get started. I hope you enjoy every part of this exciting new journey, and that you share what you have learned with others. If you would like to get more involved with our efforts to spread a healthful message far and wide, you will find plenty of resources at www.pcrm.org. I'm looking forward to working with you.

Part I

METABOLICALLY ACTIVE FOODS

CHAPTER 1

Power on Your Plate

Welcome to the Kickstart! In just 21 days, you're going to be thinner, healthier, and more energetic. As you'll soon see, the program is quite easy and very effective. You may not yet realize how powerful the foods you eat are—and what a difference a few small changes can make in your life.

There are so many different approaches to nutrition, weight loss, and health. It is important for you to know that the dietary changes recommended in this book have been carefully tested, with the results published in peer-reviewed scientific journals. Not only are they more enjoyable than other dietary methods; they are potentially more effective than any other approach ever devised.

Before jumping into the Kickstart, I thought you might like to hear how the simple changes in the program have worked for others—and will work for you, too.

Everyone knows GEICO, the car insurance company whose spokesperson-logo is a little green gecko with an English accent.

GEICO's headquarters happen to be near my office. A few years ago, the company became interested in seeing whether a plant-based diet might help its employees. Because the company provides medical insurance for its employees, every employee who starts a cholesterol-lowering drug or needs a heart bypass costs the firm money.

So my team did a research study with GEICO with just two simple steps: First, the company cafeteria included vegan options, along with the other foods it served. By the way, if this is a new word for you, a *vegan* is not a person from the planet Vegus. The word simply refers to a diverse diet that leaves out animal products. So in addition to the usual bacon-and-egg breakfast, GEICO provided an oatmeal bar and fruit. At lunch, the cafeteria served hamburgers and all the usual fare, but added veggie burgers, portobello mushroom sandwiches, red bean chili, and vegetable lasagna.

Second, employees who wanted to give a healthy diet a try were offered a one-hour group meeting once a week. The idea was to provide cooking instruction, health lectures, and time to talk together about how the diet change was going. At the GEICO site in the Washington, DC, area, sixty-eight people volunteered to try the program out for five months. They saw this as a chance to lose weight, gain more energy, and break some old habits. A separate GEICO facility in Fredericksburg, Virginia, agreed to serve as a comparison site, with no diet changes.

Hillary and Bruce worked at the Washington-area GEICO office and decided to join the study. They are real people, and those are their real names. They are upbeat and fun loving. But Bruce described their weight problems as serious and long standing, and he was not looking for excuses. "We definitely both loved our food," he said. Fast food, doughnuts, and just about everything else called to them on a daily basis. "It was really pretty terrible, the way we ate."

But solving the problem was another matter. They had tried various diets in earnest, but nothing seemed to last, and each diet failure was a demoralizing experience.

Exercise presented a different set of challenges. "You're embarrassed to go to the gym," Bruce said. "You're embarrassed to go out jogging. You really don't want to go out in public and be seen running around and jiggling everywhere."

Hillary said, "It was really difficult to find clothes that would fit and that were appropriate for work. And also knowing that it was really my fault and that there was something I should be doing about it but that I wasn't able to do—that was very frustrating."

When the GEICO study started, Bruce weighed 283 pounds, and Hillary weighed 239. But they supported each other in the change, and they put healthy foods to work 100 percent.

Weight started to melt away almost immediately. "I think eight to ten weeks into the study, I had already lost thirty pounds and had been able to go shopping for new clothes," Hillary said. "It was very, very exciting. It was also very exciting to start seeing the reactions of other people as I would attend a conference and see people I hadn't seen for several months. People really noticed. They could see that there had been a big difference in my attitude and in how I looked physically. It was very inspiring."

"The pounds were dropping like crazy," Bruce said. "My cholesterol was plummeting. It was fantastic. This was something that was working better than anything we'd tried before. And I think that we knew we were on the right path."

After five months, the study participants stood on the scale. At Fredericksburg, the average person got nowhere, of course. They had made no diet changes, and so their weight didn't fall at all. But at the Washington site, participants lost weight easily. The largest weight loss was forty-six pounds over five months; a more typical weight loss was between ten and twenty pounds. Waistlines shrank by two inches, on average, and hips slimmed by nearly two inches, too. We published the results in three scientific journal reports.[1–3]

But for Hillary and Bruce, something even more profound had happened. The short-term experience had eased them out of their routine. It had shown them a better way and had broken all their not-so-healthful habits. So when the study ended, they kept going.

Within a year, Hillary had lost eighty-five pounds, and Bruce had lost more than a hundred. They sent me a photograph showing the dramatic change. Not only were they trim, healthy, and beautiful, but I also noticed they were wearing athletic clothes—with no jiggling parts—and had numbers pinned to their T-shirts. Because their energy had come roaring back, they did something they had never done before—they signed up for a half-marathon! Changing what was on their plates allowed them to shed the weight and to gain so much energy that they *wanted* to exercise.

Today they look great, and they feel great. And eating has become a new adventure. At first, they started trying out new foods in order to participate in our program—just as you will during the next 21 days. Then as they discovered new tastes, new recipes, and new products, they gained a whole new way of thinking about food. They love their new, healthy relationship with food and their new healthy bodies, and the same is in store for you.

By the way, their tremendous weight loss started *without exercise.* They began the diet change first, and then, as their energy ramped up, they found that they *wanted* to get active. What this means is that, like Hillary and Bruce, you are about to embark on a simple but profound change, not just in weight, but in your energy level and in how you feel about yourself.

Hillary's and Bruce's story can be anyone's story. If you are looking to lose a little weight—or a lot of weight—or conquer a serious health problem, a change in diet can be powerful. It can help you gain a level of health you had not thought possible.

Not Just Thinner. Healthier, Too

Weight loss is an issue for many people and will be a central focus of this book, but it's just as important to look beyond the scale, at your overall health. And that's the beauty of the approach you're about to put to work. The menu changes that help you lose weight also have a decisive effect on health.

One of the most amazing studies ever conducted was led by Dr. Dean Ornish, a young Harvard-trained physician, who showed that a low-fat vegetarian diet, along with other healthy lifestyle changes, not only led to impressive weight loss and huge changes in cholesterol, but actually caused heart disease to reverse.[4] In other words, arteries that had been narrowed slowly but surely over decades actually began to reopen—without drugs or surgery. As blood flow improved, chest pain disappeared, and people felt young again. The heart attacks that had threatened Dr. Ornish's patients were suddenly much less likely to ever occur.[5]

At the Cleveland Clinic, Dr. Caldwell Esselstyn, MD, went a step further. In patients with severe heart disease, he prescribed an Ornish-style diet. If a patient's cholesterol level did not fall below 150 mg/dL, he added a cholesterol-lowering medication. The results were astounding. Although the patients had been very sick at the study outset, their health turned around completely. In twelve years of study, not a single person who followed Dr. Esselstyn's approach had any heart complications at all.[6]

Meanwhile, Dr. David Jenkins at the University of Toronto showed that foods alone could lower cholesterol levels nearly as well as cholesterol-lowering drugs.[7] The trick was to start with a plant-based diet, and then emphasize specific foods that have a known cholesterol-lowering ability: oats, barley, soy products, and almonds, for example. His patients cut their LDL ("bad") cholesterol by nearly 30 percent *in just four weeks*. A similar diet effectively lowers high blood pressure.[8]

Research teams have put similar diets to work for cancer patients. The idea is that vegetables, fruits, whole grains, and legumes (beans, peas, and lentils) work in three ways: First, they provide powerful antioxidants and other cancer fighters. Second, they help trim away excess weight (weight loss improves survival for certain types of cancer). Third, these same diet changes reduce the blood levels of hormones that would otherwise promote cancer growth. As it turns out, diet changes help prevent cancer; and they can also improve survival after diagnosis, reducing the risk of recurrence.[9-13]

If a look at your family tree shows heart problems, diabetes, high blood pressure, cancer, or other conditions such as Alzheimer's disease that are starting to show links with specific nutritional factors (as you will see in chapter 4), you'll want to take advantage of the health-boosting power of foods. If you already have a health problem, a diet change is often just what the doctor ordered. It not only adds years to life, but also allows you to spend those years really *living*, instead of spending your time at a doctor's office or the pharmacy counter.

It took many years for all of this research to be done. But the benefits of simple adjustments in your daily menu come surprisingly quickly. In no time, you'll be on your way to a slimmer, healthier body.

Where Did We Go Wrong?

What causes weight gain and the various health issues that go along with it? Why is it that so many people are overweight now, compared with decades past?

Researchers have been examining those questions, and we have come up with some surprising answers.

First of all, it's not a question of a lack of physical activity, at least not for the most part. It is certainly true that many people are less active than in years past. But in 2009, a team of researchers carefully examined the relationships among food, exercise, and weight, and concluded that changes in exercise habits were simply not enough to account for the rise in obesity in recent years.[14] And that makes sense. Our bodies are so efficient at holding on to fat, you could run flat-out for a mile and not burn off the calories in half an order of french fries. If we want to understand the causes of weight gain, we need to look at the input side of the equation— the foods we eat.

In 2010, I published in the *American Journal of Clinical Nutrition* a detailed analysis of how diets have changed over the past century.[15] The results are sobering.

Between 1909 and 2007, meat intake rose from 124 pounds to more than 200 pounds per person per year. That's more than seventy-five pounds of extra meat for every person every year.

What? Is it really possible that an average man or woman has found some way to eat seventy-five extra pounds of meat every year?

The answer is yes. I grew up in North Dakota, and my father's side of the family has raised cattle in the Midwest for many generations. However, our meat portions back then were more modest than portions are today. And Americans are now putting away chicken like there is no tomorrow. Convinced that chicken is somehow health food, which it is not, *Americans now eat more than one million chickens per hour.* It would probably surprise most people to learn that chicken's fat content isn't much different from beef's (about 29 percent for lean beef, 23 percent for skinless chicken breast, compared with less than 10 percent for typical vegetables, fruits, and beans).

But the rise in meat consumption is not the whole story. Back in 1909, Americans had not yet discovered cheese pizza or cheeseburgers, and an average American ate less than four pounds of cheese in a year's time. Today an average American eats about *thirty-three pounds* of it every year, nearly thirty pounds more than a century ago.

We're also tucking into greasy french fries and polishing it all off with ice cream. The average American eats twenty pounds more ice cream each year than a century ago.

And then there are beverages. When I was a child, we had sodas every few months, usually on someone's birthday or at a picnic, and they came in six-ounce bottles that are now in museums. When the first twelve-ounce cans arrived on the market, my mother wanted to find a lid to reseal them—twelve ounces, she said, was too much for one serving. Well, twelve ounces soon became sixteen ounces, and today the smallest soda bottle sold at most stores holds twenty ounces. And it's safe to say that no one saves half for the following day.

We are exporting our bad habits, too. China, Japan, India, and other countries have seen an influx of fast-food outlets unknown to them in the past. People living in those countries are tempted by burgers, battered chicken wings, pizza, and sodas, and are now suffering with epidemics of obesity and diabetes that were unknown to them before.

A meaty, cheesy, sugar-laden diet packs in calories, but it lacks the fiber that you need to satisfy your appetite. So weight gain is all but inevitable.

The good news is that you can change all this, and very easily. And you will over the next three weeks.

Go for It!

This Kickstart is based on what we've learned in our research studies. We have focused on the food choices that are most powerful for health, and how to make the switch to healthier foods easy and approachable. Our findings have been presented countless times at research conferences and have been published in peer-reviewed medical journals.

But we know that *what really counts is what works for you*. So although we document our results using statistical averages, standard deviations, regression analyses, and other scientific methods that could bore you to tears, we boil it all down to a simple, step-by-step program—the 21-Day Weight Loss Kickstart—that takes you exactly where you want to go.

This program is an easy and fun way to try out a new way of eating. Just like Hillary and Bruce and the many people we have worked with over the years, you can put foods to work to bring you a slimmer and much healthier body. When you see the numbers dropping on the scale, when people remark about how great you look, and when you feel your health getting better and better day by day, you'll really want to keep going.

And there is an extra benefit: a wonderful rebound of energy. Hollywood actor Alicia Silverstone set aside animal products in order to be kind to animals. But she soon realized that the diet change was kind to her body, too. "Within two weeks, people noticed the difference in how I looked," she said. "I felt lighter, healthier, and more energetic. It just really felt right."

That extra energy translates into feeling great, forgetting about old problems that have weighed you down, and really living again. As Alicia puts it, "This way of eating really frees you, not just from extra weight, but from having to obsess about how many calories you're eating, how many diet points you're earning, and so on. Who needs all that?"

In this Kickstart, we keep the focus on the short term—that is, three weeks—so there is never any pressure or long-term commitment. Once you've experienced the power of healthful foods, you'll never want to let it go.

CHAPTER 2

Foods That Tame
the Appetite Demons

In the introduction, I described a research study in which a group of women who had long been struggling with weight problems suddenly found themselves losing weight easily. Without any calorie limits at all, body fat melted away day after day. More than two years later, their weight had not come back. It was as if their bodies had somehow been reprogrammed.

One of our participants, named Jean, lived in Virginia, just outside Washington, DC. As a child, she had not been overweight. After high school, she married and started raising her family, and that's when everything changed. Her first pregnancy left her with an extra ten pounds, and she continued to gain weight through her twenties. Between her work and family responsibilities, she found it hard to focus on healthy foods or exercise. By the time she was thirty, she was significantly overweight.

She enrolled in a commercial weight loss program near her house that prescribed a specific nutrition system using specially packaged foods. It ended up costing more than she had bargained for, and she had little to show for it. She bought a book that advocated a low-carbohydrate diet and lost weight for the first couple of weeks. But the diet was boring and the recommended foods seemed unhealthy. After a loss of energy and a painful bout of constipation, she abandoned the diet. The lost weight promptly came back, and she felt that she really no longer knew what to eat.

As her weight continued to climb, she got scared. This was certainly not what she wanted, but she did not know what to do. Years of on-again, off-again dieting followed, but nothing got her on track.

Fast-forward to Jean's fiftieth birthday. Paging through a newspaper, she saw an advertisement about our research study. She decided this might be the answer, and she came in to volunteer. We explained the diet program and showed her how it works. The study began, and she jumped in.

Two weeks later, she had already lost five pounds. That was a start. As the weeks went by, she kept losing more and more. It wasn't tremendously fast, but it was steady.

After the first year, she had lost nearly forty pounds and looked like a different person. She was energetic and filled with life. And she lost even more in the following year.

During one of our research meetings, where our volunteers got together for cooking classes and general discussion, Jean asked a pointed question. She started by describing what she had eaten on the previous day. Breakfast had been blueberry pancakes with maple syrup (something her low-carb diet book had forbidden), with veggie sausage links on the side. Lunch was a bowl of split-pea soup, toast, and a big salad. For dinner, she'd had an artichoke appetizer, garlic bread, spinach lasagna from a recipe we had given her, and steamed broccoli, with peach sorbet for dessert. The quantity of food seemed much too generous. And yet there was no denying that her bathroom scale was getting friendlier day by day.

"So why does this work?" she asked. "It obviously *does* work, but what does the body actually do with all that food, so that you eat so much, and still lose weight?"

She had put her finger on one of the key reasons for our study. We wanted to test our theory that foods can actually control the appetite and ramp up metabolism, so that weight loss is almost automatic.

To put our theory to the test, we asked Jean and all the other participants to keep a detailed list of everything they ate. And we added up the calories. They kept track before the study began, and again after they had been in the study for several weeks.

When we added up the calories, the difference was a real eye-opener. Even though they were eating delicious food and were free to have as much as they wanted, it turned out that they were actually eating hundreds of calories less than before.

And here was what was most surprising: *They were not aware of the difference.* It seemed like they were eating the same amount as before. They liked the tastes, aromas, and everything else. As Jean pointed out, the meals seemed generous, and she was not even remotely hungry. Somehow, the participants' appetites were satisfied much earlier than before.

Rosa had a similar experience: "The weight was coming off on its own. I never felt hungry, because you're eating things that fill you up."

We have repeated this assessment many times. And every time, we have found the same result: Weight seems to come off almost automatically.

Another research participant, named Mary Ann, said how wonderful it was to lose so much weight that friends barely recognized her. And yet she did this without the slightest sense of deprivation. Everything she was eating was good for her, and it completely changed her self-image. Food was no longer the enemy. Food was actually *helping* her slim down and get healthy.

Imagine if you could turn a switch so that you not only really liked the foods you ate, but felt totally satisfied without any desire to overeat. In essence, that's what the foods that I'm going to tell you about actually do.

You Don't Need to Cut Calories

If you were to sit down with a doctor or dietitian and set out a weight loss plan, the first piece of advice would likely be to limit calories. "There's no getting around it," your adviser would tell you. "You need to take in fewer calories than you burn. Otherwise, you'll never lose weight."

And that's true enough. If you take in fewer calories than you burn, you'll lose weight.

But saying it is one thing, doing it is quite another. If your day's meals normally add up to, say, two thousand calories, a dietitian will likely trim that to about fifteen hundred. And your job is to stick with that for as long as it takes to lose the weight: six months, a year, or the rest of your life.

I am already at a healthy weight, but I recently tried a low-calorie diet to see what it was like. A dietitian sketched out my diet plan, and I got started. I was pretty good at breakfast, and not too bad at lunch. But by dinnertime, it started to get challenging. I wasn't halfway through my meal when I bumped up against my calorie limit. *No more food for you*, I told myself. With no calories left in my daily budget, I was going to bed hungry. The next day, I was only halfhearted about it, and by Wednesday, I gave it up.

The fact is, low-calorie diets get pretty old by about Wednesday for nearly everyone. Most people abandon them right away—and never lose weight—or slip away from them several weeks down the road and gain back whatever weight they have lost.

Ready for a better way? Changing the *type* of food you eat can take care of the calories for you, as you'll see in this chapter. Even if your willpower hit "empty" long ago, you can succeed, and handsomely.

Keys for Natural Appetite Control

First of all, it's clear that thin people don't count calories. They don't restrict portion sizes, and they don't buy diet drinks. Those are things that overweight people do, hoping they will help.

If you aim to trim away weight, there are four specific keys to controlling your appetite naturally. I'll share them here, and then I'll show you how they work with real foods.

Key 1. Take Advantage of Fiber

Fiber means plant roughage. It is in beans, vegetables, fruits, and whole grains. Of course, advertisers brag about the fiber in their breakfast cereals, breads, snack bars, and supplements, and how it keeps people regular and even trims cholesterol. But one of fiber's greatest attributes is its ability to tackle your appetite. Fiber signals your brain that you're full.

Here's how it works: In your stomach, fiber holds water, so it's heavy enough to trick your stomach into thinking you have eaten quite a lot. But fiber has virtually no calories. In other words, it alerts your brain that you're full long before you've eaten too many calories.

You'll find it in foods from plants. There is plenty of fiber in whole-grain bread, split-pea and lentil soups, vegetable stir-fries, and any fruit you can name. The same is true of thousands of other foods from plant sources. But you won't find any fiber at all in meats, dairy products, or eggs. They are not plants, so they don't have plant roughage.

Here's what this means in the kitchen:

Let's make chili. The usual way to make it would be to use ground beef, sometimes with added oil for stir-frying. Since beef has no fiber at all, you would likely get quite a few calories before your appetite was satisfied.

A better way would be to let beans, tomatoes, and vegetables play the starring roles, and to skip meat, cheese, and oils. It could be the most delicious chili ever served at a backyard picnic. But since it now has plenty of fiber, each bite does its part to satisfy your appetite before very many calories kick in.

If you eat meat chili, you'll get extra calories before you feel full, because there's no fiber to turn down your appetite. But if you have bean-and-vegetable chili, you'll feel satisfied before you've overdone it on calories.

You can put this same principle to work with stews, soups, salads, main dishes, side dishes, desserts, and just about everything else. Here are some examples:

- A cream-based soup is loaded with calories, but a chunky vegetable or lentil soup fills you up with fewer calories.
- A greasy meat taco can be high in calories. If you substituted beans for the meat and cheese, you'd boost the fiber and cut the calories.
- Chicken salad is high in calories, while chickpea salad is lower.

In each case, the high-fiber food satisfies your appetite with fewer calories. And you would soon notice something remarkable: You're getting lighter day by day. Nothing feels quite as good as losing weight while eating well.

Let me emphasize that you don't need to watch the calories. If your plate is filled with vegetables, fruits, whole grains, and beans, you'll get loads of healthy fiber, and the calories will take care of themselves.

Catch the Fiber!

Fiber—plant roughage—is found in all foods from plants in their natural state. The fiber champions are legumes—the group that includes beans, peas, and lentils. Vegetables and fruits come next. And whole grains are also great sources of healthy fiber.

Some foods are rich in *soluble* fiber, the kind that is especially good for lowering cholesterol. Oat cereals are well known for this benefit, but you'll find soluble fiber in beans, vegetables (broccoli, Brussels sprouts, carrots, green beans, and sweet potatoes, for example), fruits (apples, oranges, mangoes, peaches, pears, prunes, and raisins), and some grains, such as barley, which is commonly used in cereals and soups.

Key 2. Skip Fatty Foods

It pays huge dividends to avoid fatty foods. This is most important. Let me explain:

When a chicken eats a bit too much, those extra calories are stored as chicken fat. When a cow eats too much, those calories are stored as fat, too. It's the same for pigs, goats, lambs, fish, and, of course, people. That's the whole point of body fat. Nature designed it to store calories. If you eat animal fat, you're eating an animal's calorie-storage organ.

Just one gram of fat—from a chicken, a cow, a fish, or any other source—holds nine calories. Now, a gram of fat isn't much—it doesn't even fill a thimble. But every last fat gram packs nine calories.

For contrast, look at potatoes, bread, beans, and pasta. These foods have a lot of carbohydrate. But any kind of carbohydrate has only four calories per gram—less than half the calories lurking in fat.

It turns out that fats pack in the calories, while carbohydrates don't. So why did carbohydrates get a reputation for being fattening? Well, just think about how people eat them: A potato is very low in fat and naturally low in calories. But it ends up being topped with butter, sour cream, or bacon bits—all fatty toppings. Mashed potatoes have milk whipped into them and butter or gravy dribbled on top. Toast—which has very few calories on its own— is spread with butter, or maybe margarine, both more or less pure fat. Each of these foods serves mainly as a vehicle for fatty toppings that pack in the calories. If we skip the fatty additions, the foods themselves are fine.

Now let's look at things from your stomach's point of view. You've finished your day's work and are at home, having your dinner. You are talking with your family, watching television, or doing whatever it is that you normally do at dinnertime.

But your stomach has a mind of its own. Your stomach is not distracted by conversation, and it could not care less what is on television. What it is focused on is how much you've eaten. With an elaborate network of nerves, your stomach can detect how heavy and bulky your foods are. Eventually, your stomach reaches the point it has been waiting for. This is the *satiety point*—the point when you are full. Your stomach sends a signal to your brain's appetite centers that you have had enough. You put down your fork, and eventually you get up from the table.

Let's say you were to swallow a forkful of chicken. Well, your stomach knows it's there, but it's not especially impressed. The fact is, that bite of chicken does not weigh very much, and it's not very bulky, either. It is not filling you up. So you have another bite, and another. Eventually, your stomach reaches the satiety point. But all the while, each bite of chicken has been carrying in fat and calories (even without the skin, about a quarter of its calories are nothing but fat, which is why your hands feel greasy after touching it). By the time you reach the satiety point, you've gotten more calories than you bargained for.

Let's take another scenario. Let's say you have a bite of cheese. It's not very big, either. So you'll have another, and another. Even though it is not filling, about 70 percent of the calories in typical cheeses come from plain old fat. So it really packs in the calories. By the time you're full, you've eaten lots of fat and far too many calories.

Now, other foods are not like this at all. A bean, for example, is completely different from chicken fat. It is not designed for storing calories. It's just a seed, and it can't overeat. A fruit is similar. An apple, for example, has just enough calories to give apple seeds a start in life. There is no greasy fat layer on these foods. You've never seen a bean or an apple marbled with fat.

Your stomach is completely impressed with these foods. They have lots of fiber, of course, which means they hold water so your stomach's nerve network really can't miss them. But because they are so modest in fat, they are really low in calories. As a group, vegetables, fruits, grains, and legumes (beans, peas, and lentils) are naturally very low in fat. So they tend to be low in calories. With loads of fiber and very little fat, they satisfy your appetite long before you've overdone it on calories.

When you eat foods from animals, you inevitably get stored fat. When you eat foods from plants, you don't. Yes, it really is that simple!

Animal Products Versus Plant Products: What a Difference!

ANIMAL PRODUCTS			PLANT PRODUCTS		
	Fat (%)*	Fiber		Fat (%)*	Fiber
Atlantic salmon**	40%	0	Apple, 1 medium	3%	4 g
Beef, top sirloin, lean	29%	0	Beans, navy, ½ cup, cooked	4%	10 g
Chicken, white meat, skinless	23%	0	Broccoli, 1 cup, cooked	4%	3 g
Egg, 1, boiled	61%	0	Lentils, ½ cup, cooked	3%	8 g
Cheddar cheese, 2 ounces	74%	0	Rice, brown, 1 cup, cooked	7%	3.5 g

*Based on percentage of calories.

** Meat servings are 3.5 ounces (100 grams).

From the US Department of Agriculture, Agricultural Research Service Nutrient Data Laboratory, www.nal.usda.gov/fnic/foodcomp/search/index.html, accessed May 7, 2010.

To avoid fat, it pays to skip animal products; most of them, including salmon, tuna, turkey, and chicken, have more fat than is healthful. You will also want to be aware of the sources of vegetable fat: added oils, fried foods, and oily salad dressings, for starters. Also, there's quite a lot of fat in nuts, seeds, olives, avocados, and some soy products.

By now you might be wondering, *If I leave these foods out of my diet, will I really feel satisfied?* And the answer is that you're actually *replacing* foods—bringing in healthful foods that can elbow the unhealthful ones out of the way. So you'll find that your new way of eating is actually *more* satisfying than the way you are eating now. As you'll see, this is built in to the Kickstart program.

You now have two powerful keys for appetite control. By (1) sticking with high-fiber foods—that means healthful plant-based foods—and (2) avoiding fatty foods, you are likely to experience powerful and continued weight loss. You don't need to bother with counting calories, portions, or anything else. You're eating delicious food, and having as much as you want. And the calories take care of themselves.

Tricking Your Brain

Let's look at two breakfasts:

- One consists of two fried eggs, two strips of bacon, buttered toast, and hash browns.
- The other is whole wheat pancakes topped with blueberries and maple syrup, with two strips of veggie bacon.

Which breakfast has more calories?

If you guessed that the pancake breakfast must be loaded with calories, think again. At 484 calories, *it has about 50 calories less* than the egg-and-bacon breakfast (535 calories). And it has no cholesterol at all, unlike the egg-and-bacon breakfast, which has 452 milligrams of cholesterol—an astronomical amount.

If you'd like an even lower-calorie breakfast, go with old-fashioned oatmeal, along with two slices of toast, and you'll get only 440 calories.

The idea is not to actually track the calories, of course. These are just illustrations to show that when you pick foods that are high in fiber and low in fat, you may think you're getting tons of calories, but in reality these are low-calorie foods.

Okay, how about lunch? Let's say you're pressed for time and are stopping in at a Burger King. You can choose the chicken sandwich or the BK veggie burger, hold the cheese and mayo. How do they compare?

Like day and night. The chicken sandwich has 643 calories. The veggie burger is just as filling, but has only 340 calories. And it has six grams of fiber, compared with only two in the chicken sandwich.

For dinner, let's compare three different options:

- Grilled salmon, baked potato with margarine, and green beans.
- Pork chop, mashed potatoes with gravy, and corn.
- Spinach lasagna, garden salad, and crusty Italian bread.

Each one of these is a typical dinner, and they would all fill you up. But here's how they compare: The salmon dinner has 434 calories, and the pork chop dinner has 629. But the spinach lasagna dinner fills you up with only 285 calories.

Once again, I've revealed the calories in these foods just so you know what is happening inside your body. If you stick with the plant-based options and keep it low-fat, you don't have to worry about calories ever again. They will take care of themselves. All you will notice is the beautiful change on the scale.

Which brings us back to Jean. She was luxuriating in blueberry pancakes with maple syrup, veggie sausage links, split-pea soup with toast, a garden salad, artichoke appetizer, garlic bread, spinach lasagna, steamed broccoli, and peach sorbet, and wondering how in heaven's name it was possible to eat so much and still lose weight.

It's just a miracle, I might have said. But the numbers tell the real story. When I took out my calculator, her entire day's meals—delicious and filling as they were—barely reached twelve hundred calories.

So, bottom line: This is not rocket science. It is basic biology. High-fiber, low-fat foods make you feel like you're pigging out. You'll love the taste, and will lean back, slapping your belly with satisfaction. But you'll notice that your belly is shrinking, practically before your very eyes.

Smart choices signal your brain that you are satisfied. And weight loss is essentially automatic.

Does This Mean *No* Fat?

A low-fat diet is not a *no-fat* diet. There are traces of natural oils in vegetables, beans, and fruits, and these fats are important for health. Some people add other sources of healthful omega-3 ("good") fats, such as walnuts, flaxseeds or flax oil, or soy products. And some researchers have found health benefits to having a small serving of nuts each day, despite the fact that nuts are very fatty. The idea is that nuts are heart-healthy and may even prevent arrhythmias—disorders of the heartbeat.

My advice is to be cautious with these foods. They can easily impart enough fat to your menu to bring your weight loss to a grinding halt. Rather than using nuts and seeds as snack foods (where it is so easy to go overboard), you might use them as condiments or in sauces, limiting them to about an ounce or so (about one modest handful) each day.

If You Need Extra Power

Okay, so you are ramping up your fiber, and you're avoiding fatty foods. Those two steps are very powerful for appetite control. The guidelines, menus, and recipes in this book put these simple keys to work so you will feel naturally satisfied with the foods you eat and will lose weight easily.

Even so, some people need a bit more help. They find that temptations and cravings sometimes get them in their grip. It can be an uncomfortable feeling, to say the least.

Why do cravings happen? Well, some foods have specific chemical properties that make them almost addictive—rather like drugs. Other times, cravings have nothing to do with the food in front of you; rather, the cravings are triggered by a drop in your blood sugar.

Let me show you what is going on and give you two more keys that will give you extra power if you need it.

Key 3. Use the Glycemic Index

If you could monitor how much sugar is in your blood minute by minute, you would notice something striking: It is a roller coaster. Your blood sugar goes up. It goes down. It fluctuates even when you haven't eaten anything at all.

Now, your brain runs on sugar—that is, glucose. And when your blood sugar starts to run low, your brain reacts immediately. Like a highway motorist whose gas gauge is well into the "E" zone and is frantically looking for a gas station—*any* gas station—your brain goes bananas when your blood sugar runs low. Your appetite ramps up, your nerves will be on edge, and like it or not *you are going to eat something—anything*—to get your blood sugar back up. Your body insists on it.

A plunging blood sugar sparks overeating.

It turns out that this whole scenario starts with food. That is, certain foods cause blood sugar swings. White bread, for example, causes your blood sugar to rise quickly. And what goes up must come down. As your blood sugar descends, it can sometimes fall too low, triggering your appetite. And that causes the whole cycle to start again, with more rising and falling blood sugar.

Junk food can wreak havoc with your blood sugar, which in turn affects your appetite. While some people eat white bread and occasional sugary foods with no problem at all, others end up with a roller-coaster blood sugar and continual cravings. However you are affected, the answer is very simple: Use the glycemic index.

The glycemic index, or GI, is an ingenious system for rating the effect foods have on blood sugar. Some foods, like white bread, make your blood sugar climb rapidly. So these are referred to as high-GI foods. In contrast, beans have much less effect on blood sugar. They are a low-GI food.

The glycemic index was invented in 1981 by David Jenkins, a pioneering physician and researcher at the University of Toronto. Today research teams around the world test the GI values of various foods. And if you have food cravings, low-GI foods are your best friends. They tend to smooth out your blood sugar, reducing cravings. Going low-GI is also helpful for people with diabetes or high triglycerides.

So which foods have a low GI? Many books and websites provide complicated lists showing you the GI values for many different foods. But let me simplify things:

Especially good low-GI choices include beans, peas, lentils, most fruits, pasta, and all green, yellow, and orange vegetables. The main high-GI foods, and healthier replacements, are shown in the chart below.

HIGH-GI FOODS	LOW-GI REPLACEMENTS
Sugar	Most fruits
Wheat breads (white or whole wheat)	Rye or pumpernickel breads
White potatoes	Yams or sweet potatoes
Most cold cereals	Oatmeal and bran cereals

It might surprise you to see white and whole wheat bread lumped together. Whole wheat is much better, of course, from the standpoint of fiber. Whole wheat retains its fiber, while white bread has had its fiber stripped away. But both types have about the same effect on blood sugar. Both have a much higher GI than rye or pumpernickel bread.

And you might also be surprised to see that pasta has a *low* GI. Even though white bread and white pasta are both made from flour, white bread has a high GI and pasta is much lower.

Let me explain what's going on: Bread is made by combining flour, water, and yeast. Yeast, of course, causes dough to rise by creating many tiny air pockets. When you eat bread, stomach acid and digestive enzymes rush into those air pockets, quickly breaking the bread apart and releasing the natural sugars it contains.

Pasta is not made with yeast, so it does not rise. It remains compacted. No matter how much you chew it, it never breaks apart as easily as white bread. So that's really all there is to it: One food sends sugar into your bloodstream quickly, while the other does not.

At the University of Sydney in Australia, Jennie Brand-Miller has developed a comprehensive website devoted to the glycemic index, along with reliable values for the GI of many foods. You'll find it at www.glycemicindex.com.

Key 4. Treat Problem Foods Like Addictions

Les attended a lecture I gave in Chicago. He arrived early and asked if we could talk for a few minutes. He said that he already knew what healthy foods were. His problem was cravings. Every evening, around eight or nine o'clock, he had an intense craving for sugar, and especially chocolate. As cravings kicked in, he became a passenger while his stomach led him to his car for a trip to a convenience store, where he often bought one or two chocolate bars, along with a soda, and gulped it all down. He told himself that he would soon be asleep and he didn't really need his late-night binge. But he was not in control. So, his question was, is this a food addiction, and what could he possibly do about it?

It's true that some foods seem to call our names more loudly than others. Sugar and chocolate, for example. We don't eat them because we are hungry; we eat them because, for some reason, they are sending us a very insistent message.

For some people, it's cheese. For a surprising number of people, this is the one food that—damn the fat and calories—they just cannot live without.

For other people, men especially, a big chunk of meat is the food that makes them ignore their cardiologist's pleadings.

Let's face it: No one ever went to a convenience store at nine at night to buy cauliflower—or apples, oranges, or split-pea soup, for that matter. And no one ever said, "I'm so mad, I'm going to steam some green beans!" or "I'm feeling lonely; I'll go peel a grapefruit." These foods just don't hit the brain the same way that sugar, chocolate, cheese, and meat do.

What's going on? It turns out that each of these foods has a specific chemical effect within the brain. In 1992, researchers at the University of Michigan did a fascinating test using the drug naloxone.[1] Normally, this drug is used to treat heroin overdose. It blocks heroin and other opiates from attaching to receptors within the brain. The Michigan researchers wanted to see what naloxone would do, not for people addicted to heroin, but for people who binge on chocolate. They gave twenty-six volunteers a naloxone infusion intravenously, and then offered them a tray filled with various chocolate candies. And to everyone's surprise, the chocolate tended to stay on the tray. The volunteers found that it still tasted like chocolate, it smelled like chocolate, and it had the usual mouth-feel that chocolate provides. But somehow, it just was not as appealing as before.

I am not suggesting that naloxone be a treatment for chocolate addiction (although some researchers have suggested exactly that). Rather, it is a research tool that proves that taste and mouth-feel are not all there is to our attraction. Chocolate affects the brain— stimulating the same receptors that heroin reaches—and when we take away that brain effect with naloxone, much of its appeal vanishes.

Mild drug-like effects have been demonstrated, not just for chocolate, but also for sugar, cheese, and meat. And that keeps you coming back for more.

So it's not your imagination. These foods really can get you hooked. But it isn't terribly difficult to break free. On page 156, I'll show you how.

Go for the Burn

So far, you have learned how to easily control your appetite. And when you start the Kickstart program, this will pay off for you handsomely. But there is more to weight loss. In the next chapter, we'll go a step further and enhance your metabolism, so that more of the calories you take in are turned to energy, rather than being stored as fat. The combination of appetite control and burn enhancement is very powerful.

CHAPTER 3

Understanding the Calorie-Burning Secret

How would you describe your metabolism? Do you feel like you can eat whatever you want and easily burn the calories off? Or do you feel like everything you even *think* about eating turns to fat?

What if you could speed up your metabolism so that more of what you eat turns to energy, rather than being stored as fat? That would be handy, wouldn't it?

Some people seem to think that you have to exercise to speed up your metabolism. But in our research, we have found that you can do just that simply with food. By choosing the right foods, you can reprogram your cells to speed up their metabolism after every single meal. In this chapter, I'll show you how we proved this and how you can easily do the same thing.

Burning Fat

Picture a wood-burning stove. If you throw in a few twigs, you'll get a small flame. Throw in some hefty logs, and you'll get a sustained burn.

Or picture a car. If you squirt in a little gas, you can rev up the engine for a mile or two. But fill the tank with the right fuel, and off you'll go.

Your body needs fuel, too. Not logs or gasoline, of course. The main fuel your body uses is *glucose*. It powers your movements, maintains your body temperature, and keeps your organs functioning.

Glucose is actually a natural sugar, and it comes from foods. You'll find it in starchy foods, like bread, rice, beans, potatoes, and pasta, and also in fruits, such as apples, bananas, peaches, pears, and others. During digestion, glucose passes from the foods you eat, into your bloodstream, and then into your body tissues.

Metabolism is the process of turning fuel into energy. If you have a "fast metabolism," you have what is essentially a little inferno inside each cell. You're burning lots of calories minute by minute. The faster your metabolism, the faster you're burning up calories, and the less fat you're storing.

Watching Your Metabolism Change

Just looking at people, you can't tell how fast their metabolism is. But if you were a volunteer in one of our weight loss studies, we could measure your metabolism. We would ask you to lie down on a typical examination table and breathe normally. Over your head and shoulders, we would place a special see-through canopy that allows us to track how much oxygen you're taking in and how much carbon dioxide you're breathing out. With a few simple calculations, we can tell precisely how fast you are burning calories. We can also track how this changes over time.

"But what difference does it make?" you might ask. "Isn't it all genetic? I can't change it."

Well, not so fast. Hold that thought for a moment.

How Foods Affect Your Metabolism

Every time you have something to eat, almost instantly, nutrients pass into your bloodstream and then into the cells of your body, where they are converted to energy. Like throwing more fuel on a fire or pressing the gas pedal in your car, your metabolism quickens. And it stays slightly higher than normal for three hours or more, thanks to the food you've eaten. This happens more or less anytime you eat.

But is that extra burn just a little after-meal flicker, or is it a major flare? Is there a way to turn that flame higher?

In one of our studies, we measured metabolism in a group of older people with chronic weight problems. We then asked them to eat differently for the next several weeks. Specifically, we asked them to stick to entirely plant-based meals and to keep oils to a minimum—the kind of diet described in the preceding chapter. We gave everyone recipes like those in this book.

Later on, we invited everyone to come back to the laboratory, and we tested their metabolic rates again. They lay on the table and breathed into the canopy. We found that not only did their calorie-burning speed jump up after a meal—but that extra burn was significantly higher than it had been when the study started.

In other words, even though everyone gets a little calorie burn after eating, something about their special dietary plan ramped up their responsiveness, so their bodies burned calories even faster. These were the same people, in the same room, lying on the same table. We gave them exactly the same test meal. But their after-meal calorie burn was bigger. It was like turning a burner on your stove from medium to high. They were converting more food into energy, instead of storing it as fat.

On average, they were burning calories about 16 percent faster for about three hours after the meal. Now, for any given meal, that's a modest change. But if you can burn calories faster for three hours after breakfast, three more hours after lunch, and again after dinner, you're getting a bigger burn. Imagine if you were to set your car's engine to rev higher for a few hours at a time, several times a day, day after day. Over time, you would burn up quite a lot more gas. If the cells in your body rev up as well, you'll have an extra edge that helps you trim away extra weight.

The Secret Inside Your Cells

How does this happen? How can foods boost your metabolism?

It turned out that the diet adjustment our research participants had made caused a fundamental change in their bodies. It reprogrammed their cells to pull sugar out of the blood more quickly, so it could be burned.

Here are the details: Normally, the hormone *insulin* escorts sugar and protein from your bloodstream into your cells. If insulin shoots the nutrients from foods into your cells rapidly, they can be quickly converted to energy. But insulin's ability to shoot those nutrients into the cell depends on how much fat has built up inside the cell.

If you had a very powerful microscope that could look inside your muscle cells, you would see something that might alarm you. Fat from the foods you eat forms tiny droplets that seem to float inside each cell.

Now, a small collection of fat droplets in each cell is perfectly normal; everyone has some of them. But if you've accumulated quite a number of fat droplets, they interfere with insulin's efforts to move glucose into the cells.

Let me be clear. These are fat droplets *inside* your muscle cells. This is not a fat layer padding your waistline or rounding your hips. These microscopic bits of fat are lurking deep within the individual cells of your body. Scientists call them *intramyocellular lipid*, which is simply another way of saying fat inside your muscle cells.

I liken this situation to chewing gum in a lock. If some trouble-maker put chewing gum into your front-door lock, your key would not work very well. Insulin is like a key. If you have a great many fat droplets packed into your muscle cells, the insulin "key" has trouble opening the cell membrane to allow glucose inside. If glucose can't get in, it can't be converted to energy. For some people, things get even worse: The buildup of fat inside cells leads to serious *insulin resistance* and eventually to type 2 diabetes.

Those mischievous fat particles come from the foods you eat. Let's look at a high-fat meal. It might start off with a salad drenched in an oily dressing, followed by spaghetti with meat sauce topped with cheese, and fried onion rings. All these foods contribute a load of fat. And into your cells it goes, interfering with your after-meal calorie burn.

We would have done better to top our salad with a nonfat dressing or a delicious plum vinegar and to add a chunky tomato-and-mushroom sauce to our spaghetti. Instead of onion rings, we might have had steamed asparagus. We'd have cut our fat intake dramatically.

Normally, your cells can burn up some of the fat you are consuming. Each cell has tiny particles, called *mitochondria*, which are like little burners, and they do their best to metabolize fat. But when you eat too much fat, these burners no longer work very well.

Scientists in Baton Rouge, Louisiana, asked ten healthy men to eat more fat than they normally would—about half their calories came from fat, compared with the more usual fat intake, which is about one-third of calories. After three days of fatty foods, the researchers removed tiny samples of each man's muscle cells in order to examine them carefully. It turned out that the cells no longer functioned normally. The fatty foods had partially *turned off* the genes that produce mitochondria. In other words, fatty meals didn't just put more fat into the cells; they also reduced the number of mitochondria "burners" in their cells. And that makes it harder to burn away fat.[1]

What all this means is this: You want nice, clean cells, without a lot of fat inside, because a clean cell can pull in glucose and convert much of it to energy. But fatty foods can pack fat into your cells, like chewing gum in a lock. And when that happens, glucose has trouble getting inside, and your metabolism gets no boost. And it is as if your body is greedily storing fat. With fewer mitochondria to burn it up, fat continues to build up in the cell. And you're not getting the after-meal burn that you should have.

Getting Your Metabolism Back

So how can we remove the fat from our cells and get our metabolism back? Well, one way is rather drastic surgery, not that I recommend it. Researchers at Catholic University in Rome, Italy, performed a procedure called a *biliopancreatic diversion* on eight severely overweight adults. The procedure, which is more involved than stomach stapling, cuts the stomach down to a very small size and completely disconnects the part of the intestine that absorbs fat from foods. After the procedure, you cannot eat very much of anything, and virtually all the fat you eat just passes through you and into the toilet.

The result was dramatic. Not only did the participants lose weight, but the amount of fat in their cells—the intramyocellular lipid that was interfering with their metabolism—dropped by 87 percent! Needless to say, there are plenty of disadvantages to a surgical approach, and, again, I am certainly not recommending it. But this experiment proves that, if fat can no longer get into your body, it starts to leave the cells.

Happily, there is a much easier way to evict this undesirable fat from your cells. And that is to leave fat out of the foods you eat. At Imperial College School of Medicine in London, researchers looked to see whether people who avoid meat and other animal products might have less fat in their cells.[2] After all, they are avoiding all the fat in beef, pork, cheese, and other animal products.

The researchers recruited a group of people who followed an entirely plant-based diet, and measured the fat in their cells. As you might have guessed, they had about 30 percent less fat in their cells, compared with meat eaters. In other words, by skipping many common fatty foods, they had less fat in their cells.

Well, what if you went a step further? What if you not only avoided animal fats, but you also steered clear of most vegetable oils? You could choose nonfat dressings, throw out the greasy fries, and steam, broil, or bake your foods, instead of frying. That would cut even more fat from your diet. And it would probably reduce fat in your cells even more, right? Well, that is exactly what we were doing in our research study. The participants ate no animal products and kept vegetable oils to a minimum. And their after-meal calorie burn got a boost very quickly.

So the secret is this: If you take most of the fat out of your diet, each lean little cell responds to insulin much more quickly. It pulls sugar out of the blood, and converts more of it to energy. Your cells become supercharged, ready to burn off calories faster.

More than Just Weight Loss

"Wait a minute!" I hear you say. If this diet change makes insulin work better and pulls sugar out of the blood, it sounds like a good treatment for diabetes! As a matter of fact, that's what we thought, too. In 2003, the National Institutes of Health awarded our research team a grant to see just how good a diabetes treatment it is. And the results of our study changed the Clinical Practice

Recommendations of the American Diabetes Association. We'll look at the details in the next chapter. In the meantime, let me share with you an experience that occurred many thousands of miles from our research center.

The Marshall Islands are a group of twelve hundred atolls and islands—many of them very tiny, but all very beautiful—in the Pacific Ocean, northeast of Australia. Between 1946 and 1958, the US government conducted extensive atomic weapons tests in the islands, with a great many effects, all of them negative. Apart from the obvious problem of widespread radiation exposure, some residents were displaced from one island to another so the testing could go forward. And American food products became big sellers, particularly Spam. This nondescript meaty loaf in a can filled the shelves in grocery shops, along with sugary drinks and snack foods. And before you could say "intramyocellular lipid," diabetes became rampant.

In many other parts of the world, a similar scenario is playing out, except that instead of Spam, the Western import is hamburgers, chicken nuggets, cheese pizza, or fried chicken. The fatty food tsunami carries diabetes along with it.

However, there has been a bright spot between the clouds in the Marshall Islands. A medical group called Canvasback Missions gathered together diabetes experts, including John Kelly, MD, and registered dietitian Brenda Davis, to set up the Diabetes Wellness Project with funding from the US Department of Defense. And to its lasting credit, the project de-Spammed the diets of people with diabetes who visited them. The team used a plant-based diet that happened to be much more in sync with the traditional Marshallese diet—the kinds of foods consumed before the arrival of Americans, atomic weapons, and Spam.

The program made an enormous difference. People with diabetes found themselves losing weight and reducing or eliminating medications; in some cases, their diabetes was no longer detectable.

One participant was a thirty-eight-year-old pilot. Or ex-pilot, I should say. When a routine employment physical showed diabetes, it ended his career, right then and there. He was married, with two children. His work supported his family, and he loved it. But diabetes meant he was no longer allowed to pilot an airplane. Period.

Then he happened to discover the Diabetes Wellness Project, which taught him how to prepare healthy plant-based foods. And bit by bit, he started to get better. He added exercise to his regimen, and not long after joining the program, he had this to say:

> I completely changed my diet and began a daily exercise program. Upon my last physical checkup, I was told that I am fully recovered and my pilot's medical certificate was approved. My fasting sugar is below 90 mg/dL with no medications. I no longer have diabetes. I have my career and my life back.

Don't Diet

Surprising as it may sound, some dieters push their metabolism in the wrong direction without even realizing it.

Where they are going wrong is in drastically cutting calories, hoping for quick weight loss. It seems like a sensible plan. But the problem is that your body does not know that you are doing this on purpose. It misinterprets the miserly food intake as starvation. In order to stave off too much weight loss, your body automatically slows your metabolism. That is, it cuts your calorie-burning speed. If you were to do a blood test, you would find a drop in *leptin*, a hormone that normally keeps your metabolism up and controls your appetite. Diets cause leptin to plummet, and the result is a slowed metabolism.

The answer is not to diet. There is no need to anyway. If you change the *type* of food you eat, you can lose weight easily, without intentionally cutting calories, as we saw in the preceding chapter.

So now you have two powerful paths toward permanent weight control—an ability to rein in your appetite and to also boost your calorie burn. One deals with "calories in," and the other with "calories out," and they are fundamental to the success of the Kickstart. Best of all, the same foods that bring these benefits help you stay young and healthy. Let's turn to cardioprotection, the third of the Kickstart ABCs.

CHAPTER 4

Cardioprotection: Health for Every Part of You

When someone "wins your heart," they have captured your innermost being. Our hearts lend their shape to valentines, candy boxes, lockets, and so many other expressions of love, and when we are "heartsick," we are devastated.

There is a good reason why the heart is central to so many expressions of emotion. At the center of your body, it transmits life to every part of you. It sends blood, rich in oxygen and nutrients, up to your brain, down to your toes, and everywhere in between, twenty-four hours a day, 365 days a year, never taking a vacation or even a little snooze.

Every time you take a step, your beating heart keeps you going. And when your step quickens, your heart does its best to keep up. If you're good to your heart, you'll have the energy to run, dance, and play with your children and grandchildren, and you'll live longer, too.

Foods can do a lot more than trim our waistlines. If we let them work for us, they can have a dramatic effect on our health. In this chapter, we'll focus on cardioprotection. This means more than taking care of your heart. It also means being good to the miles and miles of blood vessels that radiate out from it, carrying life and health deep into the tissues of your body.

Cardioprotection means defending yourself. If you're in good shape now, I'll show you how to stay that way. If you need a bit of help, let me show you the power of foods to restore health.

When I say "power," I mean it. Let me share with you a message I received from a woman in Riverside, California. Her name is Ginny, and she approached me after a lecture. She was very worried. Her cholesterol hovered far above two hundred, and although she had already made some adjustments to her diet, she wasn't getting very far. A future of heart disease was looming in front of her, and she was skeptical that a menu change would help enough to really matter. I suggested she give our approach a try. Shortly thereafter, she sent me this message:

> I had tried for five years to lower my cholesterol with minimal success. I did not feel good on Lipitor and the oatmeal regimen was helping only moderately, moving my cholesterol down from mid 260s to high 240s. If you recall, I was moved to tears because I was so frustrated with my lack of success. You calmly suggested to try the low-fat vegan diet for 6 weeks and retest my lipids. After 2 and a half weeks, I retested with a 60 point drop to 183! Amazing! I am now a missionary for the powerful effects of the plant-based diet.

Staying Healthy

Each heartbeat propels blood into the *aorta*, the pipeline that rises from the top of the heart, giving off the arteries that go to the brain, then curves back downward to run along the front of your spine, eventually dividing to go down your right and left legs. Along the way, it sends arteries to your vertebrae, your internal organs, and most other parts of you.

If you could hop into a tiny submarine and cruise along from your heart through your blood vessels, you could see from the inside just how healthy they look. And you would notice something a bit odd. As the aorta descends and passes in front of the spine, yellowish streaks appear to be painted on the aorta wall. As your submarine driver, I can tell you that those streaks started appearing when you were a child in school. You cannot feel them, but they have been gradually growing.

You'll also notice that in a few places, these yellowish streaks have thickened up into raised patches. Some have actually started to cover the points where the aorta gives off a branching artery. Checking the anatomical chart we've brought along, you ask, "Where's the artery to my lumbar spine?"

"Covered over when you were nineteen years old," I reply.

"What? How does my spine get blood?" you ask, wondering if this has anything to do with the backaches you've been getting lately.

"There are other branches," I reply. "You've lost one or two, but some others are still open. They allow blood to detour around the blockage, at least to an extent."

I notice that you do not look reassured. Some outflow points where arteries branch off are still visible; others are narrowed, and some have been completely paved over. Inspecting the side arteries, we see that many have the same streaks and thickened walls, narrowing the passage of blood.

"But I'm still young, more or less," you protest. "These arteries look like I've got one foot in the grave!"

Surprising, isn't it?

The year before I went to medical school, I had a job as an autopsy assistant at Fairview Hospital in Minneapolis, Minnesota.

The hospital morgue was in the basement, and nobody ever visited the place unless they had to. The phone was a heavy black model that had not been replaced since the 1940s. The walls were the color of algae. But that drab and deadly quiet environment gave me an education. For most people, the idea of a stroke or colon cancer is just a vague theoretical notion. But if you are the person who runs the skull saw or who holds a colon tumor in your hand, these things become very graphic.

One day a man died in the hospital of a massive heart attack. Our job was to examine the body. The pathologist cut through the skin then, using what looked like a garden clipper, cut through each of the ribs. He removed a large pie-wedge-size section of the chest wall, setting it on the table next to the body. That exposed the heart. Knowing that I was headed for medical school, he made sure I saw everything.

"These are called *coronary* arteries," he said, "because they crown the heart." Slicing one open, he pointed out atherosclerotic plaques. "Feel them," he said. I did, and it was frightening. The plaques looked like bits of chewing gum stuck inside the artery, except that they were hard as concrete. And they weren't just in the heart. They were in the carotid arteries to the brain, the arteries to the kidneys, and all up and down the aorta, the body's main pipeline.

"That's your morning bacon, Neal," the pathologist said. "And this is your roast beef." He wasn't kidding. In America, heart disease starts in childhood, thanks to our meaty diets, and eventually kills half of us. It lurks in three-quarters of men by age twenty-three, the pathologist said—which happened to be exactly my age at the time.

After the examination, I carefully picked up the section of ribs from the table and put it back into the chest, sewed up the skin, and cleaned the table. Washing my hands, I went upstairs to the cafeteria. As I lifted the lid from the plate, what did I see but ribs staring back at me. It was an inverted chicken breast, whose exposed ribs looked and smelled very much like the body I had been working on. I stared at the meal, then put the lid back on. I simply couldn't eat it.

Not Just Your Heart

As the pathologist told me, "heart disease" is really *artery* disease. It attacks many parts of your circulatory system simultaneously. And in countries where meat and dairy products are staples, it starts early.

The process begins as cholesterol particles enter the artery wall, causing the gradual buildup of fatty streaks, then *plaques*—small bumps that narrow the passageway for blood. If one of these plaques bursts open, it can trigger the clotting of blood, which ends up plugging the artery passage. In the coronary arteries, that loss of blood flow can mean the death of a whole section of heart muscle. This is *myocardial infarction*, or heart attack.

But the artery narrowing itself can cause serious problems, even if the plaques do not burst open and form clots. In the coronary arteries, narrowing leads to chest pain. Narrowed arteries to the legs cause leg pains, called *claudication*. Narrowed arteries to the genitals cause sexual dysfunction.

That's right—in most cases, erectile dysfunction is a sign of clogged arteries. Diabetes, high blood pressure, and the medications used to treat them also contribute to impotence. Happily, a plant-based diet is good for all these conditions.

And here's another surprise: The common back pain that comes from pinched nerves appears to start out as blocked arteries to the lower back. As the back loses its blood supply, the disks that act as cushions between the vertebrae become more and more fragile, and can eventually break. Like a broken pillow whose stuffing is exploding out, a herniating disk ends up pinching a nearby nerve, causing back pain.

Here's how to protect your heart and your arteries.

Avoid Animal Fat and Cholesterol

When you eat animal fat, it causes your body to make more cholesterol. When I was a child, my mother cooked up bacon for her five children. She lifted the bacon strips out of the hot grease with a fork and set them on a paper towel to dry. Then she carefully lifted the pan and poured the hot grease into a jar to save it. But she did not bother to put the jar in the refrigerator. She simply put it on the shelf in the kitchen cupboard. She knew that, as bacon grease cools, it becomes a waxy solid. And the fact that bacon grease is a solid fat—as opposed to a liquid oil—is a sign that it is loaded with *saturated fat*—the kind of fat that causes your body to make more cholesterol.

Chicken fat, turkey fat, beef fat, pork fat—they are all waxy solids and are high in saturated fat. Dairy fat, too. You can't pour cheese like an oil; you have to cut it with a knife. It is loaded with saturated fat.

Fish fats are not so different. While some fish are lower in fat and others (such as chinook salmon) are very high, they all contribute their load of fat and cholesterol. In other words, they are more like beef or chicken than they are like broccoli.

Of course, some people eat fish specifically because it has "good fats." What they are thinking of are *omega-3 fats*, which are reputed to fight inflammation and prevent blood clots. Unfortunately, there are two problems with that thinking:

First, most of the fat in fish is actually not omega-3. All fats—including fish fats—are mixtures. From 15 to 30 percent of the fat in fish is plain old saturated fat, and most of the rest consists of various other types of fat with no health benefits at all. Their main effect is to pad your waistline, which is why salmon enthusiasts often have trouble with their weight.

Second, studies show that omega-3s may not have the health benefits people had hoped for. A detailed analysis in the *British*

Medical Journal found that neither fish nor fish oils protect against cardiovascular disease, cancer, or death.[1]

In research studies, a switch from a beefy diet to a chicken-and-fish diet lowers LDL ("bad") cholesterol only about 5 percent.[2] For comparison, an entirely plant-based diet can cut LDL by 20 to 30 percent, or even more.[3-4]

So it is important to avoid animal fat. You will also want to steer clear of cholesterol. It may surprise you to learn that cholesterol is actually not the same as fat. Fat is the yellow layer under a chicken skin or the white stripes in marbled beef. But cholesterol is not visible. Cholesterol molecules hide in the membranes that surround each cell in an animal's body, and *most of it is in the lean portion.* So if you take a bite of chicken, for example, there is fat under the skin and in between the muscle cells; the cholesterol lurks in the muscle cells themselves, packed into the cell membranes that surround each cell.

All animal products contain cholesterol. So it is in meats and dairy products, and you'll find a mother lode of cholesterol in eggs and in shellfish, such as shrimp and lobster. Plants are different. When you look at the cholesterol content of vegetables, fruits, and other foods from plants, their labels indicate a big zero. If you set aside animal products, you are getting no animal fat and essentially no cholesterol. That simple change can mean a dramatic effect on your blood cholesterol test, and can help most people avoid the need for cholesterol-lowering medications.

Avoid Tropical Oils and Trans Fats

Snack-food manufacturers sometimes use liquid oils, such as peanut or soybean oil, to cook potato chips and other snack foods. But these oils have a short shelf life; they turn rancid rather quickly. So to extend shelf life, some manufacturers use *partially hydrogenated* oils, sometimes called *trans* fats. By adding hydrogen atoms to oil molecules, the liquid oil turns into a waxy solid that has a buttery mouth-feel and a much longer shelf life. Unfortunately, partially hydrogenated oils won't help *your* shelf life at all. They are similar to animal fats in their cholesterol-raising actions.

Because hydrogenated oils have come under fire in recent years, some manufacturers have switched to tropical oils, such as coconut or palm oil. They, too, are loaded with saturated fat, and are no better than animal fats.

Keep All Oils to a Minimum

It pays to keep all fats and oils to a minimum. Yes, olive oil is better for you than bacon grease. But remember, all fats are mixtures. Olive oil is mostly made of a kind of fat called *monounsaturated* fat. The name is not important; all that matters is that this sort of fat is in no way essential for the body. It is about 75 percent of the fat in olive oil, and it's basically a source of concentrated calories. Another 11 percent is *polyunsaturated* fat, similar to the fat found in typical cooking oils (such as corn or soybean oil). This is mostly just concentrated calories, too.

So by now, you are no doubt on the edge of your seat wondering, *What is the other 14 percent?* Well, it turns out to be plain old *saturated* fat—the same cholesterol-raising, artery-clogging fat found in chicken fat, pork fat, and other less-than-healthful products.

So are there any "good" fats in olive oil? If you send a bottle to a laboratory to be analyzed, they will tell you that less than 1 percent of it is in the omega-3 form that can actually be called "good" fat. All the rest—well, it's just there to fatten you up.

As I pointed out in chapter 2, this is not a "no-fat" program. Typical vegetables, fruits, and beans contain small amounts of natural fats—usually between about 5 and 10 percent of their calories. It is odd to think that there is a tiny bit of oil in a bean or a broccoli floret. But there is, and the body needs the traces of natural oils in plant foods.

Some people seek out additional fats in the form of walnuts or other nuts, seeds, or soy products, for example. So even without pouring any oils onto your salad or into your frying pan, you will get traces of natural oils in the foods you eat. And that is good. Skip the fatty foods and added oils, and the natural oils in vegetables, fruits, and beans will take care of themselves and you.

As you check food labels on commercial products, favor those with no more than two or three grams of fat per serving.

It's Easy

I often hear from people who have tried the simple methods we have suggested and who are amazed, not only at their results, but by how easy it all turns out to be. I received this e-mail message from Ronald, whose cholesterol had been well into the danger zone, at 210 mg/dL:

> Four weeks from beginning this diet I had my cholesterol measured again. It was 153, a drop of about 25% in a month. Amazing! AND I have broken through a static position and have begun steadily losing weight again. It is EASY to lose weight this way. I can't believe this; I would have done this sooner had I known.

So many people have gotten used to the idea that menu changes produce only weak results, because they haven't tried a program that really works. And once they do, the results are often spectacular.

Emphasize Cholesterol-Lowering Foods

By now you know that a plant-based diet has a profound effect on cholesterol. And certain foods deserve special mention:

- **Oats, beans, and barley.** I briefly mentioned in chapter 2 that oatmeal and other oat cereals lower cholesterol. It's true. The credit goes to their *soluble fiber.* It traps cholesterol in the intestine and carries it out with the wastes. Other foods have soluble fiber, too. Beans, for example, work very much like oat cereals. If you include them in your daily menu, you can expect to cut a few more points off your cholesterol. You will also likely trim your LDL ("bad") cholesterol and triglycerides, and boost your HDL ("good") cholesterol.[5] You'll also find soluble fiber in barley (often used in soups or mixed with rice) and in many vegetables and fruits.
- **Soy products** reduce cholesterol, too. Of course, part of the value of a soy-based veggie burger is that it's not meat, so it has no cholesterol or animal fat. But there is more to it. Something about soy protein brings an extra cholesterol-lowering benefit.[6]

David Jenkins, MD, PhD, at the University of Toronto showed that foods alone could lower cholesterol levels nearly as well as cholesterol-lowering drugs.[4] The trick was to start by omitting animal products, and then emphasize foods with known cholesterol-lowering ability: oats, barley, and soy products, for example. His patients cut their LDL ("bad") cholesterol by nearly 30 percent *in just four weeks.*

Be a Nonsmoker

When I was in medical school, the George Washington University Hospital sold cigarettes in its gift shop. I know this because I bought them. Lining up at the cash register for Merit Menthols, I often ran into my surgery attending physician, who was there to buy Marlboros.

We were not idiots; we knew we had to quit. But we naively figured we could get away with it for a while, and then quit when our lives were less stressful.

Happily, the hospital eventually stopped selling cigarettes and banned smoking altogether. The doctors' lounge eventually aired out, and our lungs breathed a sigh of relief. But smoking affects more than your lungs. It accelerates atherosclerosis and all the problems that come with narrowed arteries—yes, that includes backaches and erectile dysfunction—and makes it much more likely that you could have a heart attack.

If you smoke, it does not really matter *how* you quit. What counts is that you do quit. Most people find that it is much more challenging to quit smoking than it is to change their diets. That was certainly my experience. I found it really tough to quit smoking, while changing my diet was really quite easy. But millions of people have succeeded, and you can, too.

Stay Physically Active

Exercise doesn't do much to lower your total cholesterol, but it can give a nice boost to HDL ("good") cholesterol, which helps your body rid itself of cholesterol particles. Exercise also helps control blood pressure.

Avoid Low-Carbohydrate Diets

Dr. Atkins and other low-carbohydrate advocates suggested that rice and potatoes were dangerous, while steak and heavy cream were healthy foods. Many people took that advice to heart, only to pay a heavy price.

Jody Gorran, a Florida businessman, started a low-carbohydrate diet hoping to lose a few pounds. By coincidence, he happened to have a heart scan just before beginning the diet; it turned out to be totally clear, and his cholesterol was enviably low at 146 mg/dL. He began the meaty low-carb diet, secure in the belief that it could not hurt him.

But two months into the diet, his cholesterol shot up to 230. Even so, he stuck with the regimen, believing that, so long as he avoided carbohydrates, as Dr. Atkins advised people to do, he would be all right. Unfortunately, his cholesterol did not return to normal.

One day, out of the blue, crushing chest pain stopped him in his tracks. Arriving at the hospital, a cardiologist found a 99 percent blockage in a coronary artery. Although he had had a clean heart scan before starting the diet, he had developed a life-threatening artery blockage. Jody needed emergency heart surgery to save his life.

Happily, he got help in time, and stopped the unhealthful diet. He then switched to a plant-based diet, which was not only good for his waistline; it also returned his cholesterol to normal. Jody's remarkable story was published as a case report in the *Journal of the American Dietetic Association.*[7]

Understanding Your Cholesterol Test

When your health care provider checks your cholesterol, the test results can be confusing. Here are the targets you'll want to aim for:

Total Cholesterol is simply all the different kinds of cholesterol added up into a single number. The US government recommends keeping your total cholesterol below 200 milligrams per deciliter (5.2 millimoles per liter). That's a good start, but many people with cholesterol levels around 200 still have heart attacks. A safer goal is 150 milligrams per deciliter (3.9 millimoles per liter). The Framingham Heart Study showed that about one-third of people who have heart attacks have cholesterol levels between 150 and 200, but heart attacks almost never occur below that 150 threshold.

Low-Density Lipoprotein Cholesterol. LDL ("bad") cholesterol increases the risk of artery blockages. So you want to keep it low

---

(think L = low). I recommend that LDL be below 100 milligrams per deciliter (2.6 millimoles per liter). Some experts suggest an even stricter limit of 80 milligrams per deciliter (2.1 millimoles per liter).

High-Density Lipoprotein Cholesterol. HDL ("good") cholesterol has been likened to tiny dump trucks that carry cholesterol away. So, unlike other types of cholesterol, you actually want it to be high (think H = high). For men, HDL should be above 45 milligrams per deciliter (1.2 millimoles per liter). For women, it should be above 55 milligrams per deciliter (1.4 millimoles per liter).

However, I have one caveat to these figures. If a healthful diet has reduced your total cholesterol to a low number—say, below 150 mg/dL—you do not have much of any kind of cholesterol in your bloodstream, and presumably you do not need so many "dump trucks" to carry it away. It appears that an HDL value below the targets described above is not dangerous if your total cholesterol is also low.

Triglycerides are fat particles in the bloodstream. They should be below 150 milligrams per deciliter (1.7 millimoles per liter).

Healing Your Heart

It was once thought that heart disease was a one-way street. Once you had it, you had it for good. The idea was that heart disease was eventually going to kill you, in all likelihood. But with prescriptions and various surgical procedures, doctors could postpone the inevitable and keep you as comfortable as possible.

In 1990, that dismal scenario gave way to a dramatically different understanding. In chapter 1, I mentioned Dr. Dean Ornish, a visionary pioneer if ever there was one. When Dr. Ornish was a medical student, heart disease was the number one killer of Americans, just as it is today. Not content with conventional approaches that often required heroic and expensive surgery, chronic medication use, and a gradual surrender to disease, he began to study a lifestyle approach that directly addressed its causes.

Dr. Ornish's program was simple. He used four steps: Starting with a vegetarian diet, he added mild exercise (a half-hour walk each day) and taught simple stress management techniques. Patients who smoked were encouraged to quit. And that was it. No drugs, no angioplasty, no stents—none of the invasive methods that are routine in cardiology today.

The program was simple, but his patients flourished. They lost weight quickly and, for the most part, permanently. Their chest pain was abolished. And when their arteries were examined by angiogram (a special X-ray of the heart), the results made medical history. Arteries that had been narrowed by advancing atherosclerosis finally began to reopen, so much so that the changes were clearly evident in 82 percent of patients in the first year. And as the years went by, their risk of any sort of heart complication was cut dramatically.[3,8]

Blood Pressure

Cardioprotection means more than just controlling your cholesterol. It is also essential to keep your blood pressure in a healthy range. Normal blood pressure is less than 120/80 mmHg.

High blood pressure isn't just rough on your heart. It also contributes to strokes and is one of the biggest threats to your kidneys—something people tend not to think about until their doctors start talking about what it means to lose them.

So how do you control your blood pressure? Well, you already know that it helps to keep your sodium (salt) intake low. If you were to add up all the sodium in the foods you eat (which you can do by reading labels), you will want to aim for a sodium limit of about two thousand milligrams per day.

But let's go a step further. It turns out that the diet changes that bring down your cholesterol do exactly the same thing for blood pressure. Here's why:

First of all, as you lose weight your blood pressure drops, too. And the diet changes you are about to make are the perfect way to lose weight.

But there is more to it. When you avoid animal fat, your blood becomes less *viscous*—that is, it's less "thick." So it is more like water and less like grease, and that means that it flows more easily through your arteries.[9]

If we were to hop back into our microscopic submarine and go scooting around in your blood vessels, we would notice that your bloodstream seems much cleaner. If it was a bit like an oil slick before, much of that grease is now gone. Your blood flows more readily through the arteries and veins, and it's not surprising that your heart does not have to push so hard to keep your blood moving.

The credit, of course, goes to the vegetables, fruits, and other plant foods you're eating now, because they don't carry the load of fat you were previously eating in meat, cheese, and so on. And for extra credit, vegetables and fruits are rich in potassium, which also helps lower blood pressure.

Researchers have found that plant-based diets reduce blood pressure quite quickly.[10] Your blood pressure will likely start dropping within the first week of the Kickstart, and you should see significant results within six weeks or so, if not sooner.

Even so, remember that high blood pressure is dangerous. It is important to have your blood pressure checked, and if you are being treated with medications, do not stop them on your own. As your diet improves and your blood pressure comes under better control, you can work with your health care provider to reduce or discontinue your medications if and when the time is right.

A Medication Vacation

When people improve their diets, they can often reduce or even eliminate medications for cholesterol, blood pressure, or diabetes. But how do you do this and when is the right time?

The answer is to work with your health care provider. If your provider feels that you have improved to the extent that you may no longer need your medications, he or she can begin what is sometimes called a medication vacation. The idea is to stop your medicines on a trial basis while keeping a watchful eye on your blood pressure (or cholesterol or diabetes, as the case may be) and to restart your medications if it turns out you are not yet ready to live without them.

Keep in mind that all of these conditions—particularly uncontrolled high blood pressure—can be dangerous, so you should never modify your medication regimen on your own, and should be guided by your health care provider. Even so, the nutritional program in this book is very powerful, and many people have been able to reduce or get off their medications.

Diabetes

Diabetes increases the risk of damage to the heart, and threatens the blood vessels to the eyes, the kidneys, and the extremities. People with diabetes lose about a decade of life, on average, compared with people without the disease. Most ultimately succumb to heart disease.

It does not have to be that way. Our research has shown that diabetes can be turned around.

When I was a child, my father specialized in diabetes treatment at the local clinic in Fargo, North Dakota. And I never once heard him say that a patient was cured. He and his patients were fighting a war of attrition, surrendering ever so slowly.

When I was a hospital intern, I shared my father's pessimism about diabetes. Patients needed endless monitoring and medications, and most seemed to wind up with serious complications—heart disease, vision loss, kidney failure, and intractable neuropathic pain in their feet.

However, in recent years, my research team has developed and tested the new approach to diabetes that I mentioned earlier. Using a low-fat, entirely plant-based diet, many of our research participants improve dramatically. In some cases, you would never know they'd ever had the disease. We have presented our findings at many medical conferences and have published them in peer-reviewed journals.[11–15] You will find the details in *Dr. Neal Barnard's Program for Reversing Diabetes*. In the meantime, let me give you the short version:

Diabetes is a condition in which there is too much sugar in the blood. This sugar—glucose—is the main fuel for the body, as you know. The problem in diabetes is that glucose cannot get into the cells of the body where it belongs. Instead, it circulates in the blood at abnormally high levels, causing all sorts of problems.

In the most common form of diabetes—*type 2 diabetes*—the problem appears to start with the buildup of tiny fat particles inside the muscle cells—the intramyocellular lipid that interferes with insulin's efforts to bring glucose into the cells, as we saw in chapter 3. A similar fat buildup occurs in the liver.

The three keys to choosing foods for diabetes are (1) avoiding animal products, (2) minimizing fats and oils, and (3) avoiding high-glycemic-index foods (as we saw in chapter 2). When people with type 2 diabetes improve their diets, their condition often improves dramatically, presumably because their cells are cleaning out some of that fat so insulin can work again.

This approach has gotten a great deal of attention in recent years, and many people have gotten in touch with our research team to let us know how it has worked for them. While more typical "diabetes diets" tend to produce weaker results, the combination of a vegan diet, minimizing fats, and going low-GI can be very powerful.

Longevity

A healthy diet does not mean we will live forever. But we certainly can add years to our lives. And more important, we can really *live* during the time we have. Rather than being hobbled by extra weight and endless health problems, we can enjoy life.

Other researchers have identified so-called blue zones—places where people live extraordinarily long lives—a concept popularized by Dan Buettner in a *National Geographic* magazine cover story in 2005. Among these are Loma Linda, California; Okinawa, Japan; Sardinia, Italy; Ikaria, Greece; and Nicoya Peninsula, Costa Rica. One of the traits common among residents of all of these places is a diet focusing on foods from plant sources, particularly legumes, rather than animal sources. They also avoid tobacco, exercise frequently, and maintain strong familial or social supports, which probably help them maintain these healthful choices.

So how many years can we add to our lives? Researcher Gary Fraser, MD, PhD, estimated that an overall healthy lifestyle, including a vegetarian diet, regular exercise, and avoiding tobacco, among other sensible choices, can extend life about ten years.[16] And during those extra years and the decades preceding them, you can aim to have a much healthier life than many people have come to expect.

As we have seen, the same dietary changes that help us slim down are also good for our hearts and the rest of our bodies, too. I hope that, if you take good care of yourself and inspire your loved ones to do the same, you'll be able to send one another valentines for many years to come.

CHAPTER 5

A Healthy Menu

By now, you know that tuning up your menu has a tremendous pay-off. In this chapter, we'll get practical. I'll show you which foods are in, which are out, and how to be sure you're starting off on the right foot. We will also take a look at complete nutrition—making sure you're getting all the nutrients you need. It's very easy, as you'll see.

The three overall principles are (1) set animal products aside, (2) keep oils to a minimum, and (3) go low-glycemic-index. Okay, so when we look at our plates, what's in and what's out?

What's In

The foods that you'll want to have front-and-center on your plate are whole grains, legumes (beans, peas, and lentils), vegetables, and fruits. These four food groups are all free of animal products, needless to say. In their natural state, most are also very low in oil and low-GI.

Let's take a closer look at these healthy staples, and then we'll see how to turn them into delicious meals. By creating delicious meals, your focus will quickly shift from what you are leaving off your plate to what you are now newly experiencing and enjoying.

The Whole-Grain Group. Bread, rice, pasta, tortillas, cereals—foods made from grains—are staples the world over. Where these foods remain a staple, people are much healthier than in places where meaty, cheesy diets have invaded.

Whole grains bring you protein, healthful complex carbohydrate, and fiber, with no cholesterol, animal fat, or other undesirables.

The Legume Group. *Legumes* is a nutritionist's word for beans, peas, and lentils—foods that grow in a pod. This group includes not only navy beans, pinto beans, black beans, chickpeas, lentils, and all their cousins, but also all the foods they can be turned into: hummus, chili, bean soups, veggie burgers, veggie hot dogs, tofu, tempeh, meatless deli slices, and many others.

The bean group brings you abundant protein, calcium, iron, soluble fiber, and even traces of omega-3 fatty acids ("good fats"). The entire legume group boasts an enviably low glycemic index, meaning these foods are powerful for keeping your blood sugar steady.

People who include beans in their routine have lower levels of LDL ("bad") cholesterol and higher levels of HDL ("good") cholesterol.[1] They are also about seven pounds thinner than their bean-neglecting friends, according to the US government's National Health and Nutrition Examination Survey, conducted from 1999 through 2002.[2]

The Vegetable Group. You know that vegetables are loaded with vitamins, and many are also rich in highly absorbable calcium, as well as iron and fiber. And although broccoli doesn't like to brag, more than 30 percent of its calories come from protein.

But what really has researchers talking is vegetables' antioxidant power. The orange color in a carrot or yam, for example, comes from *beta-carotene*. Beta-carotene and other antioxidants neutralize *free radicals*—that is, compounds in the blood that contribute to aging, DNA damage, and cancer. You'll see beta-carotene's cousin, *lycopene*, as the red color in tomatoes and watermelons; it is also a powerful antioxidant.

As you plan meals, go for color, and include more than one in a meal: green vegetables, orange vegetables, yellow vegetables, or whatever your tastes call for. They will help you get slim or stay that way, and are wonderful for health.

The Fruit Group. Fruits are not just vitamin-rich. They also have plenty of fiber to slim you down, with essentially no fat or cholesterol. And many fruits are loaded with antioxidants, just as vegetables are. So, when it comes to desserts or snacking, you can't beat fresh fruit.

Although fruits are sweet, they have surprisingly little effect on blood sugar—nearly all fruits are low-glycemic-index foods.

Turning Healthful Ingredients into Meals

These four healthful food groups give you the ingredients for a slim, healthy body. So what do they look like on your plate? The possibilities are endless:

A Mediterranean dinner might start with pasta e fagioli, followed by broccoli rabe with garlic, roasted eggplant, and a medley of strawberries and melon. Fagioli (beans) are legumes, pasta is a grain, broccoli and eggplant are vegetables, and strawberries and melon are fruits—bringing you each of the four healthful food groups.

A Latin American choice might be a corn tortilla stuffed with beans, lettuce, tomatoes, caramelized onions, and summer squash, along with Spanish rice, plenty of vegetables, and sliced papaya or pineapple for dessert.

The Southern United States might bring us black-eyed peas, corn bread, kale or collard greens, and peaches for dessert. A Boston kitchen would follow a similar menu but change the players: Black-eyed peas would become baked beans, corn bread be changed to a baked potato, and kale to Swiss chard or cabbage.

An Asian dinner might start with a savory vegetable soup, followed by tofu and bok choy in a savory sauce on brown rice. And you can read your fortune while munching on sweet orange slices.

At an Indian restaurant, delicately spiced lentils or chickpeas could be complemented by spinach and basmati rice with currants and cashew slivers, a papadum or two, along with mango slices.

You will think of countless other possibilities, and take a look at the menus and recipes later in this book. The idea is simply to let the four healthy building blocks—whole grains, legumes, vegetables, and fruits—turn into tasty meals.

What's Out

So much for the foods we want to focus on. It's just as important to set aside the foods that can cause trouble. Let's go through them. As we do, you'll probably see some that have been mainstays for you for a long time, and you might wonder what life will be like without them. For now, don't be too burdened by that thought. The whole idea of the Kickstart is to test-drive a remarkably healthy way of eating and to experience the surprising benefits it can bring. Once you've done that, you can start to think about how to approach this over the longer term. I'll help you.

So here are the foods that you'll want to skip during your 21 days.

Animal Products

As I was growing up in North Dakota, we put roast beef or pork chops at the center of the plate more or less every day. At the time, we did not make the connection between those foods and the weight problems, heart disease, and cancer that were much more common in the United States than in many other countries, and still are. But eventually researchers implicated the fat, cholesterol, and other undesirables in these foods for the health problems we have been struggling with. It is now abundantly clear that people who skip animal products are slimmer and healthier than those who eat them.

Let's take a look at a cut of meat. To state the obvious, a cow's muscles were designed by nature to move the cow's legs. A chicken's muscles allow the bird to walk and fly (although current breeding and rearing practices are such that these obese birds do not get around very well). A fish's muscles move the fish's tail. A muscle is not designed to be a nutritional supplement. It is a biological ratchet system designed for pulling. For that purpose, it is beautifully designed. Strings of protein serve as the ratchet mechanism, with fat in between them.

If meat were designed to provide good nutrition, it would have fiber to tame your appetite, complex carbohydrate for energy, and vitamin C to protect your body, among other vital nutrients. But meat has none of these things. It is mainly a mixture of fat and protein (along with the occasional parasite, perhaps).

Meat's fat packs in calories, and it adds to the fat that is collecting inside your cells—the intramyocellular lipid that slows down your metabolism, as we saw in chapter 3.

Meat's protein is a problem, too. In years past, nutrition researchers praised animal protein because it provides the amino acids (protein building blocks) our bodies need. However, it soon became clear that plants provide all the protein we need, too.

Any normal variety of plant foods provides all the essential amino acids. I'll explain more about this later in this chapter.

Plant proteins are not only free of animal fat and cholesterol; they are also free of two problems caused by animal proteins.

First, animal protein is linked to osteoporosis, apparently because it causes the kidneys to lose calcium in the urine. If you were to check urine samples from people following meaty diets—especially high-protein Atkins-style diets—you would find that they lose calcium rapidly.[3] Sodium does the same thing, as we'll see below.

Second, animal protein is also linked to gradual loss of kidney function. Harvard researchers studied a group of women who had already lost some kidney function, as many people do, due to high blood pressure, diabetes, urinary infections, or other factors. As the years went by, the researchers found that those women who tended to get their protein from animal products were much more likely to experience continued loss of kidney function.[4] Protein from plants did not have this effect. So if you get your protein from beans, grains, vegetables, and other foods from plant sources, your kidneys will breathe a sigh of relief.

Of course, people who grew up with meaty diets, as I did, are sometimes reluctant to let them go, despite the problems they cause. Whenever someone says to me, "You know, I really love meat, and I'm not sure I could give it up," I remember the words of my friend Baxter Montgomery, MD, a cardiologist in Houston. A patient had asked Dr. Montgomery for some words of encouragement to help her give up unhealthy foods. He said, "Think of it this way. What you're 'giving up' is diabetes. You're giving up high blood pressure. You're giving up the weight that you'd like to be rid of, and all those medicines you've been taking. There are delicious foods waiting for you. And when you're in a healthy body, the new foods you're eating will taste *so* good."

And I would go a step further. Although meat is one food that protests loudly when it is about to be fired, it puts up remarkably little fight once you've replaced it with other foods, especially the delicious ones you'll see in the recipe section of this book. Within a short time, you'll find you don't miss it at all.

Don't take this on faith; you'll soon see for yourself. The idea of the Kickstart is not to make any long-term diet resolutions. The idea is to try out a new and exciting approach to food and see how it goes. A focus on the short term takes the pressure off any menu change.

Let me say a word or two about chicken. In recent years, Americans have grown particularly fond of it, as I mentioned in chapter 1. But it is hardly health food. You already know that fried chicken is loaded with grease, and that grease means calories. What you may not know is that *grilled* chicken presents problems of its own.

When meats are heated at high temperatures, cancer-causing chemicals called *heterocyclic amines* form within the meat tissue. They occur as heat alters amino acids, creatine, and other compounds in animal muscle. The US government and leading cancer authorities list them as carcinogens, and there is no amount that is deemed safe to ingest. They can occur in any grilled meat, but the biggest source is chicken.

Some jurisdictions, including the State of California, require restaurants to warn their customers of the presence of cancer-causing chemicals in the foods they serve. So my research team gathered one hundred samples of grilled chicken salads and sandwiches from restaurants in California. We visited a variety of McDonald's, Burger King, Applebee's, Chick-fil-A, Outback, Chili's, and T.G.I. Friday's restaurants. And we found heterocyclic amines not only in every restaurant, but in *every single grilled chicken sample*. As a result of our action, Burger King now posts a warning about heterocyclic amines in every California store, and by the time you read this the other restaurants are likely to have followed suit.

Shortly thereafter, KFC released its new grilled chicken, trying to appeal to customers who know that fried chicken is not healthy. So we tested KFC's grilled chicken, too. And once again, we found carcinogenic heterocyclic amines. These cancer-causing chemicals commonly arise when muscle tissue is cooked at high temperatures, such as grilling.

If you were to do an experiment, grilling a hamburger, a chicken breast, and a veggie burger, what do you think would happen? Well, the hamburger is made of muscle tissue, so heterocyclic amines are likely to form. Ditto for the chicken. Chicken is muscle from a bird, so grilling it will produce carcinogens. But what happens if you grill a veggie burger? The answer is, *it gets hot*. Period. It is not muscle tissue, so it is much safer on the grill than any sort of meat.

Dairy Products

It makes sense to skip dairy products, too. If you were to send a cup of milk to a laboratory, you would soon discover that its nutrition is perfect for calves and terrible for humans. First, milk is loaded with fat to help a calf grow rapidly. Most of that fat is "bad" fat—that is, saturated fat.

Cheesemakers take advantage of all that fat. In making their product, they remove the water and concentrate the remaining fat and protein. The result is a cake composed mainly of animal fat (about 70 percent of its calories), with as much cholesterol, ounce for ounce, as a steak.

Of course, health officials are concerned about dairy fat. So dairy manufacturers offer reduced-fat products. Getting rid of the fat is certainly a good idea. But what are you left with? The most abundant nutrient in nonfat milk, believe it or not, is sugar. Lactose sugar makes up the majority of the calories in nonfat milk.

The protein in dairy products is a problem, too. Dairy products are common triggers for arthritis pain, migraines, and other conditions, as we will see on page 198. Because the problem in this case is the *dairy protein*, not the fat, nonfat versions are just as problematic as whole milk.

When you drink milk, it does in your body just what it does in a calf's body, which is something that has caught the attention of cancer researchers. That is, milk causes the amount of *insulin-like growth factor*, or IGF-I, in your bloodstream to rise. As its name implies, IGF-I makes things grow. That's great if you are a calf too small to eat grass. But it's not so good if you are an adult human. In *your* body, rapid growth can mean the growth of cancer cells.

Indeed, men with higher amounts of IGF-I in their blood have higher risk of prostate cancer. Women with more IGF-I have a higher risk of breast cancer. In two Harvard studies, men who had two or more dairy servings per day had a 30 to 60 percent higher prostate cancer risk that did men who generally avoided milk.[5-6] Studies in other locations have found a similar association. The links between milk and other forms of cancer—particularly breast and ovarian cancer—are inconclusive and still under study.

This does not mean you can't splash milk on your breakfast cereal; just make it soy milk, rice milk, almond milk, oat milk, hemp milk, or one of the other plant-based milks that are on the market these days. The variety is endless, and they are far healthier than the animal-derived kind.

Eggs

Eggs are a special case. There is more cholesterol in a single egg than in an entire eight-ounce steak. There is also a surprising load of "bad" (saturated) fat along with it. What are they doing in that egg, you might ask? The answer, of course, is that they are building a chicken.

A developing chick cannot call out for room service. Everything that is going to turn into feathers, bones, claws, a beak, an intestinal tract, and all the internal organs has to be in the egg when it is laid. Before the egg hatches, these ingredients rearrange from an amorphous mass into a complete bird body. Because cholesterol is used to build animal cell membranes, the mother hen packs an enormous amount of it into every egg she lays.

What are the numbers?

If you cracked two eggs into your skillet, you've just laid nine grams of fat. About one-third of that fat is in the "bad" (saturated) form.

And to understand the cholesterol numbers, let me give you a comparison. A Burger King Whopper has 75 milligrams of cholesterol. A McDonald's Quarter Pounder with Cheese has 90 milligrams. A *Double* Quarter Pounder with Cheese has 155 milligrams. But one large egg has 212 milligrams of cholesterol. And if you had two eggs for breakfast—well, you get the idea. Eggs are designed to build chickens, and that's it.

What about protein? Egg white is essentially solid animal protein. That is not an advantage; that is part of the problem. As I mentioned above, animal protein—including that from eggs—is hard on the kidneys and encourages calcium loss. Instead of building you up, it is gradually tearing you down. You are much better off getting protein from plant sources.

So it pays to think of bird's eggs as a wonder of nature, but not as food. When you skip animal-derived products, you skip fat, cholesterol, unnecessary calories, and a lot of health problems.

Oily Foods

Skipping animal fat is a good idea. But we want to be careful about vegetable fats, too. As you have learned, fats and oils are packed with calories. Gram for gram, they have more than twice the calories, compared with carbohydrate or protein (nine for fat, only four for carbohydrate or protein, as you know by now). Although vegetable oils are healthier than animal fats—they are much lower in saturated ("bad") fat and do not contain cholesterol—they still pack a load of calories that can get you in trouble. So it pays to learn some nonfat cooking techniques, and it turns out to be remarkably easy. In the next chapter, I'll show you how.

High-GI Foods

If you have frequent cravings, if your energy seems to come and go, or if you have diabetes or high triglycerides, there is one more group of foods to be careful with. Foods that cause a precipitous rise in blood sugar can aggravate all these problems.

Happily, there are only a few that you'll want to be concerned about. As we saw in chapter 2, the main offenders are sugar, white and wheat breads, white potatoes, and some cold cereals. We also saw that there are good replacements for each of these products.

So that's it. You'll want to emphasize whole grains, vegetables, fruits, and legumes, and all the wonderful foods made from them, and to skip animal products, oily foods, and high-glycemic-index foods. And as a quick peek at the recipe section will show, there is a huge array of delicious foods waiting for you.

Frequently Asked Questions

Let me tackle a few questions that come up very commonly.

Q: Can I drink alcohol during the Kickstart?

A: Alcohol is not restricted in the Kickstart program. In our research studies, we generally limit alcohol to two drinks per day for men and one per day for women. But there are, of course, other considerations about alcohol, particularly for women: Women who drink daily—even one glass of wine or other alcohol—have a higher risk of breast cancer, compared with women who do not drink. So if you drink, it pays to keep it modest and intermittent.

Q: How about caffeine?

A: We have not restricted coffee or other caffeinated beverages, either. This does not mean they are good for you. You may well sleep better without them, and many people find that they have better overall energy without caffeine.

Q: Is it okay to have a little meat or cheese every now and then?

A: Give yourself a complete break. That way, you'll be able to see what a really perfect diet can do for you. Also, by not teasing yourself with occasional bits of unhealthful products, you'll give your taste buds a chance to forget about them.

Q: I have a sweet tooth. Are there any treats I can have other than fruit?

A: If the usual fruits like blueberries, apples, bananas, and oranges are not doing it for you, try varieties that are a bit more special, like mangoes, papayas, bing cherries, or lychees. Or cut up chunks of cantaloupe and melon, drizzle them with lemon, and add a leaf or two of mint. Or dip strawberries in melted dark chocolate or cocoa powder. Make fresh juices. Try frozen grapes.

Or try these:

- Crispbread, water biscuits, or other low-fat crackers with jam.
- Cereal with soy milk and raisins.
- Chocolate- or vanilla-flavored nondairy milk (soy, almond, or rice milk, and the like).
- You'll find delicious desserts that are surprisingly low in fat in the recipe section.

Q: Can I have store-bought snacks like crackers, pretzels, and so on?

A: Yes. Just check the labels to be sure there are no animal products and that they are low in oil—no more than about two or three grams of fat per serving.

Q: If I do need to use oil, which one do you recommend?

A: Our goal is not to choose a different kind of oil, but to keep all oils to a minimum. There are, of course, traces of natural oils even in foods that you would not think had any at all. Vegetables, fruits, and beans, for example, all contain tiny amounts of natural oils. It's the added oils that get us into trouble with extra calories. And if you look at the recipe section, you'll see abundant techniques for cooking without oil.

Complete Nutrition

When people set aside meat, dairy products, eggs, and greasy foods, their nutrition improves dramatically.[7-8] That's important to emphasize, because some people imagine that a plant-based diet might lack the nutrition they need. The fact is, it's just the opposite.

Partly that's because of what you're not getting: animal fat and cholesterol. But it's more than that. When you replace meat with beans, vegetables, or other healthful foods, you're getting fiber to keep you slim and lower your cholesterol, antioxidants and vitamins to protect against cancer, and potassium to lower blood pressure. A plant-based diet is nutrient-rich.

In a recent study, we looked at what happens when people throw out animal products and replace them with whole grains, legumes, vegetables, and fruits. The answer is that they don't just get *less* fat and cholesterol. They also get *more* fiber, beta-carotene, vitamins C and K, folate, magnesium, and potassium.[8]

In order to measure the overall healthfulness of a diet, Harvard researchers developed the Alternate Healthy Eating Index, which rates intake of healthful and unhealthful foods. When people cut calories or count carbs, their scores don't get better at all. But when you switch to a low-fat, plant-based diet, your score improves dramatically. In other words, you are not only throwing unhealthful foods off the menu, you're bringing in the nutrients your body needs.[8]

Even so, you may be wondering if you will get adequate protein, calcium, or other nutrients. So let's walk through the common nutritional issues and see how easy it is to be sure you're getting everything you need.

Protein. Think of protein as the girders and beams that build your body. You need a certain amount of protein in your diet to repair daily wear and tear. Your body also uses it to build tiny structures: enzymes that help you digest food, for example, and antibodies that protect you from infections. The important thing to know is that a plant-based diet easily gives you all the amino acids your body needs, as I mentioned above.

Twenty years ago, when I was writing my first nutrition book, I interviewed Dr. Denis Burkitt, who became famous for identifying and then curing a form of blood cancer, now known as Burkitt's lymphoma, and then went on to establish the value of fiber in the diet, which made him a well-recognized pioneer in the world of nutrition. Burkitt argued strongly for returning whole grains, beans, vegetables, and fruits to our diets.

I asked Dr. Burkitt about protein. I knew that getting protein was not a problem, but I wanted to get his comment for my book. The more I pressed him for his thoughts about protein, the more impatient he got. He finally said, "Neal! Forget protein!" As he pointed out, if you have any normal variety of grains, legumes, vegetables, and fruits, you'll easily get all the protein you need. If you are keen on boosting your protein intake for whatever reason, you'll find plenty of it in beans and bean products, such as tofu, tempeh, soy milk, and vegan deli slices.

Fat. As you know by now, most people's meals deliver much more fat than they need. It's dripping out of burgers, oozing out of chicken salads and cheese pizza, and hidden in cupcakes and lattes. So while we are now embarking on a search-and-destroy mission to eliminate unnecessary fat from our diets, we need to remember that the body does need *some* fat. In fact, there are two kinds of fats that are critical for health. Their names are *alpha-linolenic acid* and *linoleic acid*. They are very different from the *saturated* fat that is common in animal products and that increases cholesterol levels.

Traces of alpha-linolenic acid are found in vegetables, fruits, and beans. They can supply the fat you need, even if you add no oils at all to the foods you eat. Sometimes people aim to increase their linolenic acid intake with walnuts, soy products, or flaxseeds. It is also found in flax oil, linseed oil, canola oil, and walnut oil.

Linoleic acid is widely available in foods, and there is no need to go looking for it.

Calcium. The most healthful sources of calcium are green leafy vegetables and legumes, or "beans and greens" for short. Broccoli, Brussels sprouts, kale, collards, and many other greens are loaded with calcium, and their absorption fraction—the percentage that your body can use—is actually higher than that of milk. One notable exception: Spinach is loaded with calcium, too, but spinach is a selfish vegetable; its absorption fraction is very poor.

There is also plenty of calcium in beans, as well as in fortified juices and soy milk.

Many people tend to think of milk as a source of calcium, and it certainly has been aggressively marketed in that way. But there are a couple of problems with relying on milk for calcium.

First, milk-drinking children do not have stronger bones than children who get their calcium from other foods.[9] And older women who drink milk have no protection at all against bone breaks. The Nurses' Health Study, conducted by Harvard University, which followed 72,337 women over an eighteen-year period, found that women who drank the most milk had just as many hip fractures as women who drank little or no milk.[10] The reason could be that only about one-third of milk's calcium is absorbed; the remaining calcium remains unabsorbed and passes out with the wastes. In addition, the animal protein and sodium in milk tend to increase the loss of calcium through the kidneys.

Second, milk tends to skew nutrition in the wrong direction. If you get your calcium from milk, you miss the beta-carotene, iron, and fiber that vegetables would bring you. And you would get fat, cholesterol, and animal protein, none of which the body needs.

One last point about calcium. Just as important as getting adequate calcium is *keeping* the calcium you have. It turns out that your body eliminates calcium minute by minute through the kidneys. Calcium losses are accelerated by animal protein and by sodium. So avoiding animal protein and keeping sodium low will help your bones. Exercise will, too, both in children whose bones are developing and in adults who hope to keep their bones intact.

Iron. Your blood cells use iron to build hemoglobin, which gives them their bright red color. Hemoglobin carries oxygen from your lungs to your body tissues. So where do you get iron? The most healthful sources are the same "beans and greens" that bring you calcium. Some people think of red meat as a source of iron, of course. But there is real value in getting iron from plants. Here's why:

Plants carry iron in a special form, called *non-heme* iron, which is more absorbable when your body is low in iron and less absorbable when your body has plenty of iron already. That allows your body to regulate how much iron it takes in. Meats carry iron in a different form, called *heme* iron, which tends to be highly absorbed whether you need it or not. That is not good, because iron can be harmful, if you get too much of it.

In your body, iron encourages the production of free radicals. High iron levels are also linked to heart disease, cancer, Alzheimer's disease, and aging.

So plant sources of iron are preferable. Absorption is increased when vitamin-C-rich foods (fruits and vegetables) are consumed at the same meal. Dairy products tend to interfere with iron absorption.

Zinc is involved in wound healing, immunity, and other biological functions. Hopefully, you are not lying awake at night worrying about where zinc comes from. But if so, rest easy: You'll find it in legumes, nuts, and fortified cereals (such as Grape-Nuts and bran flakes).

Vitamin B$_{12}$ is essential for healthy nerves and healthy blood cells. Deficiencies are uncommon. They are usually due to poor absorption and take years to develop. But you definitely don't want to be deficient, because the first signs can be irreversible nerve symptoms. It's really easy to avoid. Here's what you need to know:

Vitamin B$_{12}$ is not made by plants or animals. It is made by bacteria. Presumably, before the advent of modern hygiene, there were traces of bacteria in the soil and on vegetables and fruits that provided traces of vitamin B$_{12}$. Those days are long gone, of course. Animals have bacteria in their digestive tracts that produce vitamin B$_{12}$, and traces of it end up in meat, dairy products, and eggs. But there are two problems with animal sources. First, they also contain cholesterol, fat, and animal proteins. Second, their absorption is not always sufficient, which is why the US government recommends that everyone over age fifty take a B$_{12}$ supplement.

The easiest and safest thing to do is to take a supplement, such as any common daily multiple vitamin. You can also get B_{12} from fortified foods (such as fortified breakfast cereals and fortified soy milk). The amount you need is extremely small—just 2.4 micrograms per day for an adult (slightly more if you are pregnant or breast-feeding). Taking more than the required amount carries no risks.

Don't neglect this, and don't assume that the bits of garden dirt left on your vegetables contain B_{12}. They don't.

Vitamin D helps your body absorb calcium from the foods you eat, and also helps protect you against some forms of cancer, as I mentioned above.

Normally, vitamin D is made when sunlight touches your skin. Getting fifteen to twenty minutes of direct sunlight on your face and arms each day will do the job. But if you do not get regular sun exposure or live at a latitude where sun exposure is not sufficient, you'll want to take a supplement. The US government's recommended intake is 200 IU per day for people up to age fifty, 400 IU per day for those fifty-one through seventy years of age, and 600 IU per day for older people. However, because of vitamin D's possible anticancer effects, some authorities now recommend daily doses as high as 2,000 IU per day. The safety of doses above 2,000 IU per day is not clear.

The Kickstart program gives you a chance to be on as perfect a diet as is humanly possible. And that means focusing on what's in, avoiding what's out, and letting your body do the rest. In the next section, we'll put these guidelines to work.

Part II

THE THREE-WEEK PROGRAM

CHAPTER 6

On Your Marks, Get Set . . .

You are about to begin the most powerful and most life-changing three weeks ever. Most people never experience even a single day eating the foods their bodies were designed for. But now, you'll have a chance to really put foods to work and learn what they can do for you.

If old habits have sabotaged your progress, you'll be able to set them aside, and you'll see the results on the scale and in how you feel. The confidence you will gain will change your life. Here's how to start:

1. On a calendar, mark out a few days to get ready. During that time, you'll be trying out some new foods, and I'll share with you a few simple tricks that will make everything easy. That's what this chapter is all about.
2. Then, after your "get ready" days, mark "Kickstart day 1" on the date you're planning to begin the Kickstart itself.

Yes, really do it, so you treat your Kickstart experience like the important appointment with your destiny that it is. Pick a time when you're not traveling extensively or struggling with some major deadline. You want to be able to focus on *you*. That's what the following chapters are for—they will guide you day by day for 21 days.

3. On your calendar, count out 21 days, so you have a starting and ending date for the program.

4. Now walk through the seven steps in this chapter. They will give you the basics. There will be more to learn during the Kickstart itself, but this is more than enough to get you started.

This chapter will get you ready for the Kickstart. No, we're not diving in yet—this is not the time to change your diet. That's what we'll do shortly. For now, we're just putting a toe in the water. We're exploring new foods to see which ones work best for us.

Here are the seven steps that will get you set for the Kickstart:

Step 1. Food Selection: What's Your Pleasure?
Step 2. Let's Go Shopping!
Step 3. Testing Your Options
Step 4. Adapting Your Own Favorite Recipes
Step 5. Eating Well at Restaurants
Step 6. Finalizing Your Menu and Stocking Up
Step 7. Freeing Yourself from Temptations

We'll go through the steps one by one. The idea is to keep our healthy guidelines in mind as you see which foods work best for you, whether you eat at home, at restaurants, or wherever you may be. Take several days to do this. Once you know what you like, it's easy to jump into a new way of eating.

Quick Review of Our Kickstart Guidelines

Our goal now is to look for foods that:

1. Omit animal products. By steering clear of chicken, fish, dairy products, and all other animal products, you will be free of dense calories, animal fat, and cholesterol. You'll also leave plenty of room for more nutritious foods.
2. Keep vegetable oils to a minimum. By avoiding not just animal fats but also most oils, you'll avoid the real high-calorie foods. So be on the lookout for oils used in frying or baking, as well as nuts, seeds, olives, avocados, and full-fat soy products. You'll want to keep them to a minimum.

Step 1. Selecting Your Foods: What's Your Pleasure?

Take a piece of paper and jot down headings for breakfasts, lunches, dinners, and snacks. Then, under each heading, make a list of foods that fit the guidelines and that you would find appealing. You can include foods you already know and love, as well as new ones that you would like to try over the coming week. The goal is to come up with a list of foods that really will work for you when the Kickstart begins.

If you already know many foods that fit the bill, then all you need to do is to jot them down. If you need to explore a bit to find foods that will work for you, now's the time to do that. In the chapters that follow, you'll find a full set of menus and recipes that will give you plenty of ideas. Page through the appetizers, soups, main dishes, sides, and desserts. See what calls to you.

Later on, I'll also show you how to adapt your own favorite recipes. And if you don't cook—if you tend to favor convenience foods or to eat at restaurants—there are plenty of good choices, too. If you're eating at restaurants or fast-food places, you'll want to go through the same thought process: Which foods fit the guidelines and are appealing to you? You'll find more tips on dining out in step 5.

Your list is entirely up to you. It can be as simple and short as you like, as conservative or adventurous as you prefer. Just make sure the foods you pick fit the guidelines (no animal products, keep oils to a minimum) and that they really are foods you would like to eat during your 21 days in the Kickstart program.

Sample Food List

List foods you would like to try as you get ready for the Kickstart. Keep it manageable—not too short and not too long—including foods you really would like to test out.

Breakfasts
Breakfast Burrito
Oatmeal with cinnamon and raisins
Blueberry Pancakes
Veggie bacon, veggie sausage
Bran cereal with soy milk
Potato and Spinach Breakfast Scramble
Toast with jam

Lunches
Minestrone, vegetable, lentil, tomato, or split-pea soup
Chickpea-tomato salad, cucumber salad
Quick Black Bean Chili
Sandwich with vegan bologna or vegan ham
Hummus and Sun-Dried Tomato Wrap

Portobello Fajitas
Steamed vegetables with tofu
Brown rice bowl

Dinners
Rustic Tomato Soup
Green salad, sliced tomatoes
Veggie-and-mushroom pizza
Linguine with Seared Oyster Mushrooms
Portobello Fajitas
Steamed vegetables (say, broccoli, spinach, cauliflower)
Gnocchi with basil and sun-dried tomatoes
Crispy Sage Mashed Sweet Potatoes
Spanish rice
Mango slices, fresh strawberries

Snacks
Banana, apple
Cantaloupe chunks
Mali Chips
Sweet Potato Fries

Let's talk about some simple ideas. You'll find many more in the recipe section.

Breakfast Ideas

Believe it or not, people who eat breakfast are thinner than people who don't. Probably that is because they are less hungry later on, and less likely to binge on less-than-healthy foods.

Browse through the breakfast recipes in the back of this book and see which ones call to you. And here are some very simple and healthful ways to start your day:

Veggie Sausage or Bacon. If you normally eat sausage or bacon, the vegetarian versions of these foods will let you skip the fat and cholesterol while giving you plenty of healthful plant-derived protein, which is easier on your kidneys than animal protein. They are not identical to the meat varieties, but, over time, you'll come to prefer them. Try a few different brands and see which ones you like best. Read the package labels; some contain egg white, which you'll want to avoid.

Hot Cereals. Would you like a piping-hot bowl of oatmeal or perhaps cream of wheat? If so, what would you like to top it with— cinnamon, raisins, apple slices, blueberries, raspberries, or perhaps something else?

If you've never cooked oatmeal, don't be afraid of the "old-fashioned" variety. The truth is, it cooks in just a few minutes, almost as quickly as instant oatmeal. Just mix one part oatmeal with two parts water, bring it to a boil, then simmer for a few minutes. If you like it crunchier and less creamy, boil the water before stirring in the oatmeal.

Cold Cereals can be healthful choices, especially simple varieties, such as bran cereal. Skip the ones that are sugared up for children's tastes (especially if they have a toy inside!).

And top it with a nondairy milk. Soy milk is available at almost any grocery, of course, and health food stores stock endless other varieties, including rice milk, almond milk, oat milk, and hemp milk, in vanilla or chocolate, regular or low-fat, fortified or unfortified, et cetera. Try a few, and see which ones you like. And here's an odd but interesting idea: Some people like to eat their cereal with orange juice instead of milk!

Scrambled Tofu. Many people are getting away from eggs because of concerns about their cholesterol and fat. Happily, tofu is almost identical to egg white in that it has little taste on its own, but picks up flavors as it cooks. Try our Breakfast Scramble recipes, and have fun with the many varieties, such as a delicious eggless Huevos Rancheros. You'll also find boxed tofu-scrambler mixes at most grocery stores, usually shelved near rice or in the health food aisle. Nothing could be simpler: Just mix and sauté.

Pancakes and Waffles. As you will see in the recipe section, these breakfast favorites can be healthy and delicious. Try them, and you'll see what I mean.

Fresh Fruit. For health, you can't beat cantaloupe and other melons, berries, bananas, or other fresh fruit. If you find that you never seem to get around to eating the cantaloupes or melons you buy, here's a trick: When you bring them home from the store, cut them up into bite-size pieces and put them in a bowl in the refrigerator. You'll find they quickly disappear.

Breakfast Burritos. You'll find a great Breakfast Burrito recipe in the back of this book. And if you're looking for a super-quick breakfast, you can always pick up some frozen burritos. A few minutes in the microwave, and you have a nourishing breakfast. Many stores sell the Amy's brand, or you can make your own and keep them in the freezer.

Okay, you have some breakfast possibilities. Take a moment to think about what you would really like to have, and jot those ideas down. And now, let's see what you'd like for lunch and dinner.

Lunch and Dinner Ideas

You'll find an abundance of great lunch and dinner ideas in the recipe section. Here are a few to get you started:

Soups. What's better than a big bowl of hearty, hot soup? How about Rustic Tomato Soup, Sicilian Lentil and Escarole Soup, or Tuscan Harvest Soup (Ribollita)? All are simple, quick, and delicious.

An easy way to make your own soup is to start with a soup base, such as Manischewitz brand dried soup mix, and then add whatever frozen or fresh vegetables call to you. Be sure to make extra so you have some for the next day. You can also pack soup in a thermos for work or travel.

Of course, grocery stores carry lentil, split-pea, minestrone, barley-mushroom, and vegetarian vegetable soups, among other healthful choices. They are perfectly fine. You will find them in cans, and also frozen (for example, Tabatchnick brand). Low-sodium varieties are preferable and are available, especially at health food stores. For a quick meal in a pinch, it pays to keep instant soups on hand. You just open the cup and add hot water.

If you add extra vegetables, a soup becomes a stew, which is a meal in itself.

Salads can be a simple plate of greens or can be much more elaborate. Iceberg lettuce is okay, but you might also like to try romaine, arugula, radicchio, or fresh spinach. Tomatoes, cucumbers, green beans, and wax beans add flavor and crunch, and chickpeas or kidney beans add heartiness (along with protein, calcium, and iron). And top with steamed carrots, rotini, orange slices, or anything else you fancy.

You'll find wonderful salads in the recipe section: How about our Artichoke Heart and Tomato Salad or Quinoa and Red Bean

Salad? Top them with Roasted Red Pepper Vinaigrette, Creamy Chipotle Dressing, or maybe one of the many commercial brands.

All grocery stores stock low-fat, vegan dressings, which help you sidestep the fat and calories of regular dressings. And while you're there, you may wish to pick up a jar or two of three-bean salad to keep on your shelf or in your drawer at work. It's handy when you're pressed for time.

Sandwiches. Starting with a whole-grain bread, add some mustard or vegan mayonnaise (try the Vegenaise and Nayonaise brands), then add your favorite filling. How about these:

- **Meatless deli slices.** Larger groceries and all health food stores carry a variety of substitutes for bologna, ham, turkey, and the like. They have lots of taste, with no animal fat or cholesterol, and they pack easily for work, school, or travel.
- **Veggie burgers.** A veggie burger is not the pinnacle of culinary art. But it beats the nutritional socks off the meaty variety. You can make them yourself (try our Black Bean Chipotle Burger, Perfect Portobello Burger, or any of the other wonderful sandwiches in the recipe section) or pick them up at the store. Read the labels; some brands contain cheese or egg. Veggie hot dogs are great, too. Kids love them.
- **Hummus.** This traditional Middle Eastern breakfast food has become a popular sandwich filling. Made from chickpeas, it is a bit like peanut butter. If you make it yourself, you can keep the fat content very low (commercial brands tend to be a bit on the oily side). See the recipe section. Serve between slices of bread or in a pita, and add lettuce, tomato, cucumber, or whatever else your tastes call for.
- **CLT.** This is like a BLT, but its crunch comes from cucumber slices instead of bacon. It takes just a minute or two to

combine cucumbers, lettuce, and tomato with a bit of mustard, and you've got a great lunch that travels well, too. Or try our BST—a Bacon, Sprout, and Tomato Sandwich, made with tempeh "bacon." It's delicious, and so much healthier than bacon from the meat counter.

Pizza. Whether you make it yourself or have it delivered, pizza can be healthy. Let the vegetable toppings—mushrooms, spinach, peppers, onions, sun-dried tomatoes, capers, and tomato sauce—replace the meat and cheese. For an especially quick and fun meal, try our recipe for Pita Pizzas. Kids love them.

For convenience, you'll find frozen pizzas with rice crusts and vegan cheese at many supermarkets and health food stores.

If a cheeseless pizza sounds odd, let me suggest you hop the next flight to Rome. Every pizzeria in Italy includes cheeseless varieties on the menu.

Pasta Dishes. Spaghetti, angelhair, and all the other pasta varieties cook up in minutes. Try our Linguine with Seared Oyster Mushrooms; Fettuccine with Grilled Asparagus, Peas, and Lemon; or any of the others in the recipe section. They are all great.

If you're pressed for time, it's perfectly okay to use a prepared spaghetti sauce. Skip the meaty and cheesy brands. You'll find that many popular brands include varieties free of animal products. You will also want to choose those with fewest fat grams.

For a cheesy flavor with no fat, add some nutritional yeast. It is sold in the supplement or bulk aisle at health food stores. Or you might want to add roasted garlic, tomato chunks, hot peppers, or whatever else your taste calls for.

You might also try vegetable lasagna, using layers of grilled vegetables, with low-fat tofu replacing the ricotta cheese.

With a green salad and some broccoli, spinach, asparagus, or rapini on the side, you've got a wonderful meal.

Bean Dishes. Beans are nutritious—with protein, calcium, iron, fiber, and even a trace of healthy omega-3 fatty acids—and are so economical, too. Here are a few ideas for our friend, the bean:

- Black beans or pinto beans go well with rice and salsa, or rolled into a tortilla to make a burrito or enchilada. Try our Black Bean Burritos with Cilantro Lime Rice.
- Kids love vegetarian baked beans, and you can throw in chunks of veggie hot dogs.
- Try a soft taco, with beans, lettuce, tomato, and salsa.
- Bean chili is delicious, made from scratch (try our Quick Black Bean Chili) or from a box.
- Chickpeas are often used in salads, stews, and soups, and they are delicious on their own. If you like, top with a non-fat vinaigrette.

Convenience Meals. Manufacturers have responded to the demand for healthy, quick meals with a huge array of frozen dinners. You'll find pasta dishes, Asian rice bowls, bean burritos, enchilada dinners, vegan pizza, and many others. Check the labels to be sure they meet our guidelines.

Between the recipe section and the ideas above, you should have plenty of possibilities. On your sheet, jot down the meals that appeal to you. This week, your job is just to try them out.

As you do so, remember that a healthy diet will not change your personality. If you are too impatient to cook now, you are going to still be your same impatient self whatever diet you follow. So think about whether convenience foods might be better choices than more involved recipes. And think about where you'll be: at home, at work, on the road? You'll want to be sure your food choices work for you.

Snacks

Our plan won't be complete without having some snacks on hand. Healthful snacks are part of your disaster-prevention program in case the munchies arrive unexpectedly. It pays to have some simple snacks in your drawer or on your shelf. The idea is not to surround yourself with irresistible snacks that you will dip into whether or not you are hungry. Just be sure to have a few simple, healthy things nearby. Here are some ideas:

Fresh and Dried Fruit. You can't go wrong with apples, bananas, pears, oranges, grapes, mangoes, cantaloupe chunks, or any of the other seductions in the fruit section of your local grocery store. Dried fruit is handy, too. Try apricots, dates, dried plums, raisins, and cranberries.

Popcorn. The grease-covered movie variety isn't such a healthy treat. But if you air-pop it, it's perfectly fine. Have it plain or topped with nutritional yeast, lemon pepper, cinnamon, paprika, curry powder, garlic or onion powder, dried dill, or toasted sesame seeds.

Instant Soups. Stash away a few instant soup cups in your desk drawer. You'll find lentil, minestrone, split pea, and many other varieties.

Three-Bean Salad. Next to your soup cups, you might stock a jar of three-bean salad. Unopened, it keeps for months.

Sandwiches. The hummus and CLT sandwich ideas mentioned above make great snacks. Make a little or a lot.

Other healthy snack ideas include toast with pure-berry jam (skip the butter), cereal with soy or rice milk, baked sweet potatoes, rice cakes, carrot or celery sticks, and low-fat crackers.

Fill in some snack ideas on your sheet. As before, the idea is to fill in items you know you want to include in your routine, or items that you would like to try. Next, we'll go out and pick them up.

If you're looking for more inspiration, you might visit two online sites: PCRM.org and NutritionMD.org. These sites, developed by the Physicians Committee for Responsible Medicine, have hundreds of recipes for you to try.

Step 2. Let's Go Shopping!

Now that you have an idea of what you'd like to eat, let's head to the store. You'll want to get whatever recipe ingredients you'll need and any convenience foods you'd like to try.

While you're shopping, take a look at the surprising array of great food products, both at the regular supermarket and at your nearest health food store. The idea now is to experiment. Try out new flavors and new products, and have fun with it.

Here are some healthful staples and some more adventurous items to look for on your grocery store treasure hunt. A few items are usually limited to health food stores; I'll let you know which ones they are.

One word of caution: Don't go shopping on an empty stomach, unless you want to return home with the jalapeño-flavored soy yogurt and frozen garlic pancakes that seemed like such a good idea at the time.

The Produce Aisle

Vegetables and Fruits. Both are wonderfully healthful, of course. And they are also the original fast food. Pick up plenty to have on hand. While you're there, see what's new. Growing up in North Dakota, I neglected so many varieties of wonderful vegetables and fruits until I moved to Washington, DC. As I've learned, there are some real delights in the produce aisle! So if you are an apples-and-bananas kind of person, you might expand your horizons a bit with clementines, tangerines, grapes, plums, strawberries, kiwis, artichokes, Roma tomatoes, baby carrots, portobello mushrooms, endive, radicchio, and any of various spring salad mixes.

I'd suggest making a special place in your heart—and your grocery basket—for cruciferous vegetables: broccoli, cauliflower, Brussels sprouts, cabbage, kale, and so on. Dark green leafy vegetables are rich in calcium and iron, as well as folate, which reduces cancer risk. They also help protect against age-related vision loss. Pick up a lemon, too, so you can squeeze a bit of flavorful lemon juice on your green veggies.

Have a little fun in the pepper section. Nutritionally, peppers are high in vitamin C. Red peppers are really just ripe green peppers, but that extra growing time means they have double the vitamin C of a green pepper.

By the way, you can make great fajitas by stir-frying sliced green and red peppers in a dry pan with onions and mushrooms, then adding a splash of water to the pan until it evaporates. Season with fajita seasoning, and wrap in a tortilla.

Hot peppers act both as a condiment and as a medicine, in a way. They are rich in *capsaicin*, which is the active ingredient used in painkilling arthritis creams.

Take a look at the organic produce section, which is gradually becoming more generous at most stores. Buying organic is an especially good idea for vegetables and fruits that are often chemically treated on "conventional" farms: peaches, apples, bell peppers, celery, nectarines, strawberries, cherries, kale, lettuce, grapes, carrots, and pears. The difference between organic and conventional isn't as great for hardier crops: onions, avocados, sweet corn, pineapples, mangoes, asparagus, sweet peas, kiwi, cabbage, eggplant, papaya, watermelon, broccoli, tomatoes, and sweet potatoes.

Tofu. Made from soybeans, this ancient Asian food is rich in protein and extremely versatile in the kitchen. You can scramble it up for breakfast, just like eggs. You can add it to soups and stir-fries, or chop it to make an eggless egg salad. It replaces cheese in lasagna, and it will probably do your taxes, if you ask it politely. It is often shelved in the produce aisle. Take a look in appendix 1 (Ingredients That May Be New to You) for details about how to select the right variety.

Tempeh. Next to the tofu (in health food stores and some larger grocery stores), you might find tempeh, which is made from fermented soybeans and various grains. It is similar to tofu in that it has little flavor on its own. It is often marinated and used like meat in stir-fries and many other dishes. It is easy to use, as you will see in the recipe section.

Meat Substitutes. Larger grocery stores and health food stores carry deli slices that taste like ham, bologna, turkey, salami, and more, but are actually made of soy or wheat protein. They are handy when you're in a time crunch.

You'll also find many meatless varieties of burgers, hot dogs, sausage, and bacon, as I've mentioned earlier. Read the labels to be sure they aren't made with eggs or dairy products.

TVP (Textured Vegetable Protein) is made from defatted soybeans. It has a texture and flavor very much like ground beef, without the fat and cholesterol. You will find it in health food stores and online. You'll find more details in appendix 1.

Seitan (pronounced *SAY-tan*) is a high-protein food made from wheat. It has such a meaty texture, you may find yourself asking your server if your veggie fajita wasn't actually made with meat. It works great in stews, stir-fries, sandwiches, wraps, casseroles, and many other applications. You'll find it at health food stores.

The Cereal Aisle

The Many Faces of Oatmeal. Old-fashioned oatmeal is made with oats that are flattened, or rolled. Quick and instant varieties are flattened, then cut or pulverized to make them quicker to cook. But even old-fashioned is pretty quick, as we saw earlier. I highly recommend keeping it on hand. You'll also find steel-cut oats, which are cut, not flattened, so they take a bit longer to cook. Some stores carry Scottish and Irish oats, too.

However you buy them, oats are nutritious. While you're thinking of it, pick up some raisins, cinnamon, blueberries, or whatever else you'd like as a topping.

Rice Cereal. Health food stores carry a variety of wonderful hot cereals. Rice cereal is creamy and delicious. You'll also find barley, wheat, and many others.

Bran Cereal. With or without raisins, bran cereal is tasty and healthful. Other cold cereals are okay, but favor those with the fewest ingredients. Top them with soy milk, rice milk, or any other nondairy milk.

The "Nondairy" Aisle

What has happened to the dairy case? It now holds all manner of delights that never came from a cow: soy milk, rice milk, oat milk, almond milk, hemp milk—you name it. And you'll find a similar selection of nondairy yogurts.

The International Aisle

Check out all the amazing new products. There are soups, rice dishes, boxed dinners, and more condiments than you can shake a celery stick at.

The Canned Food Aisle

Canned Beans. You know about beans already; the thing to notice now is the variety: navy beans, black beans, pinto beans, kidney beans, limas, and on and on. Vegetarian baked beans omit the pork you didn't want anyway.

Be sure to hop over to the dry bean aisle, too, where there is an even grander array of beans, lentils, and split peas, and they sell for pennies. If you thought it might be challenging to soak and cook dried beans, the process requires virtually no supervision.

Chickpeas. The chickpea is a bean, of course, but it deserves special praise for its versatility. It is at home in salads, soups, and casseroles, and you could even crack open a can of chickpeas for breakfast. Chickpeas play the starring role in hummus, the Middle Eastern spread used for sandwiches and dips.

Canned Soups are handy. Try lentil, split pea, minestrone, vegetarian vegetable, and others. Read the labels; some brands include chicken stock or dairy products. Low-sodium varieties are available.

Vegetable Broth makes a great base for soups, stews, and casseroles.

The Frozen Food Aisle

Start with the basics. Frozen vegetables are very handy. They are similar to fresh in nutritional value, and they last for much longer than fresh vegetables, if you are unsure that you will be using them soon. Pick up some broccoli, spinach, Brussels sprouts, carrots, cauliflower, squash, and anything else you find. And see the condiments section on the next page for a few tips on making them absolutely delectable.

Look for frozen fruits and berries to add to cereals, desserts, and sauces.

Don't stop there, though. At well-stocked groceries and health food stores, take a look at the selection of frozen dinners, vegan pizzas, veggie burgers, burritos, and on and on. You will find many handy products here. For any product that is new to you, be sure to check the ingredient label.

Condiments

Salad Dressings and Special Vinegars. Check the great and ever-growing selection of nonfat dressings. And next to the salad dressings, you'll find balsamic vinegar, apple cider vinegar, and seasoned rice vinegar. They are delicious dribbled on salads or green vegetables.

Soy Sauce and Tamari. Soy sauce is made from soy and wheat. You'll also find tamari, which is made without grains; some people prefer it. Look for low-sodium varieties. Health food stores stock Bragg Liquid Aminos, which is like an especially savory soy sauce. It is delicious on vegetables.

Nondairy Mayonnaise. Health food stores stock Vegenaise and Nayonaise, which have all the taste of mayo, with none of the cholesterol or animal fat.

Dijon Mustard. A delicious, traditional spread that goes great on sandwiches, and is naturally free of fat and cholesterol.

Salsa. Of course! What else would you want on black beans?

Nutritional Yeast. This wonderful topping is hiding at health food stores in the supplement aisle—the aisle where vitamins are sold. It adds a cheesy taste to spaghetti sauces, soups, and casseroles.

Ask for nutritional yeast specifically, not brewer's yeast or baker's yeast. It comes in flakes and powder, and you'll find the flakes more versatile.

Grains and Pasta

Brown Rice keeps the outer coating that is removed to produce white rice. That's where the fiber is. When we get into the Kickstart program, I'll share with you a special way to cook it that preserves its flavor.

Barley is delicious and loaded with cholesterol-lowering soluble fiber. You can add it to soups or mix it with rice, cooking them together.

Pasta. Choose spaghetti, macaroni, angelhair, linguine, and any other variety that omits eggs. Whole-grain pastas are theoretically better—they retain their natural fiber—but even regular pasta is fine. As we saw in chapter 2, it has a surprisingly low glycemic index. That is, it has little effect on blood sugar.

Spaghetti Sauce. Next to the pasta, you'll want to pick up a jar of sauce for when you want a super-quick dinner. You'll find many tomato-based spaghetti sauces with mushrooms, basil, garlic, green peppers, and other ingredients. Check the labels to be sure there is no cheese or meat. It also pays to keep oil to a minimum.

Bakery Aisle

Rye and pumpernickel breads are usually free of animal ingredients. They have an added advantage of a low glycemic index compared with wheat breads. You'll also find hearty Ezekiel bread, pita bread, and many other tasty varieties.

The Bulk Section

If your grocer has a bulk section, look for brown rice, couscous, quinoa, bulgur, cracked wheat, barley, oats, wheat berries, and pasta of all kinds.

How to Read Food Labels

Packaged food products list nutrition information that helps you choose the most healthful products. Ingredients are listed in order, starting with those found in the largest amounts, by weight.

Be on the lookout for eggs, milk, sugar, oils, or whatever else you want to avoid eating. Casein, caseinate, lactalbumin, and whey are all derived from cow's milk. Albumin comes from eggs. Corn syrup, fruit juice concentrate, maltose, dextrose, sucrose, brown sugar, maple syrup, and evaporated cane juice are not forbidden in this program. But they are all simply various forms of sugar.

Next, look at the Nutrition Facts label. It lists calories, fat, cholesterol, and other useful information. Here are the key points to look for:

- **Serving size.** This reflects the amount that the manufacturer believes an average person eats at one sitting. See how this fits with how you use the product. If you normally eat twice the listed serving size, for example, you will be getting double the amount of each nutrient.
- **Total fat.** For a low-fat menu, aim for a limit of about two to three grams per serving, which should add up to no more than about twenty to thirty grams of fat per day.
- **Saturated fat.** This number should be zero, or close to it.
- **Cholesterol.** If there is any cholesterol in the product, you can assume it contains an animal-derived ingredient.

- **Sodium.** In the course of a day, your sodium intake should be roughly two thousand milligrams or less, and some authorities now suggest a limit of about 1500 milligrams.

Nutrition Facts	
Serving Size 1/2 cup (130g)	
Servings Per Container 3	
Amount Per Serving	
Calories 90	Calories from Fat 0
	% Daily Value*
Total Fat 0g	0%
Saturated Fat 0g	0%
Cholesterol 0mg	0%
Sodium 520mg	22%
Total Carbohydrate 17 g	6%
Dietary Fiber 5g	19%
Sugars 7g	
Protein 6g	
Vitamin A 4% • Vitamin C 10%	
Calcium 6% • Iron 10%	
*Percent Daily Values are based on a 2,000 calorie diet.	

You will not need to worry about total carbohydrate or protein listings. So long as your menu is made up of a variety of whole grains, legumes, vegetables, and fruits, these values will take care of themselves. By the way, even foods with no added sugar may list some "sugar." Fruits, for example, contain natural sugars.

Here is a label from a can of Heinz Beans with Tomato Sauce. The ingredients are: navy beans, tomatoes, water, sugar, glucose syrup, salt, modified cornstarch, distilled vinegar, and spices.

As you can tell, it is vegan (there are no animal products in the ingredient list and no cholesterol) and very low in fat. It does have some added sugar and salt, both of which are unnecessary but would not rule it out from the Kickstart program.

Step 3. Testing Your Options

You've come up with a list of foods that you want to try, and you've got your ingredients. So now is the time to try them out. Give them an audition, and let them do their best to impress you.

Our goal is to see which foods you want to include in your 21-Day Kickstart. Whether they come from recipes, convenience foods, or restaurant meals, you'll want to have choices for breakfast, lunch, dinner, and snacks that really work for you.

Take some time to test each one, and see how it stacks up. Ask yourself:

- How does it taste?
- Is it easy to make?
- Will people I live with like it, too?
- Could I see myself bringing it to work?

You might also try making foods in larger quantities to see how well they keep over time.

You will have some recipes or products that don't turn out to be winners. That's to be expected. In fact, that's our goal right now—to separate the winners from the losers. Just skip the foods that don't work for you and go on to the next.

You do not need to come up with hundreds of winning foods. You only need a handful. Most people have certain favorite foods that they tend to stick with. And now's the time to find yours.

Step 4. Adapting Your Own Favorite Recipes

Don't throw out your favorite family recipes! Often, all that is needed is an adjustment here and there. The idea is to change greasy or animal-derived ingredients into healthier ones, and in some cases this just requires a tweak—for example, using vegetable stock instead of meat stock, or omitting cheese or bacon bits from recipes. If you can't bring yourself to skip those tastes, stores carry "chicken" stock that is all-vegetable as well as soy "bacon" and soy "bacon bits."

Let's take a look at easy ways to replace meat, dairy products, eggs, and oils.

Replacing Meat

As you know by now, burger lovers will find many different veggie versions at regular groceries, and many more at health food stores, as well as some great burger recipes in this book. There are also replacements for hot dogs, sausages, and bacon. Check the labels to be sure there are no animal products. It also pays to keep fat to less than two or three grams per serving.

To replace ground beef in burgers and sauces, try TVP (textured vegetable protein), available at any health food store. Beans work well in stews and soups. To replace deli slices (pepperoni on pizza, ham in sandwiches), veggie deli slices work well.

Replacing Dairy Products

A great many nondairy milks, yogurts, and frozen desserts are now available at most grocery stores. See which ones you prefer.

Cheese has proven more challenging to replace. In most recipes it can simply be omitted. For lasagna, cheese can be replaced with tofu and nutritional yeast.

Replacing Eggs

When eggs are used as a binder in a recipe, sometimes you can just leave them out (in breads or pancakes, for instance). You will also find powdered egg replacer at all health food stores. Or try one of the following to replace each egg in a baking recipe:

- An egg-size piece of mashed silken tofu.
- Half of a banana (mashed).
- Soy flour or cornstarch (one tablespoon) mixed with water (two tablespoons).

When meat, dairy products, or eggs are key ingredients, you might need to make bigger substitutions. Here are some easy examples:

Breakfast

IF YOU NORMALLY HAVE:	TRY THIS INSTEAD:
Cereal with milk	Cereal with soy milk or other nondairy milk, or Oatmeal with cinnamon and raisins
Scrambled eggs	Scrambled tofu
Bacon or sausage	Veggie bacon or veggie sausage
Doughnut	Cinnamon raisin toast, or Pumpernickel toast with jam
Bagel with cream cheese	Bagel with jam or hummus
Hash browns	Oven-roasted sweet potatoes
Coffee with creamer	Coffee with nonfat, nondairy creamer
Latte	Soy latte with nonfat soy milk

Lunch or Dinner

IF YOU NORMALLY HAVE:	TRY THIS INSTEAD:
Turkey sandwich with lettuce, tomato, and mayo	Sandwich with hummus or veggie deli slices (including vegan "turkey"), with lettuce and tomato
Yogurt	Soy yogurt
Chicken noodle soup	Vegetable soup or minestrone
Hamburger	Veggie burger
Meat taco	Bean taco or burrito (hold the cheese)
Meat chili	Bean or vegetable chili
Cheese pizza	Veggie pizza (hold the cheese)
Spaghetti with meat sauce	Spaghetti with tomato sauce and chunky vegetables, or pasta primavera
Chicken fajitas	Veggie fajitas
Hot dog	Veggie dog

Minimizing Oil

It is easy to keep oil to a minimum, and your waistline will thank you. Here are some tips to help you:

- If you normally sauté onions, garlic, or mushrooms in oil, you can easily sauté them in a dry pan, as we will see on page 327. If you prefer, you can "sauté" them in water or vegetable broth. As the recipes in this book will show you, you don't need to add oil to have a delicious meal.
- Skip fried foods. Baked potato chips and baked tortilla chips are much better than their fried counterparts. Ditto for french fries. If you bake them, they are fine; unfortunately, restaurant fries have usually just been dredged up from the fryer vat, and you are better off without them. The same is true for onion rings and everything else fried. As they say, a moment on the lips, forever on the hips.
- Skip margarine (and butter, of course). There's no need to smear margarine on toast. Use jam instead. If you're thinking, *But jam has sugar!*—that's true enough. But even in its most concentrated form, sugar has less than half the calories of any fat or oil. And of course, if you buy a good bread, it tastes great straight out of the toaster or warmed in the oven, with nothing on it at all. If potatoes are your favorite margarine target, you will be surprised to find that you come to appreciate them just as well with mustard, pepper, steamed veggies, or even salsa.
- Use nonfat salad dressings. There are many to choose from. Or try seasoned rice vinegar, balsamic vinegar, and apple cider vinegar on salads and vegetables. A squirt of lemon juice works really well, too.
- When preparing vegetables, steaming is a great technique that preserves their flavor and adds no fat. If you aren't in

the habit of preparing vegetables this way, try it and see what you think.

- For packaged products, look for those with no more than two or three fat grams per serving.
- In their natural state, nearly all plant-derived foods are very low in fat. Exceptions include nuts, seeds, avocados, olives, and some soy products. If you're aiming to lose weight, you'll want to minimize these foods.

An average American swallows eighty to one hundred grams of fat each day, or even more. With these simple adjustments, you've cut that number to about twenty. Your body is breathing easier already!

Step 5. Eating Well at Restaurants

There's nothing like letting someone else do the cooking. You can just sit back and enjoy your dinner. And you can indeed eat healthfully—and heartily—while you're out on the town, even at fast-food places. Still, when you're sticking to a healthy diet, you will encounter an occasional challenge.

Several years ago, I was driving through Germany and stopped at a roadside restaurant. The menu was written entirely in German, but I noticed that they served spaghetti and what seemed like various vegetables. Despite the language barrier, I figured I had it made.

When the server came to the table, I pointed to the menu items. The server nodded, and things were working out fine. But then I wanted to ask that the spaghetti not be topped with the usual meat sauce. But I had no idea how to say "meat" in German. So very slowly, I said it in English: "May I have the sauce with no meat, please?" The server had no look of recognition at all. So I said it even slower, carefully enunciating, "May I have no meat, please?"

Still nothing. Recognizing that this was my problem and not his, I was unsure what to do. Finally, I tried French. After all, France is right next door.

"Pas de viande, s'il vous plaît," I ventured. The server still looked quizzical. So I repeated it: *"Pas de viande. Pas—de—viande, s'il—vous—plaît."* I added hand gestures for emphasis.

Suddenly the server's eyes lit up, and he stepped into the kitchen. Not long afterward, my plate arrived. The vegetables looked great. And the spaghetti was piled with more *viande* than I had ever seen. Apparently, I got the emphasis right, but some key words didn't quite make it.

Best Restaurant Choices

Now, in truth, it's pretty easy to dine out nowadays. People the world over are getting familiar with healthy choices.

If you're lucky enough to be in Fort Lauderdale around dinnertime, you're in for a treat. Step into Sublime, the aptly named restaurant that greets you with waterfalls, original Peter Max paintings, and an attentive staff. As you open the menu, you ask the server, "Which of these items can be made without meat and dairy products?" The server politely tells you that *everything* is prepared that way normally. Everything on the menu is completely free of meat, dairy products, or eggs.

Everything? Even the enchiladas? How about the mac 'n' cheese?

You've got it. This is one restaurant where the stunning decor is matched by an equally stunning menu. From cocktails to astounding desserts, every single item happens to be vegan. Sublime's creator, Nanci Alexander, wouldn't have it any other way at her award-winning restaurant.

But wait a minute, you are probably thinking. *I'm not in Fort Lauderdale. I'm staying at a motorway hotel in Newark, and wondering where to go for dinner.* Okay, let me share some tips.

When choosing a restaurant, it pays to think international. Let me offer a few suggestions:

Italian. Every city, no matter how small, has an Italian place eager to fix you pasta e fagioli, spaghetti with tomato sauce, pasta primavera, pesto, gnocchi, and plenty of fresh vegetables.

Chinese restaurants feature an entire menu section of what they call "vegetables," but are really main dishes. Spinach, tofu, broccoli, green beans, and an endless array of other vegetables are served over rice. You'll find vegetable lo mein and other noodle dishes, and an abundance of soups.

Mexican. Most good Mexican restaurants nowadays prepare beans without lard, which means their burritos and enchiladas are much more healthful than in the past. They will also cook up veggie fajitas and rice. And even if it knocks your socks off, salsa is always free of animal ingredients and oil.

American. Steak houses and other American-style restaurants serve plenty of things you won't want—as evidenced by the girth of their clientele. Still, most also take pride in their vegetables—enough to make a delectable vegetable plate (ask the server to be sure the vegetables aren't swimming in butter or oil). Many feature salad bars, pasta, and other healthful choices.

Japanese. You can't go wrong with vegetable sushi, not to mention the edamame, miso soup, and cucumber, seaweed, spinach, and other salads that accompany it.

Thai and Vietnamese. These and other Asian restaurants offer a wide selection of dishes based on noodles, vegetables, tofu, and delicious sauces.

Middle Eastern. You'll find hummus and tabouleh, along with many other tasty choices like falafel, eggplant, and couscous.

Indian. Vegetarian cuisine is, of course, traditional in India, so Indian restaurants serve a wide selection of appetizers, soups, main courses, breads, and desserts. The Achilles' heel of many Indian restaurants is the common use of dairy products and oils. Negotiating with the waiter will help.

Cuban. When I first visited a Cuban restaurant, I asked what they had for vegetarians. "Beer, beans, and salad," was the server's reply. With time, I've come to appreciate their simple black beans, salsa, healthful salads, and plantains.

Ethiopian. Some cities—Washington, DC, among them—abound with Ethiopian restaurants. Because some religious groups in Ethiopia follow vegan diets during many days of the year, Ethiopian restaurants feature delightful dishes based on lentils, split peas, green beans, cabbage, tomatoes, potatoes, and peppers, all served with a soft bread, called injera.

Enjoying the Adventure

Alicia Silverstone is especially keen on Japanese cuisine. "I love sushi, tempura, noodles, and soups," she says, "not to mention vegetable dumplings and all kinds of salads with that delicious ginger dressing." All of these—even sushi—are vegetarian when Alicia is sitting down to eat. Her husband, Christopher, loves Mexican food—bean burritos are his favorite—and they both enjoy Italian cuisine.

At most restaurants, you'll find that avoiding animal products is pretty easy. It may be a bit more challenging to convince chefs to be less exuberant with oil. Ask them to go easy or, better still, ask for items that are steamed, boiled, or roasted.

Fast Foods

What if your lifestyle or taste calls for lots of fast-food drive-thru? Well, we can still make it work handsomely. Here are some ideas:

Taco Bell. Try the bean burrito, hold the cheese, and add lettuce, tomato, hot peppers, and whatever else your heart desires. You'll also find a Seven Layer Burrito (have it without cheese or sour cream) and Mexican rice (without the cheese).

Subway and Quiznos. You'll get a great veggie sub that lets you choose all the ingredients you want, leaving off the meat and cheese. For extra credit, have it toasted. Top with vinegar, spicy mustard, or hot red peppers.

Chipotle. Compose a huge black bean burrito or taco with all the fixings. Some Chipotle restaurants serve "Garden Chicken," which is vegan.

Burger King. The Veggie Whopper serves you all the contents of the signature sandwich, minus the meat. Hold the cheese.

Family-Style Restaurants. Denny's, Bob Evans, and similar restaurants offer side vegetables that, together, make a healthy and hearty meal. You may also find a veggie burger and spaghetti with tomato sauce on the menu.

Pizza Restaurants. Ask for extra tomato sauce and all the veggie toppings: mushrooms, spinach, onions, bell peppers, hot peppers, or whatever your tastes call for. Skip the cheese.

Grocery Stores. My favorite "fast food" is at the grocery store. In the middle of the produce aisle at many stores is a salad bar.

In forty-five seconds, you can pick up three-bean salad, chick-peas, chunky tomatoes, sliced cucumbers, julienned carrots, a handsome selection of baby spinach and other garden greens, and maybe even a cup of soup.

More Dining Tips

Here are a few more strategies to make sure your dining experience is all you want it to be:

If You're Unsure, Do a Little Research. You can always call a restaurant ahead of time to ask about what they might serve you. Most restaurants also post their menus on their websites so you can peruse it ahead of time.

Let Your Mouse Do the Walking. A website called HappyCow.net can help you spot vegetarian restaurants anywhere in the world. Be sure to call the restaurant before you go, though, as restaurants are always changing.

Ask. It is surprising how many restaurants don't mention on their menus that they have all the ingredients for making spaghetti with tomato sauce, veggie burgers, breakfast oatmeal, or other things. Ask, and you may well receive.

Ask in Mandarin. At some Chinese restaurants, there is one menu for Chinese customers and another menu for everyone else. The Chinese menu often includes many delicious traditional vegetables that other customers tend to ignore. Your waiter will be thrilled to tell you about them.

Don't Fall Victim to "Just This Once." It can be tempting to break your resolve for a special occasion. The danger is that the little devil on your shoulder will now make you do so again and again. It's easier to stick to your resolve.

Look for Fat-Free Cooking Methods. Menu items often give clues to their fat content. Generally speaking, you'll do better with items that are baked, broiled, grilled, poached, roasted, steamed, or stir-fried.

Try Vegetable Plates. Years ago, when I was first exploring healthful diets, a vegetable plate really did not seem like a meal. However, as I have come to appreciate the taste and beauty of vegetables, a well-composed vegetable plate has become one of my favorites. Restaurateurs never think to suggest it, but if you ask, they are glad to serve you asparagus, broccoli, carrots, spinach, potatoes, sweet potatoes, asparagus, beets, mushrooms, endive, and whatever other delights they have on hand. Sometimes they will add a pasta salad or three-bean salad.

On the Side. For salad dressings and sauces, these are magic words.

Speaking of Dressings. Balsamic vinegar, red wine vinegar, or even lemon juice squeezed from fresh wedges can top a salad admirably.

Condiments. Mustard, ketchup, and salsa are better than mayo on your veggie burger. On toast, have jam or jelly. Skip the butter or margarine.

Don't Feel Obligated. Many restaurants feel a need to show their love with absurd portion sizes. There is no need to eat it all. By all means feel free to share or to take it home.

Step 6. Finalizing Your Menu and Stocking Up

Okay, now you're the expert. You've had a chance to try out some new recipes and convenience foods, adapt your favorite recipes, and even have nights on the town.

So now let's plan out what you really will have for breakfast, lunch, dinner, and snacks in your Kickstart program. This is exactly the same exercise we did at the beginning, except that we should do it for three days, or even more. And now, of course, you know what you like.

Take a piece of paper, and mark down your favorites. It's okay to repeat items or use leftovers.

Sample Menu

DAY 1

Breakfast	*Dinner*
Blueberry Pancakes	Green salad
Veggie bacon	Linguine with Seared Oyster Mushrooms
Coffee	Steamed broccoli

Lunch	*Snack*
Hummus and Sun-Dried Tomato Wrap	Apple
Baked potato	Sweet Potato Fries
Peaches	

DAY 2

Breakfast	*Dinner*
Oatmeal with cinnamon and raisins	Veggie-mushroom pizza
Veggie sausage	Spinach salad
Coffee	Fresh strawberries

Lunch	*Snack*
Lentil soup	Cantaloupe chunks
Portobello Fajitas	Hummus sandwich
Steamed carrots	

continued

DAY 3	
Breakfast	*Dinner*
Breakfast Burrito	Vegetable fajitas
Coffee	Spanish rice
	Mango slices
Lunch	*Snack*
Vegetable stir-fry	Banana, apple
Brown rice	Mali Chips
Chickpea-tomato salad	

Step 7. Free Yourself from Temptations

Just one last step before we start. It's a good idea to eliminate sources of temptation. After all, if you open your refrigerator door, you want to be greeted by enticing and healthy choices, not by the things you're trying to leave behind.

You can throw them away or give them away. But in any case, you're better off without them.

When it comes to dealing with temptation, let me share some advice from actress and author Marilu Henner. America first fell in love with Marilu on the show *Taxi*, and she has gone on to many more appearances on television and on Broadway. But her real passion is helping people get healthy, and she is a *New York Times* best-selling author of eight books on the subject. She has been teaching classes online at Marilu.com for twelve years and knows how important it is to avoid temptation. She puts it this way:

"Take five minutes today and go through your refrigerator. Instead of forcing yourself to face temptation, remove it. Throw out all the food saboteurs and health robbers you find in there. That means anything that's not plant-based, including lunchmeats, cheese, dairy-based salad dressings, and condiments."

If you live with others, invite them to join you as you begin the Kickstart. When Alicia Silverstone decided to change her diet, her boyfriend (now husband), Christopher, joined her gladly. But if people in your household are feeling tentative about a menu change, Alicia has a tip for you: Rather than announcing a "big change" in the family's dietary routine, she suggests simply adding more plant-based dishes to the family menu. Slowly but surely, you'll win them over. Rice is an especially useful addition. As Alicia puts it, it's a "secret weapon" that helps everyone get healthier and, over time, more open to plant-based meals.

If, for whatever reason, your family members or roommates are just not following your lead, tackle the issue head-on: Politely ask them at least not to tempt you with foods that are not part of the program. Ask for their support. It's good if their foods occupy a different part of the refrigerator and different spots on your shelves. This is not a time to try to show your Herculean resilience in the face of temptation. This is a time to minimize it.

Ready to Start

Okay, before we get started, let's run through a quick checklist:

- Have you found foods that you like that skip animal products and keep oil to a minimum?
- Have you stocked your shelves with the foods you'll need? If not, be sure to do that before you start.
- If you'll be eating at restaurants, do you know where to go and what you'll order?
- Are your shelves and refrigerator free of temptations?

If the answer to each of these questions is yes, then you are right on track. Get ready for the most healthful and eye-opening three weeks of your life. It's time to begin the Kickstart.

CHAPTER 7

Let's Go!

The moment you've been waiting for is here! You're going to Kickstart your weight loss and revolutionize your health. For the next three weeks, we'll put the very best foods to work. We'll go step by step, applying what you've learned and giving you new tricks to make your menu change easy and fun.

Now, I should say that all you really have to do over the next three weeks is to follow the diet recommendations I've already given you, using the menus you've chosen. But just to make sure you stay on track, I'm going to give you a bit of new information and inspiration every day, and I would encourage you to set aside a few minutes to read that day's lesson. It will include a nutrition topic, plus motivators and tips.

For the first week, we'll keep it very basic, mostly covering familiar ground to make sure you are totally on track. Then, in the second and third weeks, we'll take on more adventurous topics. And here are some additional features you can expect to find waiting for you:

- **A Word of Inspiration.** One of the great things about the Kickstart program is that you have many friends coming along with you, and they'll share their insights. You've already heard from Alicia Silverstone in the foreword to this book. She is 100 percent committed to what we're doing now, and she'll stay with us as we go along, sharing tips and experiences. You'll also hear from Bob Harper, Marilu Henner, Rory Freedman, Kathy Freston, and many other celebrities, elite athletes, and nutrition experts. They will keep you informed and inspired.

- **A Doctor's Prescription.** Many doctors and scientists have been studying this approach. They are leaders in medicine, nutrition, and health who have had a profound effect on me, and in the next three weeks they will share their advice with you, too.

- **Quick Kitchen Tips.** Each day, I'll share with you practical advice to make food preparation quicker, easier, and more enjoyable. Many people have shared their tips with me, and I'll pass them along to you.

As we go along, you'll have plenty of menus and recipes to choose from, and extra help if you ever encounter a challenge.

All set? Off we go! Your Kickstart begins now.

Day 1. Jump In!

When you're learning to drive, reading about it will only get you so far. At some point, you need to get behind the wheel. If you're learning to swim, sooner or later you'll need to dive into the pool. And if you want to eat really healthfully, trim away extra weight, and feel the way you've always wanted to feel, there's no substitute for actually giving it a try. Now's the time!

Staying on Track

We will do this 100 percent for the next 21 days. We're not even going to think about setting a foot wrong. This will help you in two ways:

First, you'll be able to really experience what healthy foods can do for you. Your weight loss will begin on day 1—today. At the same time, your energy will start to improve. If your digestion has been out of sorts, it is likely to correct itself almost overnight. Although you won't feel it, your cholesterol will almost certainly fall—and impressively. Ditto for blood pressure. If you have diabetes, it is likely to improve as well. If you have joint pains or migraines, they may well diminish or disappear.

Second, doing it 100 percent allows your tastes to change in a healthy direction. If you find yourself wondering whether your tastes can really change that fast, let me ask you something: Did you ever switch from whole milk to low-fat or skim milk? If so, what was the low-fat milk like at first? For many people, it seems watery; it doesn't even look right. But after a few weeks, what happens? Almost everyone finds that they are totally used to it. Then, after you made the switch, did you ever go back and taste whole milk again? What was that like? For most people, it seems too thick, like cream—almost like paint.

Well, wait a minute. For your entire life, whole milk tasted perfectly fine. But a break of just a couple of weeks is all you need to reset your tastes.

I should mention that skim milk is not an especially healthful choice, either. You would do better with soy milk, rice milk, or even plain water. But this common experience shows how our tastes do indeed change, often very quickly.

The key now is *consistency*. If you were to have a healthy meal on Monday, another one on Thursday, and maybe one more sometime next week, would you get any benefit at all? Would your tastes actually shift? Of course not. In order to change, your body—including your taste buds—needs a vacation from the foods that cause trouble. So you'll want to do this 100 percent. That means having every meal for the next 21 days be a Kickstart meal.

If we encounter any bumps in the road, we'll get past them. Speaking of which, here are a few things to anticipate:

Successes and Occasional Duds. Experimenting with new recipes and new food products means you'll have some award-winning successes in the kitchen, but an occasional meal will turn out to be less than what you were hoping for. That's what experimenting is all about. If you never have a dud, then you are not experimenting enough. So, if you do happen to try a recipe that doesn't turn out well or a food product that just isn't for you, then pat yourself on the back, and tell yourself you are a great culinary explorer.

Resilience and Temptation. Food manufacturers work long and hard to keep you hooked on unhealthful foods. Early next week, we'll take an in-depth look as to how and why we get hooked, and I'll show you how to get unhooked. For now, just be aware that temptation might raise its ugly head. For the next three weeks, ignore it.

Planning Ahead Versus Getting Stuck with Nothing to Eat. It really pays to think ahead. When you've arrived home late, you'll be glad you've already picked up the ingredients you need for whatever you're preparing. When you're racing through the airport, it's great to know you packed a healthy sandwich. There are so many moments when a bit of advance planning can make all the difference.

So that means thinking at least a few days ahead, deciding what you'll be eating, and getting the ingredients well in advance.

If you'll be traveling or planning any special events, you'll want to think them through, too.

Now, don't feel that you need to rigidly stick to the meal plan you've devised. As long as whatever you're eating is free of animal products and you're keeping oils to a minimum, you're fine. For example, if you discover that you have so many leftovers, you don't need to cook something new, that's great. In fact, I would encourage you to make extra food intentionally, so that you can just pop something into the microwave, perhaps, and don't have to cook every day. It is always okay to modify your food plan, so long as substitutions meet the same guidelines.

Social Support or the Lone Ranger. It is so much easier to stick to healthy resolutions when your friends and family join you. But sometimes they lag a bit behind and may not appreciate what you are trying to do. You'll want to ask for their support, and ask them not to tempt you with unhealthy things. And I also want to reassure you that, when you are part of the Kickstart team, thousands of people are making exactly the same changes you are.

A Word of Inspiration

You know Bob Harper from *The Biggest Loser*, from his book *Are You Ready!* and from his DVDs. Bob is kind and patient, and he is absolutely no-nonsense when it comes to respecting your body. Let me share his words of inspiration as you begin the Kickstart.

"Every day, your major focus should be trying to make the right food choices," Bob says. "Cherishing your body and treating it with respect requires a shift in thinking, one in which you create an empowering relationship with food. Very quickly, you'll feel stronger and have more energy because you're fueling your body properly. When we treat our bodies with love and care, everything in our life becomes much, much more attainable."

Bob is also keen on spreading the word about good nutrition. It is not something to keep all to yourself. You will want to help and encourage others to eat well, too.

Let me also introduce Rory Freedman, co-author (with Kim Barnouin) of the wildly successful, tell-it-like-it-is book *Skinny Bitch*. Rory is a ball of fire. She has reached millions of people through her books and lectures and has helped us in our work on Capitol Hill, striving to improve federal nutrition policies. And for your first day on the Kickstart, Rory has this advice:

"This is not a diet. This is a way of life. A way to enjoy food. A way to feel healthy, clean, energized, and pure. It's time to reclaim your mind and body. If you feel like you are 'giving up' your favorite foods, keep in mind that you're not *giving up* anything. You are simply empowering yourself to make educated, controlled choices about what you will and won't put into your body. Enjoy every second of this metamorphosis, knowing the journey is as important as the end result. And get excited; you're about to change your life!"

And what if you make a mistake? Rory says, "If you slip up and get off track, forgive yourself. It's okay to be imperfect and to make mistakes. Just dust yourself off and get back on course."

If you don't know her already, Kris Carr is an author and filmmaker whose experience with a very rare cancer was the subject of the wonderful documentary *Crazy Sexy Cancer*. Kris is always inspiring me, and here's what she would like to say to you, as you jump into the Kickstart program:

"As a result of your efforts, you're gonna twinkle from the inside out. No one can package that in a fancy French bottle! Only you can ignite the glow! Commit and try to be as consistent as possible. Your big task is to balance between pushing yourself out of your comfort zone and being gentle. There's no need to be 'in it to win it.' Be in it to do better and feel better—that's more than enough."

Over the next three weeks, you'll get a lot more help from celebrities, athletes, doctors, and other Kickstart friends. Every day, we'll pump you up and keep you going strong.

So today's your big day. Congratulations! As you move through the next several days, let me encourage you to keep notes about how you're doing. You can send them to me, if you like. I'm at 5100 Wisconsin Avenue, Suite 400, Washington, DC, 20016, or you can e-mail me at DrBarnard@pcrm.org.

Today's Quick Kitchen Tip: Getting Organized

If you'll be preparing your own foods during the Kickstart, let's take a little time to get the kitchen in shape. This means making it an organized and enjoyable place to be.

1. Make sure your utensils are ready, your spices and other ingredients are in a sensible order, and your kitchen surfaces are clean and uncluttered.
2. Stock up on the ingredients you'll need over the next few days, if you haven't done so already, and give away or throw away anything that does not fit our guidelines. If anyone else is sharing your kitchen and is eating in a less-than-healthful pattern, separate your space in the cupboards and the refrigerator, to minimize temptation.
3. Plug in a radio, if you like, so you can listen to music while you cook. You deserve to be serenaded.
4. Think beyond your kitchen about where else you'll be eating in the week ahead. If it's at work or on the road, you'll want to be sure you have what you need.
5. Plan to put everything away when the cooking is done, so you can save time later.

We Start Now

So off we go. Your job now is simple. For today, and every day for the next three weeks, every meal will be free of animal products and low in fat. That's it. You already know what you like. So jump in! And tomorrow, I'm going to ask how it's going.

Day 2. Beyond Meaty Diets

Congratulations! You've just done something that most people have never done—you've followed a really healthful menu for the past twenty-four hours! How is it going?

This is not a rhetorical question. Please do ask yourself how things are going. If you're feeling a little awkward for the moment, don't worry. Soon you'll hit your stride. And if there are any not-quite-comfortable parts of your menu so far, let's see if we can sort them out.

Many people report two experiences in the first twenty-four hours: Their energy improves, and their digestion improves, too. If you have diabetes, keep a lookout for changes in your blood sugar; it often gets better very quickly. If you happen to get stuck on anything, please take a quick step back and review the earlier chapters.

The steps you're now taking will pay off enormously. You'll want to give it your all for this short three-week experience.

Meat Replacements

In the last chapter, we briefly touched on a number of foods that are good replacements for meat. Let's go into a bit more detail here.

First of all, some people look for convenient replacements for meat dishes, like vegetarian versions of burgers, hot dogs, sliced ham, or bologna. You'll find these meatless products and many more at many regular grocery stores and all health food stores.

But the fact is, you don't need to have a literal replacement for meat, in which you take the roast beef off your plate and add something else in its place. If you were to have veggie lasagna, pizza, a vegetable plate, or spaghetti, you might not think about needing anything meaty in the meal. You'll get more than enough protein from grains, beans, and vegetables.

If your tastes call for high-protein foods, you might favor beans, tofu, tempeh, and seitan. Take a look in the recipe section, and give them a try. Let me add a few comments about a couple of them in particular.

The Humble Bean. Beans are a nutrition powerhouse, with plenty of protein, iron, calcium, fiber, and other essentials. And of course, they are completely free of cholesterol and animal fat. Your body will thank you when you switch from meat chili to bean chili, or from a meat taco to a bean burrito. You'll find them dried or canned, and they are nutritious either way. If you would like to reduce sodium from canned beans, rinse them, or look for low-sodium brands.

Tofu or Not Tofu, That Is the Question. Many people are intrigued by tofu, but are a bit shy about actually trying it. It is, of course, entirely optional. However, many people quickly come to adore it, and it has major health benefits, as I'll describe in a minute.

One easy way to get to know tofu is to have dinner at a Chinese restaurant, especially one specializing in Szechuan or Hunan dishes. The savory Asian sauces really bring it alive, and you will see why it is so popular. Another way is to pick up baked tofu at a health food store and add it to a stir-fry or wrap. It is firm and flavorful (having marinated in various sauces and spices), and makes a great replacement for meat.

Not too long ago, some food industry groups looked sideways at soy products, saying the new kid on the block could create all kinds of biological mischief. Websites sprang up suggesting that soy products were unhealthful. Here's what they were getting at: Soy products contain natural *isoflavones*, which are similar in some ways to hormones in the human body. Scientists wondered whether these isoflavones would affect cancer risk. The answer is that soy products actually *reduce* cancer risk.

Girls who include soy products in their routine—say, one cup of soy milk or about one-half cup of tofu each day—have about a 30 percent less risk of developing breast cancer as adults, compared with those who have little or no soy in their diets.[1] There also seems to be a benefit for women who have been previously treated for breast cancer; they have about a 30 percent reduction in risk of recurrence if they consume soy regularly.[2] Similarly, men who include soy products in their routines have less risk of prostate cancer.[3] So soy products appear to be beneficial for both cancer prevention and survival.

That said, tofu and other soy products are by no means essential. If they are not your thing, there are plenty of other great choices.

A Doctor's Prescription

There is one more reason you'll be glad you're setting meaty meals aside.

Every time your heart beats, it sends a wave of blood into your arteries. As that pulse hits your arteries, the artery walls flex a bit. They expand and contract in order to safely carry blood and oxygen to every part of you. However, people on meaty diets tend to have stiffer artery walls, meaning that they have lost their flexibility, a precursor to high blood pressure and artery blockages.

Researchers at the University of Maryland Division of Cardiology actually measured artery flexibility in people following a meaty Atkins Diet and in those who had adopted a vegetarian diet, based on the guidelines of Dr. Dean Ornish. The Atkins Diet made their arteries stiffer. The vegetarian diet made their arteries more flexible.[4] But here's what is especially frightening. This effect occurs *after a single meal*.[5] The saturated ("bad") fat that is common in animal products and tropical oils tends to stiffen the arteries almost immediately after you've swallowed your burger and milk shake, and they stay that way for hours after the meal.

Many people pummel their arteries every single meal. But every plant-based meal helps your arteries regain their youthful resilience and helps your body heal.

Today's Quick Kitchen Tip: Replacing Meat

Meat replacements can be extremely varied. You can use mushrooms, hearty vegetables like eggplant, or one of the meat alternatives presented in this book. But what can you serve to that dyed-in-the-wool meat eater who is just not going to go for mushrooms, tofu, or the very-best-cooked bean?

The Gardein company of Vancouver, Canada, has you covered. It has come up with an ingenious line of products that will have your guests thanking you for the delicious Tuscan chicken with a garden fresh salad, or the chicken breast with garlic mashed potatoes and green beans. They'll never know that the "chicken" is actually an entirely plant-derived product. Gardein offers other products that turn into stroganoff, tacos, stews, potpies, scaloppine, and many other dishes. You'll find them at your local grocery or at www.gardein.com.

Day 3. Beyond Dairy Products

Today we're going to give a bit of extra attention to dairy products and how to replace them. But first, let me take your temperature, so to speak. How are you doing so far? Are you feeling confident about the changes you've made so far? Can you see a slimmer, healthier you on the near horizon?

Dairy Replacements

Several years ago, a man approached me after a lecture at a health conference. He had been raised overseas and came to the United States to go to college. Soon after his arrival, he began to have intestinal symptoms—gas, bloating, cramps, and diarrhea. He went to the doctor for an evaluation. The most likely culprit, the doctor thought, was a parasite he must have picked up back home and carried with him to America. But a series of tests revealed nothing. And his symptoms continued.

He was sent to various specialists. A detailed evaluation, including a colonoscopy, turned up no explanation for his problems. As the symptoms carried on, the young man was miserable and had no idea what to do. Finally, after two years of struggling with his intestinal problems, a new doctor asked him a few simple questions about his diet:

"Did you drink milk back home?" the doctor asked. The answer was no. Aside from breast-feeding, milk was not part of his culture.

"Have you been drinking milk since you came to the United States?" Yes, he lived with other college students, and there was always milk in the refrigerator. He thought it must be good for him.

The doctor suggested he stop drinking milk. And that was it. Within two days, his symptoms vanished.

In retrospect, the diagnosis was obvious. He had lactose intolerance. The *lactase* enzymes that digest the lactose sugar in milk normally disappear after the age of weaning. For some people, they disappear in childhood; for others, later on. But when they are gone, a glass of milk is likely to cause gas and pain.

In some people, including most whites, these enzymes persist well into adulthood, and so they tend not to have intestinal discomfort after drinking milk. And until 1965, American medical textbooks described lactose intolerance as a rare condition. But once scientists began testing larger groups of people, they discovered that it is not only common, it is the biological norm. Most people develop lactose intolerance sooner or later.

In other words, Mother Nature designed humans to be breast-fed and then to be weaned after infancy. Drinking milk after infancy is not what Nature had in mind, and it has caused all manner of problems.

Healthier Choices

We discussed this in chapter 5. But it bears repeating: Regular milk is loaded with fat, and most of that fat is *saturated* fat—the kind that raises cholesterol. And nonfat milk has problems of its own: Its main nutrient is sugar—that is, lactose.

Cheese is even worse. Nearly all common types are around 70 percent fat, most of which is *saturated* fat. The enormous rise in cheese consumption in recent years is almost certainly one of the key reasons for the obesity epidemic in North America.

Aside from their contribution to weight gain, dairy products are also linked to arthritis, migraines, and prostate cancer, as we saw in chapter 5. Their nutritional selling point is calcium, of course. But there is plenty of highly absorbable calcium in green leafy vegetables, beans, and fortified foods.

Replacing Milk and Yogurt

As you have probably already discovered, the number of nondairy milk products is growing by leaps and bounds. Even Starbucks features soy lattes. The various nondairy milks vary in taste and texture, so try a few to see which is best.

It should be said that you don't really need any sort of milk. After the age of weaning, the only beverage your body actually needs is water. Even so, if you're looking for something to splash on your cereal or to add to a recipe, you'll have no trouble finding a nondairy milk that you like. Nondairy yogurts have also become popular. You'll find them at regular groceries, and a wide selection is available at health food stores.

Replacing Cheese

If you're looking for a cheesy taste in a recipe or a cheesy texture on a sandwich, there are many healthier choices.

Nutritional Yeast. In the grocery shopping section of the last chapter, I introduced you to nutritional yeast. By all means, give it a try. It provides a cheesy flavor with virtually no fat and no cholesterol. It is much higher in protein than cheese, and much lower in calories. Some brands (such as Red Star Vegetarian Support Formula) are fortified with vitamin B_{12}.

Dairy-Free Cheeses made of soy, rice, or other ingredients are available at health food stores. You'll even find a vegan substitute for Parmesan cheese. They vary in quality, and really should be thought of as a bridge to healthier eating. That is, they are certainly better for you than dairy-based cheese, yet they do not have the health power of vegetables, fruits, beans, or whole grains. Read the package label and choose those with no animal ingredients (many include casein, a milk derivative) and the least amount of fat.

Tofu. If you're making lasagna or stuffed shells, you'll find a delicious Tofu Ricotta recipe on page 299.

You can often just skip cheese and cheese substitutes altogether. Pizza is fine without it. Just add extra sauce and all the veggie toppings. The same is true of sandwiches and many other foods. Just leave it out. If cheese happens to be a central ingredient in a recipe, you'll want to pick another recipe.

Marilu Henner told me, "Many people have no idea how good they are going to feel when they get away from dairy products. For me, it was like night and day. So many people find that, as soon as they get off dairy, their skin clears up, they become more regular, their headaches and sniffles are gone, their snoring stops, their joint pains vanish—not to mention having a much easier time staying in shape!"

A Doctor's Prescription

At Harvard University, Walter Willett, MD, DrPH, has led some of the largest and most influential research studies ever conducted. Carefully tracking the diets of tens of thousands of research participants, his team teases apart how food choices lead to good health or to problems.

One of the questions Dr. Willett's research team has examined has been what effect milk has on bones. Does it help? Does it hurt?

"Although many people have assumed that milk maintains strong bones, our research has shown that people who don't drink milk are no more likely to break a bone, compared with people who do," Dr. Willett says. "There are, of course, many foods that can supply calcium, and it is good for people to get to know them."

We *do* need calcium, of course, along with all the other ingredients for building a healthy body. As we saw in chapter 5, the healthiest calcium sources are green leafy vegetables and beans, and there are many other sources as well.

Today's Quick Kitchen Tip: Replacing Cheese

We've already covered great ways to replace cheese in recipes. But there is one more important technique.

A great way to replace the flavor of cheese is to use entirely different, but equally delicious flavors. For example, instead of loading enchiladas with cheese, you can fill them with smoked zucchini, roasted shallots, and a sprinkling of pine nuts for a lush texture and wonderful flavor. For a thick creamy texture in a dish, you can use soy milk or other nondairy milk thickened either with flour or with mashed potatoes. Give a few of your favorites a spin and have fun!

Day 4. Keeping It Low-Fat

How are things going? The changes you're making are great for slimming down, of course, and they also bring many other benefits. They are powerful for controlling cholesterol and can actually help narrowed arteries to reopen. That's important not only for your heart, but also for your brain, your extremities, your private parts—everywhere blood flows.

As you enter the second half of your first week, start thinking about the week that is coming up. You'll want to look at the recipes or convenience foods that you'll be eating, and be sure to stock up well in advance. Empty shelves are dangerous, so be sure yours are well stocked with healthful choices.

Minimizing Vegetable Oils

Today I'd like to focus a bit on minimizing oils. Yes, vegetable oils are healthier than animal fats. They have much less saturated fat, and they never have cholesterol. But there are a couple of reasons for keeping them to a minimum.

The first is the Olive Oil Syndrome. Do you know people who just adore olive oil? They slather it on their salads, pour it into recipes, or soak it up with chunks of bread. Ask yourself, how is that person's weight? Fats and oils—wherever they are from—are the densest source of calories in any of the foods we eat. So you want to steer clear of not only chicken fat, beef fat, and greasy cheese, but all oils as well. If you also minimize oils, your waistline is suddenly free to shed the weight.

People who eat salmon regularly often have trouble controlling their weight (salmon is very fatty, and most of that fat is *not* "good fat" at all), and those who get a bit too enthusiastic with olive oil tend to have the same problem.

But olive oil is natural, you might say. I would ask, what is natural about taking thousands of olives, discarding all the fiber and pulp, and using only the fattiest part?

The second issue is that all fats are mixtures. As you'll remember from chapter 4, olive oil is a mixture of various fats, including about 14 percent *saturated* fat—the kind that raises cholesterol levels.

One more thing: Our arteries are lined with an extremely thin protective layer of *endothelial* cells, like a cobblestone street. This layer is just one cell thick. But these cells have a vital function. They produce a compound called *nitric oxide*, which keeps our blood vessels flexible, prevents artery blockages, and counteracts inflammation. When our meals are laden with oils, dairy products, and meat, these cells gradually lose their capacity to produce sufficient nitric oxide. On the other hand, when we build our menu from vegetables, fruits, beans, and whole grains, we can protect and restore these vital cells.

So skipping fatty foods, including added oils, is a good idea. Remember the recommendations from chapter 6? Skip fried foods, avoid adding oils to foods, and look for packaged products with no more than two to three grams of fat per serving. Nearly all vegetables, fruits, whole grains, and beans are almost fat-free.

A Doctor's Prescription

Let me quote Caldwell Esselstyn, MD, whom we met in chapter 1. Dr. Esselstyn showed that a plant-based diet can stop heart disease in its tracks. So, I asked him, how much oil should we use? And what are the best kinds? He said, "I encourage people to just throw their oils away. You don't need to cook with it. You don't need to dribble it on your salad, and you're better off without it. I never use oil in anything. Not a drop."

Now, if that sounds like tough love, you should know that there are still traces of healthy fats in vegetables, fruits, and beans, so you'll get all that your body needs. When you follow Dr. Esselstyn's advice, what you'll miss is virtually all the "bad" fat and a boatload of calories.

Today's Quick Kitchen Tip: Cooking Without Oil

You already know that every gram of fat or oil has nine calories, so skipping oil means you avoid a lot of calories. But there is also a culinary reason to break up the love affair with grease. Oil can interfere with other flavors. Leaving it out allows more flavors to come through.

In many recipes that call for oil, it can easily be done without. You may be amazed to discover that sautéing—or even stir-"frying"—can be done in a dry pan, often faster than if oil was added to the pan. If you are adding oil to sauces for richness or smoothness, these qualities can be achieved with other ingredients.

Day 5. Quick Breakfast Ideas

You're now well into your first week. I'm hoping that healthy eating is starting to feel comfortable, and that you're continuing to branch out and explore new tastes. As always, we're not even considering setting a foot wrong. We're giving this program our all.

As we reach the end of the first week, let's talk about how to take stock of our progress:

I would suggest that you weigh yourself about once a week. Assuming weight loss is one of your goals, a week is more than enough time for the scale to start showing results. How fast should your weight loss be? Everybody is different, but as long as the number is going down, you know you're heading in the right direction.

If your weight is not budging, something is wrong. Do not rationalize that you're losing inches, not pounds, or that the problem is a lack of exercise. If you're not losing weight after a week, we need to identify the problem and fix it. Take a quick look back at the preceding chapters and see if you can pinpoint the issue.

For cholesterol, you'll need more time. Although changes occur within the first week or two, it takes about two to three months to see the full effect. For blood pressure and diabetes, improvements can start right away, but you can continue to keep improving for quite some time, particularly if you are continuing to lose weight.

And a quick reminder: Next week is coming soon. Be sure to think about what you're going to eat, and stock up on anything you might need.

Super-Quick Breakfasts

Today I'd like to zero in on breakfast. A healthy breakfast gives you the nutrition you need, and it insulates you against the cravings that can crop up if you set off from home on an empty stomach.

If you're asking yourself, *What can I make that's healthy and really, really quick?* we've got you covered. We offered many breakfast ideas in chapter 6. Here are some especially quick ones for you to try:

Fruit. The original fast food is still the best: bananas, cantaloupe, apples, pears, prunes, and anything else. For speed and ease, remember you can cut up the fruit the night before so it's there waiting for you. Fresh and dried are both fine.

In Praise of Oatmeal. It's quick, it's healthy, and it tastes like whatever you add to it: cinnamon, raisins, blueberries, raspberries, strawberries, marmalade—you name it. Personally, I have it just plain. Instant is okay, but why not have the "old-fashioned" variety? It cooks nearly as fast and has a lower GI—that means more appetite-taming power.

Is it still old-fashioned if it's microwaved? Yes, it is. Just put one part oatmeal and two parts water (the actual amounts depend on your appetite) into a microwavable bowl, turn on the power, and you'll have breakfast in about three minutes. Oatmeal expands as it cooks, so be sure to use a big enough bowl.

Cold Cereal. Skip the sugary cereals. But you'll still have a wide selection to choose from. Serve with nondairy milk, sliced bananas, blueberries, or other fresh fruit.

The World's Fastest Smoothie. Rory Freedman taught me this one: Toss a handful or two of frozen fruit into a blender with a cup of your favorite nondairy milk (soy milk, rice milk, what have you), and push the button. That's all there is to it. It works great with bananas, strawberries, peaches, or anything else.

Berry Shake. Here's the nonfrozen version: Just combine 1½ cups soy milk, a banana, and a cup of berries (perhaps a mixture of strawberries and blueberries, or whatever you like), and into the blender they go.

Toast or Bagel. Plain, or spread with hummus or applesauce.

Rice Pudding Express. This one is so fast, it could be illegal in some parts of town. Just take some leftover rice from your refrigerator, warm it in the microwave for thirty seconds, then stir in rice milk with raisins, mangoes, or other sweet fruit, plus a touch of cinnamon.

Bring Home the Smarter Bacon. Veggie bacon, veggie sausage, and similar breakfast foods are very quick and far healthier than the meaty fare they replace.

A Word of Inspiration

There is no reason to feel stuck in the usual breakfast rut. Your morning meal can be whatever you want it to be. Let's take a lesson from Alicia Silverstone. Alicia's parents are English, and, as you may know, a traditional English breakfast features toast, tomatoes, mushrooms, and baked beans, not to mention bacon, sausage, and eggs. Now, some of these are not exactly the foods that Americans are used to starting their days with. But when Alicia and her husband, Christopher, visit her parents, they prepare an English breakfast—and they do it vegan-style.

Other days, Alicia's breakfast might include miso soup and steamed leafy greens, in addition to a more traditional porridge.

The moral of the story is that breakfast can be whatever you want it to be. Not only can you throw out the bacon and eggs—you can throw out the rule book.

No matter how rushed I am, I always make time for breakfast. It starts the day off right, keeps cravings at bay, and helps you stay slim.

Today's Quick Kitchen Tip: Perfect Brown Rice

Brown rice is a wonderfully healthful staple. But many people find that their best efforts at cooking brown rice yield something suspiciously like wet newspapers.

Here's a better way: Start with organic short-grain brown rice. All health food stores have it. Put about a cup of rice into a saucepan and rinse it briefly with water, then drain away the water completely. You are now left with damp rice in a pan. Put the pan on high heat and stir it dry, about one or two minutes. This imparts a lovely toasted flavor.

Then add three parts water for every one part rice you began with. Bring to a boil, then simmer until it is thoroughly cooked, but still retains just a hint of crunchiness—about forty minutes or so. Then drain off the extra water (do not cook it until all the water is absorbed). Serve topped with soy sauce, sesame seeds, or the topping of your choice. It will be the best brown rice you've ever tasted.

Day 6. Mastering Social Situations

Today we'll look at social situations—eating at work or at parties, dining with friends, and getting together for holidays. These are times when health considerations sometimes take a backseat, only to lead to regrets later on. I'll give you some tips that will get you through.

But first, how are things going? If you're finding plenty of good things to eat, and have set unhealthy things aside, you're doing great. If you have goofed up at any point, don't dwell on it—and definitely don't use it as a reason to abandon your healthy plans. Just dust yourself off and jump back on the wagon.

At Work

Whether you eat at your desk, in a company cafeteria, or in a nearby restaurant, you should have very little trouble keeping to the Kickstart program. You might even entice some of your co-workers to join the team!

At Your Desk. If you have access to a refrigerator and microwave, the possibilities are unlimited. With a glass bowl and fitted lid, you can bring leftovers from home and put them into the microwave (you'll find handy one-quart bowls at Pyrexware.com). Anything and everything you've cooked at home will work.

I often prepare two or three bowls in advance, each with a layer of brown or wild rice, then a green vegetable, like kale, broccoli, or bok choy, and a top layer of tofu, tempeh, or chickpeas, drizzled with soy sauce, spicy Thai sauce, or whatever. Each bowl is a lunch for one day. With a couple of them in the work fridge, I know I'm set.

You can also keep frozen products on hand. The Amy's brand includes vegan burritos, pizzas, potpies, and many other convenient products. Hummus works very well (it is much lower in fat if you make it at home, compared with commercial versions). Spread it on bread with sliced tomato and lettuce or baby spinach; if you prefer, you can use it as a dip for rye crackers, water biscuits, rice cakes, or crudités.

You can also keep soups in your desk drawer: dry soup cups, low-fat ramen, or canned soups that you can pour into a microwavable bowl. Stock up, and you'll never be caught without a healthy meal or snack.

It's great to keep fruit on hand: bananas, apples, pears, or whatever your taste calls for. Stock enough to share.

In the Cafeteria. If your company has a cafeteria, you may be in luck. As I mentioned in chapter 1, we worked with GEICO to provide healthful foods at two of its corporate sites. Here's what they served:

Cereals: Old-fashioned oatmeal, grits
Soups: Lentil, vegetable, split pea, and bean chili
Salad Bar: Fresh greens, tomatoes, chickpeas, three-bean
    salad, couscous
Sandwiches: Vegan burger, portobello sandwich
Fresh Fruit: Bananas, fruit salad

If your selections are limited, have a word with the cafeteria manager. Let him or her know that if a small green lizard can do it, others can, too! Be ready to make suggestions, and also be sure to promote the healthful new offerings to your co-workers, so that the cafeteria will see the demand. Managers want to please their customers, especially if it means luring in a larger clientele.

Work Celebrations. If there is a work party or picnic, bring something you can eat (maybe some hummus with crudités or soy ice cream) that will provide a healthful counterpoint to the usual cupcakes.

Out to Lunch. If the office employees are headed out to a restaurant (or if you are collectively ordering food), see if you can
suggest the place. Italian, Chinese, Mexican, Thai, and Japanese
restaurants all have healthful choices. You can even make it work
at a pizza place—have your pizza made without cheese. Review
the section on restaurant dining on page 112.

Magic Words

Once in a while, when you are trying to eat healthfully at work,
you'll find yourself to be the recipient of unwanted attention or
even a bit of teasing from your friends and colleagues. And the
more they like you, the more they lay it on. Of course, they don't
mean any harm, but they are not making it any easier for you to
stick to your guns.

Here's how to handle it. Ask a co-worker *individually* (not in a
group) to help you. Say, "I'm really trying to eat better, and it's hard
for me. I could use your support. All that means is just to pay no
attention to what I'm eating, and not to tempt me with anything.
You've always helped me in other ways, and this would really
mean a lot to me." Do the same with whomever else you need to,
and you will soon find that not only will your co-workers not tease
you; they will bring you fruit, articles about health, and their own
personal confessions about dietary missteps, all unsolicited.

Finally, let your co-workers know about the Kickstart. Give them
a copy of this book. So many people change their diets *together*,
and that is really a recipe for success.

Parties and Dinner Invitations

Many people approach social situations with trepidation, fearing
that they will (a) fall off their healthy path, (b) inadvertently insult
their hosts by turning down what is offered, or (c) become the
focus of attention or the recipient of endless unsolicited advice.

For starters, keep in mind that *lots of people* are working on improving their diets and many more wish they were! Chances are, other guests are, too—and your hosts might even be making changes in their own lives. Dinner conversation almost routinely gets around to food and health. The point is, many people are trying to eat healthfully, and your hosts will certainly not be surprised.

Here are a few tips that will let you master social situations:

Offer to Bring Something. When I am invited to dinner, I always call the host and say something like this: "I'm following a vegan diet, and I don't want to put you to any trouble. May I bring something? I have a great dip (or casserole) I'd love for you to try."

The answer invariably is "No, there's no need to bring anything. There will be lots to eat."

Now, you have no idea what they were really thinking. But you've just done your hosts a huge favor. You've alerted them to your needs and left them plenty of time to deal with it. This is *much* kinder to your hosts than saying nothing. Let me illustrate.

My father worked at a large clinic in Fargo, North Dakota. One day, he brought home three dinner guests. They were physicians visiting from India, and they managed to squeeze around the dinner table with the seven Barnards. We had a great discussion about how Indian medical practice differed from that in the United States, among a wide range of other topics. We hit it off well, and as they left, we were delighted to have passed such a pleasant evening.

About half an hour later, my mother slapped her palm against her forehead and said, "Oh my gosh!"—which is strong language in Fargo.

"What's the matter, Mom?" we asked.

And she slowly replied, "They are from India."

"Yes," we answered. "So what's the problem?"

"I served roast *beef*!"

And we all fell silent, trying to replay the evening in our minds.

They had all taken some, and they had all eaten it, or most of it, it seemed.

"Oh, my!" Mom said, "Should I call them? What should I do?"

To make a long story short, my father apologized to the doctors the next day. And they reassured him that it was perfectly all right. But we never did know what they had thought of our gaffe, and the event stuck in everyone's mind for years.

Bottom line: It's nice to be polite, but being politely straightforward sometimes prevents serious embarrassment later.

Bring a Gift. It's nice to arrive at your hosts' home with a healthy gift: a fruit basket, a healthy dip or salsa, a loaf of unusual bread, or some other treasure you might find at the store. Your hosts will feel honored, and you'll have something to eat.

Don't Arrive Ravenous. The object of a party is to see your friends, not to line up at a feeding trough. So if you're starving, have a snack before you go, so that hunger is not propelling you toward less-than-healthy offerings.

Dealing with a Smothering Host. Hosts want to be *good* hosts. That means having an abundance of food and encouraging guests to eat it. In turn, guests sometimes don't know how to say no if there's something they'd rather not have.

Let me share an important secret: Hosts don't actually care if you eat. They just want to be good hosts. They like to fill empty hands, and they thrive on praise for the wonderful spread they've prepared.

So if you're trying to avoid making a false step, carry a plate with a few small items. And then, if the host or other guests push you toward the wrong kinds of foods, use some carefully practiced lines. Start with a word of honest praise. Then, take the focus off you, and put it on the food instead:

"Wow! This is wonderful. Did you make those? How do you do it?"

"This is an amazing spread! What are those called? Are they hard to make?"

As time goes by, more and more people are eating more healthfully. It seems like everyone is either trying a vegetarian or vegan diet or knows someone who is. Perhaps one day in the not-too-distant future, a meat eater arriving at an office lunch or dinner party will have to apologize to the other guests, all of whom changed their diets long ago, "Excuse me, I'm still a carnivore. I hope you don't mind if I indulge my habit today." And of course, you can be magnanimous and let him know that you once had the same habit yourself, and you'd be glad to help him out whenever he's ready.

A Word of Inspiration

Let me share with you a few words of inspiration from Alex Jamieson. You may have seen Alex in the documentary *Super Size Me*. She stood by her boyfriend (now husband), Morgan Spurlock, through his all-McDonald's-all-the-time experiment. As Morgan chowed down on burgers and fries day after day, his waistline expanded, his cholesterol rose, and he rapidly developed signs of liver disease resulting from his high-protein, high-fat diet. Moviegoers were unsure whether to laugh or shriek as Morgan supersized before their very eyes.

After the thirty-day ordeal ended, Alex guided him to a vegan diet, helping him shed the weight and health problems the experiment caused. Alex has some words of encouragement for the Kickstart team. When things are going well, healthful eating is easy and rewarding. But what if your friends and family don't see things the way you do?

"It isn't always easy," Alex says. "Every relationship is about giving and receiving, and sharing food is one of the most intimate things we do with the people we love and live with. The key is not to let their habits become yours. Be patient, and as time goes on, your good example—and the good food you prepare—will help them enormously."

Today's Quick Kitchen Tip: Share the Love

Cooking is more fun when you work as a team. It's good to ask the other members of your household to help with shopping or cooking, or to handle the cleanup. Small children can tear up lettuce, husk corn, and do other simple tasks, and older children and adults can help you do everything else.

The key to success when others help you in the kitchen is to let them goof up. If they make the occasional mistake, just look the other way. The cooking process is best when it is enjoyed by everyone. You may not end up with the perfect meal, but the overall experience will be much better.

Day 7. Eating for Energy

Congratulations! You've completed week 1! How has the week been for you?

As you look ahead, what does the next week hold? Are any challenges looming—such as travel or an unusually busy work schedule? You'll be able to conquer all of them, but you'll want to be sure to plan for what's ahead. Now is the time to stock up on any foods you might need, if you haven't done so already. Think day by day, and be sure you have everything you need.

You might also want to think about any times that were challenging for you this past week or that might require a little extra planning this coming week. For example—if you're eating at work or on the go, are there any problems there? If so, what can you do to solve them? Are there any issues with loved ones in your home? Now's the time to address them. Take another look at the discussion in yesterday's lesson, and see if you find the answers you need.

Eating for Energy

Many people find that a plant-based diet makes them feel lighter and more energetic. Their moods are better, too. Hillary and Bruce, the couple we met in chapter 1, experienced exactly this change dramatically as they joined our GEICO study. We guided them through the same diet changes you're making, and Bruce noticed a huge change: "We both have a lot more energy. We work out all the time, and we were sedentary before. We never moved. We just sat on the couch, ordered food in, and conked out."

What is it about a plant-based diet that turbocharges your energy? Presumably, it is because these foods have almost no *saturated* fat—the thick, waxy fat that is so common in meats and dairy products. Without that fat, your blood is less *viscous*—that is, it's less like grease and more like water. So you have better blood flow, better oxygenation of body tissues, and more overall energy.

Also, some credit may go to a more stable blood sugar. Certain carbohydrate-containing foods—beans, lentils, pasta, sweet potatoes, and most fruits, for example—tend to keep the blood sugar stable: neither too high nor too low.

Athletes have noticed the difference. Among the world's elite distance runners is Brendan Brazier. Brendan began running in 1998 and soon began conquering ultramarathons and triathlons. As his training progressed, Brendan came to an important realization: All serious runners can push themselves to train hard. What separates the winners from the rest of the pack is *recovery*. The quicker the recovery after training, the sooner an athlete can lace up his sneakers and start training again.

Brendan knew he didn't want lawn-mower oil in his arteries. He wanted the very best fuel, both during the race and afterward, when his body was rebounding from a punishing event. So he adopted an entirely vegan diet. And he had more energy than ever, with quicker recovery times.

Perhaps the world's most amazing athlete is Scott Jurek. Growing up in Duluth, Minnesota, Scott entered his first ultramarathon—a fifty-mile race—at age twenty, and came in second. From there, his drive and talent exploded. In 1999, Scott entered the Western States Endurance Run. It extends, believe it or not, for one hundred miles. That's a hundred-mile run *in one stretch*. It is a grueling test of human endurance. But Scott set off, and dominated the race. He came back and won again the following year. And the next year, and the next. Scott won the race *seven years in a row*. And no one has ever beaten Scott's time.

Apparently, a hundred miles was not quite long enough for Scott. The Badwater Ultramarathon extends 135 miles from Death Valley to Mount Whitney in California. Scott entered the race and again conquered the field. He then entered the Spartathlon, a 153-mile race from Athens to Sparta in Greece, winning three years in a row.

Where does Scott get his superhuman performance? He fuels his body just as Brendan does—without a scrap of animal products. Like a stallion, Scott follows an entirely vegan diet.

If You Need Extra Energy

Most people feel energized by a plant-based diet. But if, for some reason, that feeling has passed you by, let's diagnose the problem.

- Are fatty foods creeping into your routine? Fat can leave you feeling sluggish. Take another look at page 137 for tips on reducing fat in your foods.

continued

- Is sugar or white bread dominating your diet? These can push your blood sugar up—and what goes up must come down. Sometimes a crashing blood sugar can leave you feeling drained. Good choices for stable blood sugar include beans, lentils, pasta, most fruits, rye or pumpernickel bread, and old-fashioned or steel-cut oatmeal. For more details, see chapter 2.
- You might also try putting higher-protein foods at the beginning of your meals, particularly at breakfast. Here's why: Starchy foods can sometimes cause the brain to produce more serotonin—the natural brain chemical that is involved in mood regulation and sleep. That's great for late in the evening, but not necessarily so great for the morning hours when you want to be alert. This serotonin-producing effect is blocked by protein. So if you start your meal with, say, scrambled tofu, beans, veggie sausage, veggie bacon, or some chickpeas—the kind you might sprinkle on a salad—you'll feel awake and alert.
- And if you want to choose foods to help you unwind or to go to sleep, do just the opposite: Starchy foods like bread or rice are great choices for the evening.

A Word of Inspiration

I asked Scott Jurek to share a few words for the Kickstart team:

> The key to quality nutrition is spending time on food preparation and cooking. Plan ahead. Make a grocery list so your kitchen is stocked with essentials. Check out the farmers' markets in your area. Then get in the kitchen and experiment with new foods and ethnic cuisine!
>
> Think about what you eat, rather than what you don't eat. Many people eliminate foods from their diet without finding healthy alternatives. I try to eat organic, locally grown,

seasonal foods as much as possible. Focus on eating healthy fats, whole grains, beans, soy protein, nuts, seeds, fruits, and vegetables.

And here are some words from Brendan Brazier, starting with a quick tip for athletes, and then some advice for the rest of us:

Within forty-five minutes after a workout, eating an easily digestible snack is key. Comprised of primarily simple carbohydrates, such as fruit and a small amount of plant-based protein, the post-workout snack will speed recovery. Better recovery will allow workouts to be scheduled closer together and therefore more training done in less time. This will directly translate into better performance.

At fifteen, I decided I wanted to be a professional Ironman triathlete. This led me to look at the importance of nutrition. I found a plant-based whole-food diet to be a significant advantage. Many people associate the word *diet* with a restrictive way of eating. It doesn't have to be. A vegan diet can be one of inclusion. When you add healthy plant-based foods in your diet, you'll find there won't be room left for the unhealthy ones. Considering what you're gaining, taking this time to transition is a worthwhile investment. The payback is higher-quality living, and greater all-around performance.

And one more thing. Brendan and Scott feel the sense of community as a race begins—thousands of people at the starting line, all headed for the same goal, and knowing there will be challenges along the way. That's what we are doing here. We are working together to get healthy or stay that way, and to help others do the same. And you're an essential part of that team.

Today's Quick Kitchen Tip: Can You See the Beans?

Soybeans are a common choice these days because they are high in protein and turn into a miraculous range of healthful foods. When choosing soy products, there is some value to going for the ones that still look like beans—that is, the least processed varieties. Edamame and tempeh, in particular, are made from soybeans that are left more or less intact. Edamame, of course, is barely processed at all—a light boil and a sprinkle of salt is all it gets. Tempeh is fermented.

On the other end of the spectrum is soy protein isolate— extracted soy protein that is packed into shakes, puddings, power bars, and simulated meats. The protein content is extremely high— higher than you actually need—and you're leaving behind the fiber and minerals of the intact bean. So while these are okay for occasional use—and certainly much better than the meaty products they replace—the best soy products let you see the beans you're eating.

Okay, congratulations on completing your first week! On to the next!

CHAPTER 8

Getting in Gear

As we begin our second week, let me thank you for joining me in this nutritional adventure. Many people are doing it with you, and I hope you have been discovering many new things about foods and about your body. We're now starting a new week, and now's the time to step on the gas a bit, and accelerate our progress.

If you haven't already weighed yourself, let me suggest that you do. If you have lost weight—whether it's a little or a lot—you're doing great. If, for whatever reason, you have not lost weight, take another look at the preceding sections, especially those about replacing animal products and minimizing oil. Even though weight will bounce up and down slightly from day to day, you should see a definite trend as the days go by.

I hope you have had a chance to tell others about the program you've begun. Hopefully, they will want to try it, too, and you can share recipes, favorite restaurants, or new products that you find. This is a journey to be shared.

Week 2 begins right now!

Day 8. Tackling Cravings and Destructive Eating Habits

Before we get into today's topics, let me make another pitch for planning ahead. It can make all the difference between an easy, fun experience and one that involves a lot of last-minute scrambling.

And the planning is simple. You don't need aerial photographs or an MRI. All you need to do is to think about the upcoming week, day by day. If you're making recipes, pick up the ingredients well in advance. If you'll be on the road, make a plan for what you'll eat. It's very simple, but so helpful.

Quieting Cravings

Today let's take a look at cravings—those times when foods call our names so loudly that our resolve can be shaken. When you understand what cravings actually are, it is much easier to get a handle on them.

Cravings are not a character flaw. They do not mean you had a bad childhood or that your self-discipline is somehow lacking. The fact is, cravings are simple biology. Just as alcohol, caffeine, and nicotine affect your brain, certain foods do, too, albeit in a more subtle way. So if you want to blame anyone for cravings, blame the food. It is the chemical makeup of certain foods that causes the craving.

We crave only certain foods. We may appreciate apples, peaches, or strawberries, but we don't binge on them. The foods we crave are (1) sugar and starchy foods that turn to sugar, (2) chocolate, (3) cheese, and (4) meat. Each of these foods triggers an opiate effect in the brain that peaches and apples just can't match. Let's take a quick look at each one.

Sugar. Do you sometimes feel that sugar is calling your name? It can certainly be insistent. The fact is, sugar has a mild drug-like effect that can be demonstrated on the first day of a baby's life. If a hospital nurse is planning to get a blood sample, say, through a heel-stick, the baby will cry, of course. But if the nurse were to dribble a bit of sugar water into the baby's mouth first, the baby would cry much less.

The sensation of sugar on your tongue triggers the release of opiates in your brain. These opiates are natural painkillers, rather like the endorphins that are responsible for the "runner's high" that some people experience after extended exertion. In turn, the opiates trigger the release of *dopamine*, a brain chemical that is responsible for the feeling of pleasure. It makes you lick your lips and remember the experience fondly. Whatever you were doing just as dopamine was released becomes a new favorite activity. So right around the same time tomorrow, an alarm clock inside your brain will remind you about sugar. And having sugar again resets the alarm to go off again the next day.

All recreational drugs do the same thing. Did you ever wonder why people smoke tobacco or marijuana leaves and not elm or maple leaves? Why do people inject the extract of poppies and not acorns? Or become addicted to the fermentation products of grapes and not plain grape juice? The answer, of course, is that tobacco, marijuana, heroin, alcohol, and every other drug of abuse triggers the release of dopamine within the brain. Foods or drinks that can trigger dopamine become wildly popular.

By the way, if it's bread and bagels you're craving, this is likely because your digestive tract breaks the starch into sugar. But, as you have probably noticed, you don't crave just any kind of starch. Your taste buds are calling for cookies, bread, crackers, cold cereals, and the like, not beans, macaroni, yams, or fruit. Here's why:

Your taste buds learned a long time ago that beans and fruit release their natural sugars only very slowly. That's great for energy and endurance, but it doesn't give you a sugar high. White bread, on the other hand, digests quickly, releasing glucose into your bloodstream within minutes.

The question is, does it matter? I would argue that a spoonful of sugar here and there doesn't matter. The problem is that sugar is a stealth nutrient. *It dissolves.* So you can pour 250 calories' worth into a soda bottle, and you can't see that it's there. You can bake it into cookies and cakes, and you'll never see the calories adding up.

Sugar-fat mixtures—cookies, cakes, fudge, glazed doughnuts—seem to have an even more powerful opiate effect than sugar itself. And that's an especially dangerous combination, because the sugar lures you in, and the grease fattens you up.

Chocolate has opiate effects, too, as we saw in chapter 2. But there is more to chocolate than just opiates. It also contains stimulants called theobromine and phenylethylamine, along with traces of caffeine.

So is it bad? Not necessarily. Some people argue that a little bit of dark chocolate might even have health benefits. But if a little becomes a lot, your thighs are expanding before your very eyes, and your tastes have turned to the milky varieties of chocolate that can trigger the various symptoms related to dairy proteins (such as migraines or arthritis), then it clearly is a problem.

So what to do? I'll show you. But first, we need to describe two more seductions.

Cheese. We have helped people to transition to healthy plant-based diets in many research studies with tremendous results. And the one food that really seems to linger on in people's minds, oddly enough, is cheese. Strange, isn't it? It smells like old socks. It can be pockmarked with blue speckles, loaded with cholesterol, and nearly as greasy as Vaseline. And yet we can't seem to get enough of it.

I experienced this during my own transition to healthier eating. Gooey cheese melting over a pizza was really my idea of a meal. And so many other people feel exactly the same way. I have spent a considerable amount of time trying to understand why cheese—even more than ice cream or other dairy products—tends to get us hooked.

The reason, I believe, is a group of chemicals called *casomorphins*. If I were to feed you a serving of cheese and then pass a tube down into your stomach (don't volunteer for this), we would find that your digestive tract is full of them. Casomorphins are opiates. So how did they get there?

The main protein in milk and other dairy products is called *casein*. You may have seen this word on package labels. Like all proteins, casein is like a long string of beads. Each bead is an amino acid—that is, a protein building block. In the digestive process, these "beads" come apart and are absorbed into your bloodstream.

But as casein digests, the beads don't entirely separate. Some of them stay attached in strings of four, five, or seven amino acids, for example. These protein fragments can attach to the opiate receptors in your brain. As the name implies, casomorphins are casein-derived morphine-like compounds.

You may have experienced cheese's opiate effect without knowing that that's what it was. If you ever lingered too long over the cheese buffet, you may have been constipated the next morning; cheese's constipating effect is very much like that of a narcotic drug. Opiate painkillers that you might have after surgery are very constipating, and cheese can slow down your digestive tract in much the same way.

So why would Mother Nature build opiates into dairy proteins? You can see the answer every time you look into the face of a nursing baby. The baby nurses intently, then collapses into a beautifully deep sleep. Of course, we attribute that sleep to lullabies, cooing, and maternal warmth. At the risk of sounding coldly biological, the fact is we've just drugged the baby. The natural opiates in mother's milk seem to be part of the basis for the mother-infant bond.

So why do we crave cheese more than milk or yogurt? That's an easy one. As milk is turned into cheese, the water and whey protein are removed, leaving casein and fat—the most concentrated form of casein in any food.

If nature builds opiates into milk products, it also builds the weaning process into the maturation sequence of all mammals, including humans. Weaning, of course, ensures that no one would be exposed to milk as an adult. But, like a restless adolescent climbing over a fence onto train tracks, we humans keep trying to subvert nature's rules that would guard us from danger.

Meat. Some people—men, in particular—say that meat is the food they crave most. And here, too, opiate effects rear their ugly head.

An English research team gave opiate-blocking medications to a group of volunteers, finding that their desire for meat fell off substantially.[1] The implication is that it's not grill marks or grease that attract us to meat. It's an opiate effect that keeps us coming back. Of course, meat eaters pay a price, with far more weight problems than their vegetarian friends, as well as higher risk of heart disease, diabetes, cancer, hypertension, and many other problems.

So What Do I Do?

If you've decided enough is enough, let me offer some suggestions. First of all, most people find that it's easier to just steer clear of a craved food than to tease yourself with small amounts. In other words, if you can manage to avoid whatever your problem food is for several days, cravings diminish. And the reverse is true, too: We tend to crave today what we had yesterday.

But let me offer seven other practical steps:

1. Have a healthy breakfast. Hunger fuels cravings. If you avoid excessive hunger, cravings tend to stay at bay.

2. Eat foods that keep your blood sugar steady. These are the low-glycemic-index foods that you read about in chapter 2.

3. Don't restrict calories. Low-calorie dieters are more likely to binge.

4. Break craving cycles. If cravings kick in at about the same time each day, schedule an activity that is inconsistent with eating. An evening at the gym, for example, can prevent the snacking that can occur if you were at home.

5. Get plenty of exercise and rest. Vigorous exercise not only gives you an opiate effect of its own, but also helps you sleep, boosting your resistance to cravings.

6. Take advantage of social supports. Let your family and friends know that you are trying to start some healthful habits. They can help you resist temptation.

7. Use other motivators. Some people get away from sugar or chocolate, not because of the harm these foods do to their weight or their health, but because their moods are so much better without them. Some people avoid cheese or meat because they have learned about how animals are treated on modern intensive farms. Many people aim to eat better because they have a personal obligation to stay healthy for the sake of their loved ones. Whatever your motivations are, they can help you stay on the straight and narrow.

A Word of Inspiration

"I just *knew* that I absolutely, positively could never give up cheese."

Those were the words of Ginnifer Goodwin, the young actor who shined in the Oscar-nominated movie *Walk the Line* and many other films, as well as in HBO's acclaimed dramatic series *Big Love*.

But that was then. When Ginnifer decided to dump *all* animal products, including cheese, she was surprised to find it actually wasn't hard at all. It turned out to be really easy.

"Not only was I absolutely, positively wrong about myself, but now two of my four parents have gone vegan. They see the impact a plant-based diet has had on my life and want to live more healthfully and happily, too.

"If you're anything like me, you'll enjoy food more: Your taste buds will awaken, and you can eat more without gaining weight."

A Researcher's Prescription

Dr. Hans Diehl heads the Coronary Health Improvement Project, an intensive program for people who want to lose weight and get healthy. The program includes lots of instruction and an entirely plant-based meal plan, and results come very quickly. Dr. Diehl has begun programs throughout the world.

Needless to say, as people are changing their diets and throwing out junk food, some have cravings for sugar and other foods during the first few days. And I have always remembered Dr. Diehl's simple three words of advice for a sweet tooth: "Have it pulled!"

He's not being harsh. What he means is that some people try to negotiate with cravings. That is, instead of abandoning the unhealthful foods that got them into trouble, they try to include small portions of them every now and then, hoping things won't get out of control. But they soon learn that foods are stronger than they are. Many end up right back into the same old rut.

Dr. Diehl feels—and I agree—that we do best when we simply ignore cravings. It's not always easy. But just as quitting smoking is actually easier than trying to cut down, if we don't keep reminding our taste buds about unhealthful foods, sooner or later the cravings just quiet down.

It bears repeating: We crave today what we ate yesterday. And if we skip unhealthy foods altogether, cravings fade away.

Today's Quick Kitchen Tip: Make It Special

The chef's trick to limiting the damage that cravings can do is summed up in three words: *Make it special*. The idea is that you can start with something that could be fattening—say, chocolate—but you present it in such a delicate way that the diner is delighted with a very modest serving. This is the same theory that brings you a tiny shot of espresso, accompanied by an even tinier specimen of lemon rind.

Here are a few examples:

- Chocolate-dipped strawberries or cantaloupe.
- A delicate square of cake (see the Wacky Chocolate Cake recipe), topped with a mint leaf.
- Orange slices. An orange is humble. But Chinese restaurants learned that a slice of orange, served with its peel partially tucked under, is special. There's no calorie issue with oranges, of course. This is just an example of presentation winning the day.

These presentations work very well if you are serving others or preparing a social function. The only one at risk is the chef (who has a kitchen full of cake and chocolate).

Some people tackle sugar cravings by using a sweetener that has such intense flavor, the taste buds are satisfied with a smaller serving than they would be with regular sugar. If you would like to try this approach, here are two sweeteners to think about:

- **Maple syrup.** You know about using it on pancakes and waffles, of course, but it also works in cereals. Chemically, it is essentially the same as regular sugar, but people who typically add tablespoon after tablespoon of sugar to their morning cereal are likely to be much more modest with maple syrup.
- **Molasses.** Unlike other sweeteners, molasses actually has some nutritional value, being rich in iron and vitamin B_6. Some varieties (such as blackstrap molasses) are rich in calcium. Use it on toast or oatmeal.

Day 9. Heart Health

Earlier, I described Dr. Dean Ornish's approach to heart health. His pioneering research showed that we can conquer this disease, using simple diet and lifestyle changes that anyone can implement.

I want to revisit this topic today for three reasons. First, heart disease is the biggest health issue in North America and most other parts of the world; if you're wondering what is likely going to kill you one day, this is it. Second, it's already started. Most people reading this book have significant buildup of plaque in their arteries right now. Third, you are now on day 9 of the program that is going to stop the damage and save your life.

The beauty of Dr. Ornish's approach was its simplicity. There was no need for a prescription. No need for surgery. He just used very simple steps: a low-fat vegetarian diet, a half-hour daily walk, and stress management. Smokers were encouraged to quit. With this simple program, 82 percent of his patients reversed their heart disease. The damage done by years of bad habits started to melt away.

When Dr. Ornish published these findings, most doctors came to accept that the program would work, but many were convinced that no one would be willing to follow what they saw as an austere regimen.

So I decided to see what Dr. Ornish's patients had to say about that. I flew out to California and had the opportunity to meet many of them and to interview them about their experiences. It was amazing to hear them describe how their weight fell away, their chest pain vanished, and their energy rebounded.

One of the reasons people stuck with the program is that it turned out to be a phenomenally easy way to lose weight. Some of the patients were already at a healthy weight. But others were quite overweight, and the average patient lost twenty-two pounds in the first year. Although typical weight loss diets are usually followed by weight regain, back to and beyond the starting weight, Dr. Ornish's patients still kept much of their weight off five years later.

I vividly recall one patient telling me how angry he was that other doctors were eager to prescribe endless medications, send patients to the operating room for major heart surgery, risk dangerous and sometimes deadly side effects, and charge them tens of thousands of dollars, without so much as a whisper that the disease could be improved by lifestyle changes. Happily, things are changing. More and more doctors are recognizing that diet and lifestyle are the main *causes* of the disease; changing these factors is the key to treating them.

As Dr. Ornish's studies progressed, he showed that it did not matter how old you were, how long you had been sick, or whether your home was in California or West Virginia. In his study of 2,974 people in twenty-four different locations, he showed that people reap enormous benefits.[2]

One important side note: Diet and lifestyle changes have a profound effect, not just on the body, but on the mind, too. Many people with heart disease are burdened by depression. Their lives seem to be on a shorter and shorter tether, and their futures have lost their promise. Because of their weak hearts, they are often unable to exercise to any great extent. But in a large research study, Dr. Ornish found that people suffering with depression who got their diets in gear, began modest physical activity, and learned stress management techniques had a dramatic lift in their moods. As their health rebounded, life suddenly felt worth living again. Patients described how their sleep habits and appetite finally got back to normal. Hopelessness was replaced by a future filled with plans, projects, and activities. The tether was finally broken.

A Doctor's Prescription

Geetha Raghuveer, MD, is a pediatric cardiologist in Kansas City, Missouri. She took a look into the arteries of seventy children, aged ten to sixteen, using a noninvasive ultrasound technique. What she found was shocking. The children had the typical signs of artery thickening that we would expect to see in a person forty-five years old. In other words, just a few short years of an unhealthful diet is all it takes for artery disease to start. Just as a smoker's lungs turn black, a person following an unhealthy diet ends up with diseased arteries, and the process is fast.

The good news is that the Kickstart program incorporates exactly the sort of diet that helps the arteries clean themselves out. And, like quitting smoking, you'll want to do it all the way. If the disease process starts quickly, it may reverse just as quickly.

Today's Quick Kitchen Tip: Let Stress Go

Dr. Ornish helps his patients manage stress in order to ease the burdens on their hearts. But reducing stress does not mean eliminating challenges from your life. Rather, it means putting you in charge and taking on challenges you can manage. Think of the difference between leaping off a mountaintop and, on the other hand, taking the same leap with skis on your feet and negotiating your way to the bottom. One is stressful, the other is exhilarating.

Let's take this in the kitchen. If you're stressing about every last detail as you're preparing food, let me reassure you. The fact is, most recipes were devised by chefs who never even measured their ingredients. The amounts they wrote down in recipes were actually just their best guesses. So if they weren't measuring things precisely, you don't have to, either. They are similarly lax with many other aspects of food preparation.

Now, there are some exceptions. If you're making oatmeal, for example, getting the right consistency depends on the proportion of oats to water. And if you're cooking pasta, you'll want to be sure you're making enough—not just throwing in "a handful," hoping it will expand in the boiling water. But most recipes are very forgiving.

It's not essential that everything be perfect. After all, it's just food! And the pleasure comes not just from the meal, but from the preparation and the companionship, too. It's your time, and it's okay to play a bit.

How about turning on some music? Let the stress go, and have fun with it. A relaxed approach in the kitchen is perfectly fine—in fact, it's just what the doctor ordered.

Day 10. Convenience Foods

We're now reaching the halfway point in our three-week program. Time goes fast, doesn't it?

Today let's look at convenience foods. There are plenty of occasions when you do not have the time to fire up the stove and spread out over the kitchen counter. Sometimes you just want something quick. For times like that, what have you found that works for you?

Last week, on day 5, we looked at quick breakfasts. Let me share some simple and quick ideas for lunches, dinners, and snacks:

Pasta and Spaghetti Sauce. Spaghetti and other pastas keep basically forever, and when you're in a pinch, you can just boil them up and pour on some sauce from a jar. Of course, you'll want to read the label to be sure the sauce has no animal products and is low in fat.

Couscous. The world's smallest pasta is also the quickest to cook. It's wonderfully easy. Just add 1 cup couscous to 1½ cups boiling water, then turn off the heat and let it sit for a minute or so. Fluff with a fork and top with garbanzo beans, spices, and a dash of hot sauce. Or treat it like the pasta it is, and top with a tomato-based spaghetti sauce. Very quick and easy.

Frozen Meals. The old TV dinner has been eclipsed by an amazing range of frozen meals: vegan pizza, burritos, enchiladas, Indian dinners, rice bowls, and many others. You will find them in the freezer case at most regular groceries and all health food stores.

Canned or Instant Soups. What could be simpler? Just heat 'em and eat 'em. It pays to keep soup on hand, whether canned, frozen, or instant. For instant soup cups, Dr. McDougall's is a particularly good brand—it comes as lentil, minestrone, split pea, black bean, tomato, and other flavors developed by John McDougall, MD, and available online at www.rightfoods.com.

Veggie Dogs and Veggie Burgers. These ubiquitous products are easy and quick to serve, no matter how many people you're cooking for.

Frozen Vegetables. It is good to keep a stock of frozen vegetables on hand. They are as healthful as fresh vegetables with a much longer shelf life, and so easy to prepare.

Canned Beans. Pinto or black beans heat up in a flash and go great with rice or tortillas, topped with salsa. You'll find them at every grocery, along with vegetarian baked beans and many others. Low-sodium brands are available.

Red Lentils. These little legumes cook in ten minutes flat. They can serve as a soup base, or you can mix them with rice or other grains. For extra credit, stir in some kale or broccoli, and you've got a hearty meal in no time.

Precooked Rice. Personally, I prefer to cook rice from scratch. But if you are in a hurry, you can buy frozen precooked brown rice. Just heat and serve.

Soy Yogurt. Yogurt lovers will find no shortage of soy brands at health food stores and many larger groceries.

Super-Quick Sandwich. Top bread with lettuce, tomato, vegan deli meat slices, and mustard. Tasty and much healthier than typical deli fare.

Power Bars. Clif Bars, Lärabars, and the like are not one of life's essentials, but they are quick and handy. You'll be glad to have some in your desk drawer or in your luggage while traveling.

Grapes. Have them as is, or frozen like little Popsicles.

Dried Fruit. Raisins, apricots, figs, apples, and other dried fruits wait patiently on your shelf or in your desk drawer, ready to give you a burst of energy when you need it.

A Word of Inspiration

On the rare occasions when my parents went out to enjoy the Fargo nightlife, our babysitter, Mrs. Franek, came over to look after their five children. Arriving at our front door, Mrs. Franek carried under her arm an appliance that was about the size of a toaster. She went into our den, set it down on the floor, plugged it in, and sat down on it. It whirred into action. As it jiggled her bottom, she explained that it was going to help her lose weight. Needless to say, we couldn't wait to have our turns sitting on the amazing vibrating stool.

It was a poor man's version of the vibration belts that were popular at gyms in the 1950s. People stood up to a machine and wrapped a wide belt around their backsides, then flipped a switch. As it vibrated their bums—making them feel like a huge milk shake—they hoped that their fat would magically vibrate into oblivion. They soon discovered that the machines were lots of fun, but completely useless for weight loss.

So why am I telling you this, you might ask? Here's why: People have always looked for shortcuts. And there has been no shortage of manufacturers ready to sell them. But once we recognize the power of foods, it becomes clear that they provide the biggest shortcut of all. Properly chosen, they slim us down, protect us from toxins, and nourish us in every sense of the word.

So a vibrating stool is a very convenient way to entertain children. And healthy foods are a wonderfully convenient way to slim down.

Today's Quick Kitchen Tip: Keep It Simple, Keep It Quick

In line with today's theme of convenience and saving time, let me share a couple of ideas for speeding up food preparation.

First, there might be some things you are doing in the kitchen that you don't need to do at all. For example, do you peel potatoes? How about carrots? Do you de-seed tomatoes? Perhaps you try to get every seed out of every pepper that you use. While those steps have occasional merit, in most cases they simply don't affect the taste or presentation at all. Here are a few things you may have been doing that you don't need to worry about:

- Removing the seeds from tomatoes. You also don't need to remove the tops if the tomatoes are going to be cooked down into a sauce.
- Peeling potatoes. There is no need to, even if you're making mashed potatoes.
- Removing every bit of skin from a roasted pepper.
- Peeling carrots.

- Getting exactly the right cut on your veggies.
- Soaking lentils before cooking.

And once foods are on the stove, sometimes it's best to just leave them alone. Onions and carrots need the direct heat of the pan to fully develop their flavors, so leave them to it. Stirring them doesn't just waste your time; it momentarily removes them from the heat. So don't stir until you see your ingredients begin to transform. Unless an ingredient is volatile, like garlic or spices, constant stirring is rarely necessary. Sometimes saving time can make an even better meal.

Day 11. Travel

You are now officially past the halfway point in the Kickstart. Congratulations on sticking with your healthy plan! Still, now is not the time to slack off on the program or, for that matter, to make any long-term decisions about what you will or will not eat. For now, you're still exploring—getting to know new foods and the benefits they bring.

Speaking of exploring, today let's focus on travel. Getting out and about can be enormously fun and a little challenging at the same time. As you widen your radius, you discover tastes, restaurants, products, and cultural practices that can enrich your life.

Growing up in North Dakota, I knew all about roast beef and burgers, and I could tell you exactly what a sugarbeet plant smells like. But there were quite a few things I didn't know about. For example, in the heart of New Mexico and Arizona, beautiful dishes are made of traditional corn, beans, and squash. In France and Italy, vegetables are presented with the respect and care they deserve. In Africa, grains and legumes provide wonderfully healthful meals. In Japan, the vegetables of the sea are harvested and presented as delightful parts of the menu. In India, idli sambar—a spicy soup served with cakes made of lentils and rice—is a perfectly routine breakfast, while oatmeal is unheard of.

You'll find a similarly wide range in mealtime customs. At a coffee shop in Boise, our waiter Brian introduces himself in a loud and friendly tone of voice and scrawls B-R-I-A-N in crayon across the tabletop. In France, servers stay out of sight, trying not to intrude on your meal until you signal them. In America, being vegetarian is becoming trendy. In India, being nonvegetarian is becoming trendy, as is diabetes (much to the consternation of public health officials).

For the traveler, the biggest problem is that healthful foods sometimes seem to be in short supply. At first glance, there's nothing healthy at the airport, and there's nothing at all on the plane. The hotel menu looks like it is trying to drum up business for the local cardiologist. Miscommunications with waiters are pretty much routine, and temptations are everywhere.

Well, yes. That's all true. But you can do more than survive as you travel. You can thrive, and really enjoy it. One of the keys to eating well on the road is planning ahead. There will be any number of things you cannot foresee. But most problems are predictable and avoidable.

Nanci Alexander, the owner of Sublime, the premier Fort Lauderdale restaurant, has these tips for travelers:

- **If you're flying.** When you travel, be sure to request vegan meals on flights that offer meals, as most international flights do (call at least forty-eight hours in advance). On flights that do not offer meals, pack a healthful snack: How about a hummus, lettuce, and tomato sandwich? Or instant soup cups, fresh fruit (mandarin oranges, tangerines), dried fruit, applesauce or fruit cups, baby carrots, sliced cucumbers, small soy milk or juice cartons, or low-fat granola bars.

- **At the hotel.** Arriving at your hotel, you can request a mini fridge and even a microwave, which will allow you to cook up a bowl of oatmeal for a quick breakfast and heat up convenience foods. Some hotels—especially the less expensive ones, for some reason—provide these appliances routinely. For extra points, you might even get a kitchenette.
- **Visit the local grocery.** A ten-minute stop at the local grocery can mean you'll have not just your oatmeal and bowl, but also microwavable frozen dinners, fresh fruit, instant soups, canned beans, or whatever else you would like.
- **At a restaurant.** Expand your horizons with world cuisine. International restaurants often have healthy vegan menu items. There may even be some in your neighborhood. Try Mexican, Chinese, Italian, Middle Eastern, Japanese, Thai, Ethiopian, or Vietnamese.

And don't forget that you can easily "veganize" meals at almost any restaurant. Many menu items are already vegetarian and can be made vegan by simply leaving off eggs, cheese, or other dairy products.

I love Nanci's suggestions and would add a couple more:

At any good restaurant, the menu is really just a suggestion. Ditto for room service. The chef may well be able to serve all kinds of things that aren't listed on the menu: oatmeal for breakfast, and spaghetti with tomato sauce, a vegetable plate, or veggie burgers for later in the day, for example.

If you're headed out on a long road trip, you can certainly stop at the fast-food places along the way, picking from the options we highlighted in chapter 6, choosing the veggie burger instead of the hamburger and the bean burrito instead of the meat taco. But you'll also want to think through what you can bring with you in the car. Spread up sandwiches before you go, or pack any of the following:

- Fresh fruit (apples, bananas, mandarin oranges, tangerines)
- Dried fruit
- Applesauce or fruit cups
- Baby carrots, sliced cucumbers
- Rice cakes and bean dip
- Soy milk and juice cartons
- Luna Bars, low-fat granola bars, or trail mix

A Word of Inspiration

Let me share some tips and encouragement from Kathy Freston. You know Kathy as the author of the best-selling *Quantum Wellness* and *The Quantum Wellness Cleanse*. Kathy is always in the air or on the road, it seems, so I asked her what tips she would share with us about travel:

> I travel a lot, and so I'm always confronted with how to eat a healthy diet while on the road. It took a bit of planning the first few times, but I think I've got it down now.
>
> If I'm flying, I'll try to swing by a health food store or one of my favorite healthy restaurants to pick up a meal to bring on the flight. I sometimes feel guilty when I open up my delicious Mediterranean platter of hummus and tabouleh when the guy next to me has something that looks inedible.
>
> If I'm driving, I bring some soy creamer (creamer mixes better with tea or coffee than regular soy milk, which may or may not be offered at the hotel) for my morning beverage.
>
> I always enjoy searching a new city for local health food stores and cool little vegetarian restaurants in my spare time; this makes my trips richer and gives me a reason to explore a new town and find new foods that are local to that particular spot.
>
> To guard against the possibility of not finding healthy things to eat, I pack what I jokingly refer to as my "feed bag" at home

before I leave. In a tote bag, I put some baggies of various kinds of nuts and seeds, some of them mixed with dried fruits; some breakfast bars; packages of soy protein powder that I can just shake up in a small bottle of water (I roll up a piece of paper into a funnel so the powder doesn't spill all over the place); vegan jerky; a couple of apples; and maybe a few other snacks that I pick up at the health food store. This can last me as filler, along with whatever fare is offered at my destination, for a good couple of weeks.

I've noticed recently how things are changing; I even saw a tofu sandwich offered at the airport the other day. Next thing you know, we'll see quick-serve vegan restaurants sprouting up all over. I know that day is coming and I look forward to it!

Today's Quick Kitchen Tip: Try Something New

Want to take a trip right in your own kitchen? Many cultures have tried-and-true veggie-centered recipes, with treasures you'll want to get to explore. Did you ever want to cook authentic Italian meals? How about Mexican, Chinese, Japanese, Thai, Vietnamese, Indian, Pakistani, Ethiopian, Portuguese—there are so many to try. But how do you get started? Here's an easy way:

1. First, try out a restaurant that serves the cuisine that intrigues you. Make a note of the dishes you like. If the restaurant isn't busy, you might also ask your server or even the cook about the ingredients or techniques.
2. You'll easily find recipes for the foods you've chosen online or in a bookstore. Note down the ingredients, techniques, and special equipment, if any. Keep it simple for starters.
3. To pick up what you need, check a well-stocked grocery, health food store, or specialty market if there is one near you. Online purveyors are very convenient, making virtually anything available anywhere.

4. Then fire up the stove and have fun!

5. Don't forget that many cuisines have discovered time-saving mixes, frozen products, and even convenience versions of traditional foods. You'll see them at health food and specialty stores.

Day 12. Fighting Cancer with Food

Of all the health concerns that loom in front of us, one of the most worrisome is cancer. Every woman of any age wants to prevent breast cancer and the other common forms of the disease. Men are at risk for prostate cancer; their doctors are taught that *every* man will eventually get the disease, if he lives long enough. Happily, that turns out not to be true. But the condition is so common that an ounce of prevention goes a long way.

It may surprise you to learn that foods play a decisive role in preventing cancer. During the Kickstart program, you are learning about the very foods that can reduce the chances of you ever developing this disease. For people who have been diagnosed with cancer, these foods can also improve survival. Today I'd like you to have the details.

Research teams have long noticed that population groups with different diets have very different cancer rates. For example, breast cancer was historically rare in Japan, where traditional diets are based on rice, but very common in North America, where meatier diets prevail. And then, as fast-food chains and meaty business lunches invaded Japan toward the end of the last century, cancer rates rose dramatically. Obviously, genes did not change. What changed was diet, and the changes were profound.

So why should foods affect cancer risk? Part of the issue is body fat. As meaty, cheesy diets fatten us up, that extra body fat is not simply a dormant storage organ. It is living tissue, and one of its jobs is to build hormones. The more body fat you have, the more your body produces *estrogens*, the female hormones linked to cancer of the breast and uterus.

In 2007, the World Cancer Research Fund and American Institute for Cancer Research summed up the evidence, showing that, indeed, if foods fatten you up, your cancer risk rises, and not just for breast and uterine cancer. Extra body fat increases our risk of cancer of the colon, rectum, esophagus, pancreas, and kidney, too.[3] The good news is that the reverse is true: As we slim down, cancer risk falls.

But body fat is not the only issue. Even women who are not heavy, but whose diets are high in animal products and low in fiber, tend to have more estrogen in their blood, compared with women on more plant-based diets. This may be why Westernization of the diet in Asian countries has been accompanied by an increase in hormone-related cancers, such as breast cancer. Something similar happens for men. A meaty, low-fiber diet tends to increase testosterone. It does not make you more macho; it increases your risk of prostate cancer.

Red meat is linked to colorectal cancer, and possibly to other forms of the disease. This is especially true for processed meats—bacon, sausage, ham, bologna, et cetera.

Grilled chicken contains carcinogens, called heterocyclic amines, linked to breast cancer and many other forms of the disease. As we saw in chapter 5, these carcinogens are found in essentially every grilled chicken sandwich or grilled chicken salad. And you'll also recall from chapter 5 that several studies have linked dairy products to prostate cancer. Milk-drinking men appear to have 30 to 60 percent higher risk, compared with men who avoid milk. We also noted in chapter 5 that regular alcohol use increases the risk of breast cancer.

But the food news is not all bad. Vegetables, fruits, whole grains, and beans are cancer fighters. Their healthy fiber that fills you up and satisfies your appetite also helps protect you against cancer. The same is true for the beta-carotene that gives carrots their bright orange color and the lycopene that lends a red color to tomatoes and watermelon. They are powerful antioxidants.

So what this means is that the diet changes you've made— setting aside animal products and bringing in the vegetables, fruits, whole grains, and beans—will do more than help you fit into your jeans. They can cut your cancer risk.

Survival

What has been especially intriguing is to see how foods can help people who have already been diagnosed with cancer. One of the first studies to show the power of foods was called the Women's Intervention Nutrition Study (WINS).[4] Nearly twenty-five hundred women who had previously been treated for breast cancer were asked to reduce the fat in their diets. After five years, the risk that their cancer would come back was cut by 24 percent.

Another investigation, called the Women's Healthy Eating and Living (WHEL) Study, tested the benefits of increasing fruits and vegetables.[5] After seven years, it turned out that women who ate five fruit and vegetable servings daily and who were also physically active cut their risk of dying by half, compared with women who did not get as many fruits and vegetables or who were physically inactive.

These studies show that foods are important not just for preventing breast cancer, but also for containing it once it has struck.

Men benefit, too. After Dr. Dean Ornish proved that a plant-based diet, along with other lifestyle changes, could reverse heart disease, he tested a similar program for men with prostate cancer.[6] The effect was dramatic and rapid. Prostate cancer is tracked with a blood test called prostate-specific antigen, or PSA. If PSA rises, that can mean that cancer is spreading. In the group of men who followed Dr. Ornish's regimen of a vegan diet, exercise, and stress management, PSA actually *fell* over the ensuing year. After two years of follow-up, the benefits still held for nearly every patient.[7]

The lesson from these studies is that a prudent approach to cancer is to not only take advantage of whatever tests and treatments your doctor recommends, but to also put foods to work. Trimming away extra weight, keeping fat low and vegetables and fruits high, avoiding animal products, and boosting physical activity—these steps shore up the body's natural defenses.

A Word of Inspiration

Ruth Heidrich, PhD, is an author, health expert, and amazing athlete, with an important personal story to share:

> I was 47, living in paradise—that is, Hawaii—and working on my PhD in psychology. One day, while in the shower, I felt a lump in my right breast. Needless to say, I was worried, and so I got right in to see a doctor. But he just remarked, "Oh, you're too young for breast cancer." He did, however, order a mammogram, "Just to be sure." The mammogram was negative, which was reassuring. And so he told me that, to be safe, I should get yearly checks. And the next year's test was also negative. The third year, however, the lump was clearly visible. The doctor looked shocked and ordered an immediate excisional biopsy.
>
> It turned out that the mammograms had been wrong all along. Not only was it cancer, but there were no clear margins.
>
> Of course, I was devastated. I felt betrayed by my body. I had been an active runner for 14 years and had even run marathons. I was the most physically fit person I knew. I had been following what I had thought was a healthy diet. And yet I had cancer. It was unbelievable!

Ruth had to have more surgery in an attempt to get all the cancer. But it was too late. The cancer had already spread to her bones and to her left lung, and her liver enzymes were elevated, meaning it had apparently spread there as well. With no hope of removing the metastatic cancer, she was offered chemotherapy and radiation. Neither one promised a cure; they were a way to buy time, nothing more.

I dreaded chemotherapy, but was terrified not to have it. In addition to the hot spots in my bones, I was having serious bone pain that medication could not relieve.

But in what I consider one of the best strokes of luck ever, I happened to see a blurb in the paper about research being done to investigate the role of diet on the spread of breast cancer. I literally ran to the phone to contact the researcher, Dr. John McDougall. He explained that he was investigating whether a completely vegan diet could be more effective in reversing cancer than chemotherapy or radiation. Given the options, it was a no-brainer. With great relief and a little trepidation, I turned down chemo and radiation and chose diet instead. And it turned out to be exactly the right decision. No "transitioning" for me—I went vegan that very day!

I found the diet amazingly easy to follow. I already loved brown rice, whole grain breads, and oatmeal; I just had to replace the chicken, fish, and dairy with vegetables and fruit, and throw out all the oils.

When I returned to the oncologist, I told him what I was doing. He responded by saying that diet had nothing to do with my getting breast cancer, and that I couldn't possibly get enough protein, calcium, and essential fatty acids. I made a mental note to look into his concerns, but I stuck with my new diet, after being reassured by Dr. McDougall that I would get more than enough protein, calcium, essential fatty acids—and everything else!

The second major stroke of luck at that time was seeing the Ironman Triathlon on television. I was captivated by the idea of going beyond a 26.2-mile marathon. The triathlon was a 2.4-mile swim, followed by a 112-mile bike race, and then the marathon! When I found out that no cancer patient nor any woman as old as I had ever completed what was considered one of the most grueling races in the world, I found my challenge.

I was especially excited to find that my new diet gave me more energy and faster recovery times. It got me back to running very soon after the surgeries and I added swimming and cycling to my daily training.

The triathlon was every bit as grueling as advertised, and as I looked around and saw all these young, fit bodies, I wondered what I'd gotten myself into. Then I recalled my mission: to show people how powerful this vegan diet was. I did have to dig deep, however, as I was challenged like I'd never been before! Crossing that finish line 14 hours later, I experienced indescribable feelings—a mix of joy, empowerment, exhilaration—and total fatigue! I could not have gone another step!

Meanwhile, I was being monitored to check the status of the cancer. Within two months, the hot spots in my bones began to fade. My body actually encapsulated the lesion in my lung, and my liver enzymes normalized. I felt healthy and strong. And I have remained healthy for 28 years.

I also wanted to show that my completing the Ironman wasn't a fluke. So, since my diagnosis, I've done the Ironman six times, have run 67 marathons, and set a number of world age-group fitness records in the process!

Today's Quick Kitchen Tip: Vegetables Show Chemicals the Door

If you are thinking about which vegetable to serve for dinner tonight, think about broccoli, cauliflower, cabbage, or kale.

In addition to all their other benefits, they have special cancer-fighting power.

Each of these is a *cruciferous* vegetable, a name that refers to their cross-shaped flowers. In your body, these vegetables stimulate your liver to make enzymes that detoxify and remove chemical pollutants. That's important because all of us are exposed to various chemical pollutants in the air, water, and sometimes in foods. Some of these chemicals can damage your DNA, leading to cancer.

Common Cruciferous Vegetables

Bok choy	Collards
Broccoli	Kale
Brussels sprouts	Radish
Cabbage	Rapini (broccoli rabe)
Cauliflower	Watercress

Within forty-eight hours of eating broccoli or its cruciferous cousins, your liver is making more of the enzymes that remove cancer-causing chemicals from your body. Cooking them does not destroy their effectiveness.

Day 13. Our Friend, the Bean

"I would like to thank my producer, my director, all the little people who made this film so wonderful, and I would especially like to thank our friend, the bean."

I dream of the day when beans get the gushing praise they deserve. One day, they will be the focus of a national holiday, or perhaps a television spectacular. Today we'll tip our hat to one of the most nutritious—and yet most neglected—foods: the humble bean. Beans have so much going for them, and now's the time to show how much we appreciate them. They are rich in protein, highly absorbable calcium, iron, fiber, and even a trace of omega-3 fatty acids ("good fats"). The only thing they are missing is a good PR agency singing their praises.

Here, let me lay it out for you:

WHAT BEANS HAVE	WHAT BEANS DON'T HAVE
Protein	Cholesterol
Calcium	Saturated fat
Iron	Trans fat
Fiber (soluble and insoluble)	
Omega-3s	

In countries other than the United States, beans do seem to get their due. Throughout England, many people start their day with beans on toast. Ditto for Australia. Hummus, the spread made from chickpeas, is a traditional breakfast food in the Middle East. In Latin America and the Caribbean, pinto beans and black beans are everyday staples. Many Native American tribes, particularly in the Southwest, have traditionally cultivated beans as a principal food, although they lost much of their prominence as other foods came into the picture. Returning them to their former glory makes a lot of sense.

Calcium and Iron in Beans (milligrams per cup)

Beans are great sources of both calcium and iron. Here are a few examples to show how common types stack up.

continued

	CALCIUM	IRON
Chickpeas	80	4.7
Great northern beans	120	3.8
Navy beans	126	4.3
Pinto beans	79	3.6
Soybeans	175	8.8
Tofu	506	4.1

Source: USDA National Nutrient Database for Standard Reference, Release 22 (2009).

Digestive Problems?

If beans give you a bit of a digestive challenge—that is to say, a little gas—let me remind you of two quick tips.

First, start small. If you had thought that an enormous steak needed to be replaced by a similarly gargantuan plate of beans, the fact is, a little goes a long way. Start small, and work your way up.

Second, cook them well. Beans should be really soft, never al dente. Some canned-food manufacturers understand this, while others do not.

And different varieties have different effects. For example, you might be fine with chickpeas, but have trouble with navy beans. This can change over time as you adapt.

Try Them All

- **Chickpeas** deserve a special word of praise. Many people have never gotten to know them. But they are extremely versatile. They are great in salads and soups, mixed into hummus, or even as a breakfast food.
- **Navy beans** are the famous baked beans that every kid will gladly eat.

- **Pinto beans** are the basis for much of traditional Southwest cooking, particularly for the misnamed "refried beans."
- **Black beans** are great in soups, burritos, and even in cold salads mixed with corn or other grains.
- **Lentils** are a staple for soups and are used in Indian cooking, Italian cuisine, and many other traditions. You can even make your own veggie burger by combining cooked lentils with brown rice.
- **Split peas** are delicious in soups and are a staple of African cuisine.
- **Soybeans** are eaten intact as edamame, and are converted into everything from bacon and sausage substitutes to milk, cheese, and yogurt.

Buy them canned, if you want convenience. Buy them dried, if you prefer to cook them up from scratch. They have the same nutrition either way, with the exception of sodium, which is often added to canned beans, unless you get the no-salt-added brands.

A Word of Inspiration

A bean plant may seem a rather humble part of a modern garden. But beans have a history that goes back thousands of years. Along with corn and squash, beans make up what are called the Three Sisters—three plants that have traditionally been planted together by Native Americans in a system that began in Mexico and swept upward throughout much of North America. As corn grows, it provides a trellis for the bean vines. In turn, beans fix nitrogen in the soil—nitrogen that corn needs. As squash grow around them, the broad squash leaves shade the ground, inhibiting weed growth. And the spiny squash vines discourage nocturnal nibblers.

Nutritionally, the Three Sisters provide abundant nutrition. And without getting overly poetic, the three plants living together in perfect harmony provide a role model for us humans who seem to have trouble doing the same.

Today's Quick Kitchen Tip: Bean Tips

In appendix 2, A Primer of Basic Cooking Techniques, we'll cover the basics of getting legumes ready for the table. But here are two quick tips for today:

- Baking soda helps beans cook. You just add about 1¼ tablespoons per cup of dried beans to the soaking water and cooking water. It reduces the cooking time and softens the beans. This is particularly noticeable with chickpeas, fava beans, and pinto beans. Do not add more than that amount.
- If you are simmering beans, be sure to cover the pot. In an uncovered pot, heat is conducted mainly through the bottom. But a lid traps heat on the top, creating a second heat source. And as liquid turns to steam, it creates pressure that accentuates the heat. You won't see a marked difference if there are only a couple of cups of liquid in the pot, but you will if you are making larger servings.

Day 14. Choosing Good Carbohydrates

Congratulations! You've completed two weeks of the Kickstart program. As I've said, most people never experience even a single day eating the foods their bodies were designed for. But you've given your body a chance to test-drive what is as close as humanly possible to a perfect diet.

We're not done yet, though. You've got another week to make things a little more solid, and there are more benefits to experience. So that's what the next seven days are all about.

And as our third week approaches, this is the time to look at what you'll be eating in the next several days to make sure you have the ingredients you need. Remember, empty shelves are the playground for cravings. Be sure to stock up on healthful foods that will help you stay on track.

Today let's say a word about carbohydrates. There is probably no part of the diet that is more misunderstood. So let's make it easy. And let's also nail down how to separate healthful carbohydrate-rich foods from less-than-healthful ones. Here's what you need to know:

As you will remember from chapter 3, the human body runs on glucose. This simple sugar is the gasoline that powers your cells. And that glucose comes mainly from carbohydrate that you eat. It passes from your digestive tract, into your bloodstream, and then into your muscles, brain, and all the rest of you. So carbohydrate-rich foods are good for health.

However, some people have tried to paint a dim picture of carbohydrate. Rice, potatoes, beans, and so on got a bad rap from Dr. Robert Atkins and other low-carbohydrate diet advocates. Their thesis was that when people avoid bread, cereal, fruit, beans, pasta, and everything else with carbohydrate in it, they lose weight. That's true enough. But what they missed was that leaving out *any* large part of the diet is likely to cause weight loss. Carbohydrates are about half of the American diet, so leaving them out is bound to make you lose some weight—that is, unless you make up for it with some other food. Which is exactly what a lot of people did. And indeed, people who skipped the carbs and dug into meat and cream often found their overall calorie intake did not fall at all, and they didn't lose an ounce.

Worse, some low-carb advocates tried to maintain that high-cholesterol, fatty foods weren't really dangerous. But their own studies proved them wrong. About one in every three low-carb dieters has an increase in LDL ("bad") cholesterol, sometimes to a dangerous degree.

Perhaps most important, the thinnest people on the planet are those who eat *the most* carbohydrate. People in Japan and in much of the rest of Asia were thin as long as they stuck to a rice-based diet. But as the influx of meaty diets caused rice intake to fall in Japan, waistlines expanded rapidly.

Good Carbohydrates

So carbohydrates are certainly not unhealthy. Just the opposite; they are the body's number one fuel.

That said, some food choices are better than others. When it comes to carbohydrate-containing foods, there are actually three ways of separating the wheat from the chaff, so to speak: Do they have their natural fiber? Do they have a low glycemic index (that is, only a small effect on blood sugar)? Are they *simple* or *complex* carbohydrates?

These are all very simple concepts. Let's look at each one:

Fiber. Why is whole wheat bread more substantial than white bread? Because it contains natural fiber. It's the same with brown rice, compared with white rice. To turn whole wheat bread into white bread, the grain's tan outer coating is stripped away, revealing the pearly white color beneath it. That outer coating is where the fiber is. So you want to keep that fiber. It controls your appetite, keeps your digestion working right, and helps you in many other ways.

The average American gets only about ten to fifteen grams of fiber each day, which is why pharmacies offer so many brands of laxatives. A healthy diet should have around forty grams. It's easy to get there:

- Include beans, peas, and lentils in your routine. A half-cup serving of typical beans gives you a good seven grams of fiber.

- Fruits and vegetables are fiber-rich, too. They have roughly three and four grams of fiber, respectively.
- Favor whole grains, such as brown rice and whole-grain bread, over refined grains (white rice, white bread).

Simple, isn't it?

Glycemic Index. In chapter 2, we looked at the basics of the glycemic index. It is a simple way to separate foods that can spike your blood sugar from those that are gentler on your blood sugar.

Foods that have a high GI value—wheat breads (white and whole wheat) and baking potatoes, among others—are not necessarily bad. Many people do perfectly well with them. But if you tend to suffer from cravings, or if you have diabetes or high triglycerides, you might profit from sticking to low-GI foods. That means beans, peas, and lentils; green, yellow, and orange vegetables; fruits (yes, they are sweet, but they have little effect on blood sugar); rye and pumpernickel bread; bran cereal; pasta; and oatmeal.

Simple Versus Complex. You have probably heard people talk about "complex carbohydrates" and how they are better than "simple carbs." Let me explain what they are getting at. But let me also point out that, if you understand fiber and the glycemic index, you don't need to think very much about simple versus complex. Here's what it's all about:

The story starts with sugar. Sugar molecules are obviously sweet to your taste buds. If two sugar molecules happen to connect together, they still taste sweet. These sweet molecules are referred to as simple carbohydrates.

Now, if you were to examine the starch in a potato or a piece of bread under a powerful microscope, you would discover that it consists of hundreds of sugar molecules joined together in long chains. These long chains don't taste sweet; they taste starchy. Because they are long chains, rather than tiny molecules, they are called complex carbohydrates.

So, which is better—simple or complex? Well, the complex carbohydrate in beans beats the nutritional socks off table sugar—it is really gentle on your blood sugar. But there are plenty of exceptions. The simple sugar in typical fruit, for example, actually has less effect on your blood sugar than the complex carbohydrate in a potato.

So my bottom line is this: Pay attention to fiber and to the GI, and leave it at that.

A Doctor's Prescription

Are carbs good or bad? The question has been the subject of water-cooler debates—and entire medical conferences—for decades. Some have argued that carbohydrates are fattening. Others have pointed out that they are just what the body needs to stay slim over the long term.

The problem, of course, is that the group of foods we call "carbohydrate" is so broad that it includes jawbreakers, pumpernickel bread, and everything in between. Whether they are good or bad depends on which ones you are thinking of.

In 1981, David J. A. Jenkins, MD, PhD, came up with a remarkable system that suddenly made sense of it all. He fed various carbohydrate-containing foods to volunteers and then took blood samples over the next two hours. He found that some foods had a huge impact on blood sugar, while others had no effect at all, and still others were between the two extremes. He standardized the testing method and gave it the name glycemic index.

Dr. Jenkins did not stop there, however. After showing how the glycemic index (GI) could be used to help people with diabetes, he then showed how healthy food patterns could have dramatic effects on blood sugar, cholesterol, and many other aspects of health. Following an entirely vegan diet himself, Dr. Jenkins asks whether our food choices are not just healthful, but also humane and sustainable. Are they environmentally sound? In the process, he has guided government bodies and the food industry to healthier policies.

So, are carbs good or bad? The answer is that carbohydrate-rich foods are healthful as a group. They supply the energy our bodies need, and the best of them have a low GI, along with their natural fiber. But when they are overly processed, as in the case of white bread and french fries, they lose much of their health value.

Today's Quick Kitchen Tip: GI Combinations

Not too long ago, I visited France. The baguette in the breakfast basket was still warm and smelled wonderful. I cut a six-inch piece and poked my finger in the end of it, making a little trough. Opening up a can of lentils I had bought at the store, I spooned lentils into the bread, making a lentil sandwich.

I tell you about this odd little experiment to illustrate a point. When you combine two or more foods, the GI of the combination is simply the average of the two. So white bread's high GI is balanced by the low GI of lentils. In England, breakfast beans on toast accomplish the same thing. The low-GI beans counterbalance the high-GI bread.

When you buy rye or pumpernickel bread at the store, you will see a similar principle in action. Many brands are actually mixtures of rye and wheat. Since rye has a low GI and wheat is higher, the actual GI of the bread ends up between the two.

One more tip: When Italian chefs keep their pasta al dente—that is, cooked just enough and not too much—they are actually maintaining its healthful low GI. The longer you cook it and the softer it becomes, the higher the GI.

Celebrating Our Progress

Let me share with you a few comments from Kickstart participants. Next week, I'll share their long-term successes, but I thought you'd like to hear what they are saying in the first week or two. These are real experiences of real people who are doing exactly what you are doing.

Lori from Austin wrote, "I have lost 5 lbs in the first 4 days without doing anything physical. So far, so good. I hope that I end up losing 15 more lbs."

Another Kickstart participant wrote, "I have only been on the program for one week and have already lost 6.5 pounds. This is a much healthier way to eat and honestly I am not hungry between meals. It's true this type of diet makes you feel fuller and it stays with you. I feel like I can really succeed with this lifestyle change."

Another Kickstart friend wrote, "I wanted to share my excitement at losing 2.8 pounds from a week ago, 7.4 pounds over the course of two weeks." She mentioned that her diet had been reasonably good before the program started, but tuning it up made all the difference. "I am very encouraged to see weight coming off, and I am hoping to lose at least 3 pounds this week as well."

As I've mentioned, weight is not the only issue for the Kickstart program. Jen from Boston wrote, "I cannot believe how my acne has cleared up, skin tone is more even and brighter. Healthier looking. I have had someone ask me what products I am using on my skin. (I haven't been wearing makeup for 3 days!)"

CHAPTER 9

Going to the Max

Congratulations! If following this program has led you to this page, that means you've reached your final week!

By now, you might be getting comfortable with this new way of eating. Or perhaps there are still some things you are sorting out. Or you might be feeling that you have only just gotten started, and you're a bit nervous that we're already nearing the end!

Whatever you're feeling, there is still much, much more ahead. For most people, the third week is when everything starts to come together. The bathroom scale really becomes your friend. Your energy is better than ever. Health problems are fading away. And you suddenly find that your tastes have begun to change as old and unhealthful habits fade away.

Day 15. Protecting Every Cell, and Slowing the Aging Process

What is it that causes the aging of our skin—or the aging of other parts of the body? Is there something we can do to slow down the aging process?

It turns out that the aging process has very little to do with time. It is caused by the persistent attack, day by day, of *free radicals*, those mischievous molecules we briefly touched on in chapter 5. Just as pollution in the air gradually damages stone buildings, these destructive molecules take their toll on our bodies. Fortunately, we have built-in defenses, and foods can strengthen them.

Understanding the Enemy

Every minute of every day, you breathe in oxygen. It passes through your lungs, into your bloodstream, and ultimately to every cell in your body. Oxygen is life giving. But it is also very unstable. As oxygen molecules course through your bloodstream and in and out of your cells, it is easy for them to become altered or damaged. This altered form of oxygen is called a *free radical*. And unlike normal oxygen, which is life giving, free radicals are like sharks, attacking anything in their path.

Free radicals attack the cell membranes that surround your cells, causing skin wrinkling, for example. They can even damage the DNA deep inside the cell's nucleus, sparking the changes that lead to cancer.

Strengthening Our Defenses

Our bodies have shields against free radicals. Beta-carotene, for example, is the orange pigment in a carrot. But it is much more than an attractive color. As you eat a carrot, these protective molecules pass into your cell membranes. If a free radical attacks, it damages your beta-carotene shield instead of your cell membrane.

Slice open a bright orange yam. The same beta-carotene color is there, too. Ditto for butternut squash and cantaloupe. Some foods also have hidden beta-carotene. Did you ever neglect a stalk of broccoli until it was too late to eat it? Did you notice that it starts to reveal an orange color as the green starts to fade? That's beta-carotene that was hidden by the chlorophyll. Just as green leaves turn orange in autumn, many vegetables show their other pigments when their chlorophyll is gone.

Am I suggesting that green and orange foods can fight free radicals—and even fight the aging process to a degree? Yes, that's exactly what I am saying. But there is much more to it than that. Your biological defense system has many other parts. They are not perfect, but it is important to put them to work.

Vitamin E parks in your cell membranes, just as beta-carotene does. You'll find it in soybeans and other common beans (pinto beans, chickpeas), sunflower seeds, almonds and other nuts, and many other foods.

Selenium is a mineral that works with vitamin E. Selenium is found in a great many foods, including oats, rice, wheat, corn, soybeans, walnuts, and plenty of others.

Vitamin C plays a special role. While beta-carotene, vitamin E, and selenium shield your cell membranes, vitamin C patrols the watery parts of your body between the cells, looking for free radicals and knocking them out.

Beta-carotene, vitamin E, and vitamin C are called *antioxidants*; they fight free radicals. And they have a great many allies. Take a tomato, for example. That bright red color is *lycopene*, a cousin of beta-carotene. You'll also see lycopene in watermelon and pink grapefruit. It turns out that there are hundreds of similar compounds in other fruits and vegetables.

And that is actually the key fact. Some people take a beta-carotene or lycopene pill, hoping to build their antioxidant defenses. But what they are missing is that there are actually hundreds of antioxidants packed naturally in fruits, vegetables, and their botanical cousins. If you take just one or two of them in pill form, not only are you missing all the other parts of your antioxidant army; you are creating a nutritional imbalance.

When you shop for groceries, start at the produce aisle, and notice the bright colors, signaling the presence of antioxidants. If an abundance of vegetables and fruits, along with beans and whole grains, make their way into your shopping cart, you will get the protection you need.

Here is what to look for:

Orange, Yellow, and Green Vegetables. Carrots, yams, squash, broccoli, kale, and many others bring you beta-carotene and its carotenoid cousins, as well as vitamin C.

Fruits. Oranges, papayas, strawberries, and mangoes bring you vitamin C. Tomatoes, watermelon, and pink grapefruit bring you lycopene.

Beans, Nuts, and Seeds. Vitamin E is found in many legumes (that is, the bean group). So those chickpeas you're putting on your salad don't just bring you protein, minerals, and a hearty texture; they also add some vitamin E. Nuts and seeds have vitamin E, too. But go easy. Because nuts and seeds tend to pack in fat, an ounce per day is more than enough, and you're better off using them in sauces and toppings, rather than eating them as a snack, where things can easily get out of hand.

Aiding and Abetting

Just as some foods are your allies in the battle against free radicals, others work against you. Certain foods actually *encourage* the production of free radicals:

Iron. If you were to leave a wet cast-iron pan in your sink for a day or two, what would happen? It would rust—that is, it oxidizes. A similar process happens to the iron inside your body: Iron encourages the production of free radicals, as we saw in chapter 5.

You do need a small amount of iron in your diet. Your red blood cells use it to make the hemoglobin that transports oxygen from place to place. And you can get the iron you need from green vegetables and beans. Where people run into trouble is with meat or iron supplements; they often end up getting too much iron, setting themselves up for free radical attacks. You already want to avoid meat, of course, because of its fat and cholesterol. Iron supplements should only be used if your health care provider has specifically recommended them.

Alcohol encourages the production of free radicals. It also depletes your body of antioxidants, which may account for why people with alcohol problems sometimes look older than their years. If you drink, it is a good idea to keep it modest and intermittent, rather than daily.

Oils encourage the production of free radicals, too. Fish oils, for example, are highly unstable, and encourage the formation of free radicals as they degrade. You can get the healthful omega-3 fats your body needs as a natural part of fruits, vegetables, and beans. There are also natural omega-3s in walnuts, soy products, and flaxseeds.

A Word of Inspiration

Just as aromas attract us to foods, colors can, too. Brenda Davis, RD, says, "When you plan a meal, think in every color of the rainbow." Brenda is a dietitian and author who has been influential in nutrition policies in the United States and Canada. She points out that those colors are not there just for fun:

The amazing color pigments in plants are phytochemicals that are there to protect the plant. Fortunately, when you eat them, they help to protect you, too. Many are powerful antioxidants; some fight cancer, others help to protect against diabetes, high blood pressure, or heart disease.

If your plate is mostly brown and white, it's time to color it up. Each color offers unique protection. Aim for at least three green (e.g. broccoli, leafy greens, asparagus, peas, honeydew), one red (e.g. red pepper, cherries, red apples, tomatoes, watermelon), one purple or blue (e.g. purple grapes, eggplant, purple cabbage, blueberries, blackberries), one orange-yellow (e.g. carrots, squash, yams, mango, pineapple) and one white fruit or vegetable each day (e.g. onion, garlic, cauliflower, bananas, mushrooms).

Today's Quick Kitchen Tip: The Quick Cut

So you're looking at that beautiful mango, tasty and full of beta-carotene, wondering how to slice it open. Don't spend all day trying to carve it. The trick is to turn it inside out.

Just slice it in half and remove the pit. Set the mango on your cutting board and, with your knife tip, cut a grid into the flesh, like a big tic-tac-toe design. Then just pop it inside out and little cubes of mango will jump up, ready for you to cut them off.

Speaking of cutting things up, let me share a tip for garlic. When you slice garlic, does it cake up on the knife and on your fingers? Here's the answer: Just dribble a few drops of water onto the garlic clove before you slice it (or dip your fingers in water), and it will be much easier. For extra credit, add a bit of salt. Salt "digests" the garlic as you cut it, and if you mince it very fine, it turns into a very handy garlic paste. Try it. You'll see.

Day 16. Foods That Conquer Pain

To feel your best, you'll want to get rid of everyday aches and pains. So today, we will look at how foods can help. It is surprising to imagine that foods could cure joint pains or headaches. But they can. Today we'll look at foods that help and hurt.

But first, let's see how you are doing. How is your weight? Is it going in the right direction? Are you feeling comfortable with the foods you're eating, and are they giving you the rewards you are looking for? If so, you are right on schedule. If you are having any troubles, it's always good to review our basic guidelines, and make sure you're not missing anything.

Okay, on to today's topic.

Fighting Pain with Foods

We all have aches and pains from time to time. That's normal, of course. But if pain is ongoing or recurrent, you should know how foods fit in. As a physician, I was surprised to learn that foods play a key role in back pain, joint pain, and headaches. I also discovered, quite accidentally, that diet changes can alleviate menstrual cramps.

Because these problems are so common, I wanted to share this information with you. As you will see, the dietary prescription for each of these resonates strongly with the Kickstart program you are already familiar with. But there are some important extra steps you can take, as we will see. For many people, simple diet changes lead to amazing relief.

But first, one important note: See your doctor. This is important. Many types of pain reflect serious underlying conditions. It is essential to have a thorough evaluation of your pain and to understand the appropriate treatments. It is a serious mistake to simply make diet adjustments without knowing what sort of condition you are dealing with.

Joint Pains. If you have rheumatoid arthritis, a diet change could help you, and perhaps even eliminate your pain entirely. In research studies, many people who eliminate certain trigger foods find that their pain improves or goes away. The reason, presumably, is that certain foods spark inflammation in the tissues lining the joints. When those foods are gone, so is the inflammation.

Not everyone has an identifiable diet trigger. In research studies, about half of people with typical rheumatoid arthritis improve with a diet adjustment. Here are the most common triggers for joint pain:

Common Triggers for Joint Pain

Dairy products	Potatoes
Corn	Tomatoes
Meats	Nuts
Wheat, rye, oats	Coffee
Eggs	Sugar
Citrus fruits	

Typically, it is just one or two of these foods that causes the problem. The question, of course, is which one? Here's how to find out:

Start with the basic Kickstart diet. We've already eliminated dairy products, meats, and eggs, which are three of the top triggers. If your joint pains are starting to improve, you may have already solved your problem. If you need more help, I suggest you eliminate all the triggers listed above for about one month. If your joint pains improve or disappear, the next step is to reintroduce each trigger food, one at a time, starting at the bottom of the list. As you do so, have a generous amount of each one for about two days before introducing the next item. So you would have sugary foods for two days. If no symptoms recur, go on and have coffee for two days, then nuts, and so on. Skip any foods that you do not wish to include in your routine. If a food causes symptoms, omit it for several weeks before trying it again.

Migraines. If you have headaches, and your doctor has diagnosed migraines, you might see what a diet change can do for you. Many people with migraines are able to reduce or eliminate their headaches using exactly the same technique described earlier for joint pains. The main difference is in the list of common triggers.

Here are the most common triggers for migraines:

Common Triggers for Migraines

Dairy products	Nuts
Chocolate	Tomatoes
Eggs	Onions
Citrus fruits	Corn
Meat	Apples
Wheat	Bananas

Back Pain. As we saw in chapter 4, back pain may be related to food, too. Surprising, isn't it? The problem, it appears, is poor circulation. Just as a meaty diet and smoking can constrict the arteries to the heart, they do the same thing to the arteries to the spine, particularly the lower back. When that happens, the leathery disks that act like cushions between the vertebrae start to become fragile. A fragile disk can break open, like a pillow that loses its stuffing. The soft core of the disk then squeezes out and can pinch a nerve, causing pain that extends all the way down your leg.

The menu changes that are part of the Kickstart program are ideal not only for reopening arteries, but also for trimming away excess weight that can aggravate back pain. If you suffer from chronic back pain, I would encourage you to stick with this program and see how things go.

Menstrual Cramps. Several years ago, a young woman called my office in misery. She could barely get out of bed. The problem was severe menstrual pain. Most young women experience cramps to some degree, but for about one in ten, they are really off the scale.

For a day or two every month, life can be pretty tough, and that is what she was going through. She asked for painkillers so she could function.

I agreed to give her a prescription for painkillers to ease her immediate symptoms. But as she was talking, I got to thinking. We know that foods can influence sex hormones. After all, cancer researchers noticed long ago that women on mainly plant-based diets had lower—that is, healthier—levels of estrogens in their blood and much less risk of breast cancer, compared with women eating meaty diets. Maybe a plant-based diet would also reduce the risk of other hormonal problems. Problems like menstrual cramps.

So I suggested an experiment. I asked if, over the next month, she would eliminate animal products and oily foods and emphasize whole grains, vegetables, fruits, and beans. She agreed to give it a try. And to her amazement, when her period arrived the following month, she had virtually no pain at all. Her period just sneaked up on her with no problems.

I then decided to test this approach in a larger group of women. We found that, indeed, it reduces the intensity and duration of menstrual pain, sometimes knocking it out altogether. We published our findings in the journal *Obstetrics & Gynecology*.[1]

If you have bothersome cramps, try it out for yourself. The key is to keep it vegan throughout the month, keep oils to an absolute minimum, and emphasize natural high-fiber foods. That means plenty of vegetables, fruits, beans, and whole grains. The fiber in these foods helps your body eliminate excess estrogens. When your next period arrives, see how you feel.

Whether you suffer from joint pains, headaches, back pain, or cramps, foods may be a big part of the solution.

A Word of Inspiration

I recently spoke at a nutrition conference in Monterey, California, invited by Dana Armstrong, a registered dietitian. I asked Dana what had led to her interest in a plant-based diet. She told me that she had started to experience neck pain a couple of years earlier. At first, she thought she might need a new pillow. But then the pain began to spread throughout her body. It became clear that this was not ordinary stiffness. She soon had a diagnosis of rheumatoid arthritis, and her form was especially severe. One morning, after having had a long drive the day before, she could not even get out of bed. She was only forty-nine years old. She started taking steroids and other powerful drugs, but was still in pain.

Although most physicians treat joint pain with medications, research has shown that foods play a role, as you now know. A 2002 study showed that a very low-fat vegan diet can have a dramatic effect on even severe rheumatoid arthritis, and several other studies have shown similar results. Needless to say, vegan diets omit some of the particularly common triggers.

Dana learned about how nutrition could help, and threw out the animal products. Almost immediately, her symptoms started to improve. Before long, she had not only recovered from arthritis but also lost forty pounds and found that her acne cleared up! "I also sleep very well now," Dana says. "Apparently I didn't need a new pillow!"

Many people have never heard of the power of diet changes. But those who have had a chance to try this approach often report stunning success.

Today's Quick Kitchen Tip: Healthful Omega-3s

If you sprinkle some flaxseeds on your salad or serve yourself a bowl of edamame (soybeans steamed in the pod), you're thinking about taste. But what you might not know is that these foods contain traces of a natural anti-inflammatory compound called ALA, or alpha-linolenic acid. It is an essential omega-3 fatty acid—that is, a "good" fat that your body actually needs—and it helps combat the inflammation of arthritis. There are traces of it in many vegetables, fruits, and beans, and you'll find an abundance of it in flaxseeds and soy products.

As you know, a key part of the Kickstart program is to get away from the oily foods that are such a big part of many people's diets. I think of ALA not as a food, but as a natural medicine. In fact, health food stores sell it that way—not just as flaxseeds, but as bottles of flax oil.

There are also other, less common, oils that have shown value against arthritis pain. Borage, black currant, and evening primrose oil contain GLA, or *gamma-linolenic acid*. These are not cooking oils. They are on the supplement shelves at health food stores.

If you are thinking of using these oils against arthritis, let me encourage you to start with a menu change first. You'll want to see if you can identify a food trigger, following the guidelines on page 200. Then, if you'd like to add modest amounts of healthful oils, here is a typical regimen. You take *each* of the following every day with your evening meal:

1. Flaxseed oil, one tablespoon.
2. Borage, black currant, or evening primrose oil, 1.4 to 2.8 grams of GLA.
3. Vitamin E, four hundred IU, or one hundred IU for people with high blood pressure (vitamin E protects against oxidation of the oils).

Day 17. Eating Your Way to a Good Night's Sleep

Today, let's talk about sleep. For two reasons:

First, one of the benefits of a healthy diet is that you sleep better.

Second, one of the benefits of sleeping better is that it helps you stick to a healthy diet. The fact is, if you are sleep-deprived, you'll eat almost anything just to get through the day. But if you are well rested, it is easier to say no to temptation.

Do you remember when you were little? Chances are, you ran around during the day, then when bedtime came, you collapsed into sleep. Next morning, you woke up filled with energy. You didn't need coffee or an energy drink. You were energetic naturally.

As we get older, things change. Increasing responsibilities and some not-so-healthy habits start to get in the way of a good night's sleep. And that can cause problems you're not expecting.

First of all, you might have trouble with your weight. Surprising, isn't it? In the 1980s, US government researchers surveyed a large group of Americans about their sleep patterns as part of the National Health and Nutrition Examination Survey. It turned out that those who slept only five hours a night were 60 percent more likely to be obese, compared with people who got seven to nine hours. People who slept only two to four hours per night were more than twice as likely to be obese. Other researchers found exactly the same thing. People who don't sleep much have trouble managing their weight.

How can this be? Well, one reason is obvious: You can't eat when you're unconscious. But there is actually more to it. As you sleep, your brain produces leptin, the appetite-control hormone. Sleep also strengthens your emotional equilibrium and brings back your energy for physical activity. If you are sleep-deprived, you will have poor appetite control, higher stress levels, more impulsivity, and no energy to exercise. You are set up for eating junk food of all kinds.

It will not surprise you that chronically sleep-deprived people are more likely to develop diabetes and high blood pressure.

So let's see what we can do to get our z's back. If you've lost track of how to get a good night's sleep, here are some simple tips:

Increase Physical Activity. The more physically active you are during the day, the better you'll sleep at night. The fact is, sleep rests your body *and* your mind. So if you have been vigorously active during the day, your body demands sleep. If you have been sedentary, a few push-ups or similar muscle-stressing exercises—whatever you can do within the limits of safety—before bed can help.

Avoid Caffeine. You know that caffeine is a stimulant. What you might not know is that as much as one-quarter of the caffeine in your morning coffee is still circulating in your bloodstream twelve hours later. Different people eliminate caffeine differently, so pay attention to how it affects you. You may do well to break a caffeine habit altogether.

Avoid Alcohol. A mixed drink or glass of wine lulls you to sleep. But soon, alcohol transforms into related chemicals, called aldehydes, which are stimulants. At four thirty in the morning, they will wake you up, and all the problems of the previous day will descend.

Stretch and Yawn. Before you lie down to sleep, do what you did as a child: Make a big stretch and yawn. These routines get your body ready to sleep, and you'll notice that stressed-out people tend not to do them. So even though it sounds a bit silly, go through the same motions: Stretch and make a big yawn, even if you have to fake it. Do it four times. Eventually, a genuine yawn will follow, and you'll find your body starting to relax into sleep.

When you wake up tomorrow, you'll be better rested and ready to take on the new day and new challenges.

A Word of Inspiration

Let me share a tip from Bob Harper, the charismatic fitness trainer from *The Biggest Loser*. You may have already discovered that you are not just getting healthier *physically*. A menu change also affects how you feel about yourself and about the world around you. And things work in the other direction, too: A good attitude toward health can help your physical transformation.

Bob starts a nutritional makeover from the inside out—that is, he starts by building the right attitude. "When you pay attention to what you eat, it becomes easier to understand your relationship with food and how it affects your day-to-day life," he says. "When you really start to respect your body, your body starts taking care of you."

Okay, but if we're dissecting everything we eat, and trying to squeeze exercise into an already busy schedule, will we end up getting so stressed out that we'll just defeat our purpose? The answer is no, as Bob points out: "Health, happiness, and peace can be achieved simultaneously—and are really at the root of learning how to take care of ourselves."

Today's Quick Kitchen Tip: Keep High-Protein Foods Earlier in the Day

Beans, lentils, tofu, and other high-protein foods can be very nutritious. But if you are not sleeping well, try shifting these foods to earlier in the day. These and other high-protein foods block your brain's ability to produce serotonin, the neurotransmitter that helps you sleep.

On the other hand, if you are trying to sleep, starchy foods—like bread, potatoes, and pasta—are just what you need. They cause your brain to produce more serotonin. With high-protein foods early in the day and starchier foods (rice, pasta, and so on) in the evening, you'll be alert when you want to be, and can unwind as night approaches.

By the way, the idea that turkey is good for sleep is a myth. Years ago, health writers said that turkey contains the amino acid tryptophan, which is converted to serotonin in the brain. Well, turkey *does* contain tryptophan. But it contains many other amino acids along with it, and all of them compete with tryptophan to get into the brain. So turkey eaters actually get *less* serotonin, not more. The reason people feel sluggish after their Thanksgiving dinner has more to do with the greasy meal, not any serotonin effect from turkey.

Day 18. Play with Your Food

By now, you've got the basics down. Hopefully, you have found plenty of meals you enjoy and they are beginning to work their magic for you. Today, I'd like to ramp it up just a notch. There are a million ways to add something a little special to food and its place in our lives. Let me share some of my favorites:

Special Toppings. There is almost nothing as healthful as green leafy vegetables, like broccoli, kale, and spinach. But if their nutritional power is not quite enough to seduce your taste buds, try a special topping.

Apple cider vinegar, for example. It is unassuming on its own, but sprinkle it on greens, and an amazing alchemy turns them instantly sweet and flavorful. Seasoned rice vinegar does the same thing with an Asian twist. Bragg Liquid Aminos is *the* topping for steamed kale, and it works great on Brussels sprouts, broccoli, and other greens, too. Or dust your veggies with nutritional yeast for a mild cheesy taste without cheese's fat or cholesterol.

Perfect Pizza. A couple of simple tricks can make pizza truly spectacular. Yes, you want to skip the cheese and make up for it with extra tomato sauce. But let's make it special. Sauté some onions (see the technique in appendix 2). As they caramelize, they become the perfect topping. Do the same with mushrooms and spinach, then sprinkle on nutritional yeast for a cheesy flavor. If you'd like a little zip, add a few jalapeño slices, and you are headed for pizza nirvana.

The Cool Cookout. Grilling isn't just for meaty tastes anymore. Anyone can chip in. Corn on the cob, asparagus, portobellos, and veggie kebabs are all great, not to mention veggie burgers and veggie hot dogs.

Turbocharge Your Salad. Turn a simple salad into a delicious main dish by adding flavored tofu, beans, nuts or seeds, and fruit (sliced strawberries, cubed mangoes, chopped apples, or dried cherries, for example).

New Foods. A few years ago, I had the chance to visit Corsica, a Mediterranean island that has been part of France for the past two centuries. The countryside is rugged, and the coastal towns and beaches are spectacular. But what really got my attention was the *blette*—a green leafy vegetable that appears on menus and turns up in soups all over Corsica. It looked a bit like spinach, but sturdier and very tasty. Unfortunately, I could not for the life of me figure out what it was or how I might find it at the Safeway back home. So I measured it, photographed it—everything short of a biopsy.

After arriving home, I happened to notice that Swiss chard bears a suspiciously strong resemblance to a *blette.* And, of course, that's just what it is. I had never tasted chard back home, but I was now in love with it.

The lesson I learned is that venturing into the uncharted regions of the produce aisle can be an adventure. Not only are there *blettes* (chard to you), there are a zillion other fruits and vegetables to try.

Juicing for Variety. In the early 1990s, a Juiceman juicer arrived in my mail, unsolicited. Apparently, the company wanted me to test out its product, which was being sold on television.

I had tasted carrot juice once or twice, but it really didn't do it for me. Before giving the juicer away, though, I decided to give it another try. I bought some carrots and a couple of apples and stuffed them in. And to my surprise, it turned out to be very tasty. I tried it again and before long, I became a kid with a chemistry set, whipping up all kinds of juice combinations from carrots, apples, celery, spinach, beets, oranges, and everything else. It was fun, healthy, and really delicious. And I found that organic baby-cut carrots meant I didn't even need to spend time washing and peeling.

Now, the dietitians I work with at the Physicians Committee for Responsible Medicine remind me that the process of juicing discards much of the fiber from a vegetable, and so I should really be eating the whole thing. And of course, they're right. But as a special treat, a glass of carrot juice beats the socks off a doughnut, and it's a great way to add variety to your menu. It also makes a fun party for your family or friends. Especially for anyone who is a bit reluctant to take advantage of vegetables, juicing is a handy trick.

Cereal That Tastes Homemade. I learned this one, and the next, from Brenda Davis, RD: If you'd like to ramp up your morning cereal, you can replace processed boxed cereals with homemade muesli. Just mix old-fashioned rolled oats with fruits, nuts, and seeds and soak it overnight in nondairy milk and/or nondairy yogurt.

Delicious Desserts. You can make your own frozen dessert with frozen bananas, along with other frozen fruits such as mangoes or berries. Add them to a blender, along with just enough nondairy milk so it will blend.

Or try blending frozen bananas with a touch of maple syrup, pecans or walnuts, and vanilla. Out of this world!

Exploring New Cuisines. Growing up in Fargo, our idea of dining out was dinner at The Bowler after playing a couple of lanes. We didn't know much about Italian food or Chinese food, let alone Thai or sushi. The closest we got to ethnic cuisine was lefse, a flat Norwegian potato bread that appeared on North Dakota tables every Christmas, which we smeared with butter and sugar.

When I started to rethink my diet, I first discovered Italian plum tomatoes and fresh basil, which were delicious on angelhair pasta. And then I discovered that Chinese menus had a special section beyond beef, pork, chicken, and fish—a huge list of vegetable main dishes I had never heard of. And that led me to Hunan and Szechuan dishes. Eventually, I stumbled into Japanese food, with wonderful soups, salads, and vegetable sushi. Mexican, Salvadoran, Thai, Vietnamese—there were so many to explore. I felt like Dorothy in *The Wizard of Oz*, whose world turned from black-and-white to color when her house plunked down in the Land of Oz. For me, a vegan diet did not mean restrictions. Just the opposite: It meant that the world of culinary delights was opening up.

So if you need a short vacation from the usual, why not try a new cuisine? If you are near any major North American city, you'll find endless possibilities that let you take a culinary trip to East Asia, India, South America, or Africa. In Washington, DC, Ethiopian cuisine is all the rage (and the flat injera bread is surprisingly similar to lefse!).

If your restaurant choices are limited, you can still travel the world through the recipes in this book and in the array of international cookbooks you'll find online and in bookstores.

Asian Grocery Stores. If you have never been to an Asian grocery store, you are in for a treat. The range of new and exotic vegetables and fruits is stunning, and there are endless packaged foods to try as well. Of course, Asian groceries favor many different traditions—Indian, Korean, Japanese, Chinese, Vietnamese, and many others, depending on where you go. But you will soon find that you are opening many new doors, and the range of new tastes is practically endless.

Start with the vegetables. You'll find a huge array of greens, all of them worth trying. Look at the exotic mushrooms, interesting fruits, and wonderful seasonings.

A Word of Inspiration

A great many people have given a gift of good health to themselves and their families. The great physicist Albert Einstein was one of them. In a letter dated December 27, 1930, he wrote, "It is my view that a vegetarian manner of living by its purely physical effect on the human temperament would most beneficially influence the lot of mankind." It took him a while to get there himself. But on March 30, 1954, he wrote, "So I am living without fats, without meat, without fish, but am feeling quite well this way. It always seems to me that man was not born to be a carnivore."

Today's Quick Kitchen Tip: Be Careful About Freezing Foods

Okay, so we've got lots of interesting new fruits and vegetables on our kitchen counter. And we have a take-home bag from our dinner out. Let me share a quick tip about freezing foods:

Some foods freeze very well, and others don't. Here's why: Freezing creates ice crystals that burst the cellular structure of your ingredients, making them soft. So you've cut up your salad, fruits, or uncooked vegetables—maybe some zucchini, asparagus, or plantains. If you were to pop them in the freezer, they would come out soft and even mushy.

But if foods are already soft or are liquid, like soups and stews, that's okay. Into the freezer they go. And foods that contain very little water, like nuts and seeds, tend to freeze very well. But if your meal needs a crunchy or firm texture, don't freeze it.

Day 19. Extra Motivators: Environment and Animals

When we change our diets to improve our health, some of us stick with it really well. But others need a bit of help. The fact is, people who develop motivations beyond their personal health often find it much easier to stay on the straight and narrow. Take committed environmentalists, for example. Knowing how the livestock industry affects the planet, they wouldn't think of eating meat, and knowing what pesticides can do to the waterways, they always favor organic produce. They have the weight of the world on their shoulders.

If you have young people in your home, you know that they are not even remotely concerned about atherosclerosis, diabetes, or prostate cancer. A teenage boy does not have a prostate, so far as he knows, and will not become aware of it for quite some time. But many young people care passionately about the environment or about animals. So if you are encouraging them to jump with you into a healthier way of eating, let me share some facts that might be meaningful to them.

Before I do, I have to confess that, when I moved from the Midwest to Washington, DC, to go to medical school, I did not have a thought in my head about any of these things. I was training to become a doctor, hopefully a very good one, and that was it. I cared about the environment in a generic sort of way and I believed in kindness toward animals. But that did not keep them off the menu. I hunted with my father and brothers and knew a bit about the cattle business. As time has gone on, I have come to learn a bit more, and this chapter will share some of these basics.

Livestock Feed

When I was growing up in North Dakota, cornfields were a common sight. Corn grows as far as the eye can see. But essentially none of it is going to be eaten by a human being. It is feed for cattle, hogs, and chickens.

Now, a stalk of corn looks innocent enough. But each cornstalk in those fields is like a domino—one knocks down the next, and the next, and so on. I don't mean that the cornstalks actually fall. What I mean to say is that, when they are used for animal feed, they set in motion a series of events that add up to a real catastrophe. Let me explain:

First of all, it takes about a million gallons of water to grow an acre of corn. Irrigation uses far more water than watering our lawns, washing our cars, brushing our teeth, cooking, or any other routine human activity.

As that water trickles into rivers and streams, it carries fertilizer along with it—fertilizer that the farmers had applied to their fields. That fertilizer makes algae overgrow in the waterways. And as algae decomposes, it uses up oxygen in the water—oxygen that fish need to live. The fish die, along with all other life-forms in what is known as a dead zone—an area where aquatic life simply cannot survive.

This may sound like no more than a theoretical problem. But the Mississippi River collects water—and fertilizer—from a huge section of North America, depositing it in the Gulf of Mexico. And long before British Petroleum fouled the Gulf of Mexico with oil, there was already an eight-thousand-square-mile dead zone below Louisiana and Texas, all thanks to American agriculture.

Here is what matters: It takes about three pounds of feed to produce a pound of poultry meat. It takes even more—seven to thirteen pounds of feed—to produce a pound of beef. If people actually ate plants, instead of feeding them to animals, the amount of land we would need to feed ourselves would be minuscule compared with what we are using today. Our need for irrigation and fertilizers would be reduced, too. Our waterways would be spared.

These observations are certainly not news. In 1971, Frances Moore Lappé made exactly this argument in a book called *Diet for a Small Planet*. That year, 1971, was also the year I graduated from high school. My light blue pants had grease stains that came from the McDonald's on University Drive in Fargo, where I cooked french fries, made milk shakes, and worked the cash register. The hamburger chain proclaimed "*You* Deserve a Break Today," and I was entirely unaware that the Earth needed a break, too.

Greenhouse

In case I haven't depressed you entirely, let me share a couple of other facts. First, cows are big. Each one is as big as a sofa, and the combined mass of the hundred million or so beef and dairy cattle on US farms easily outweighs that of the entire human population. Every last one of them is busily belching methane into the air— methane that is produced as the feed in their stomachs ferments. Methane is a greenhouse gas—a much more potent greenhouse gas than carbon dioxide. At any given time, the result is an enormous invisible methane cloud.

What about fish, you might ask. Are they any better, environmentally? Well, to meet the world's demand, fishermen do not wait for fish to jump into their boats. They pull them in with nets that trap the target fish and any others nearby—dolphins along with tuna, for example. Bottom trawling is a method that drags a huge net across the ocean floor, catching any and all species that can be scooped into the net and destroying coral and everything else in its path.

Here's the good news: Switching to a plant-based diet reduces your carbon footprint to the size of a baby bootie. Now, you could argue that the raising of crops can be harmful to the environment, too, and you would be right. Produce demands irrigation and fertilizer, and farmers who are not using organic techniques apply pesticides and other chemicals. The difference is one of scale. Growing grains simply to feed them to animals is enormously inefficient, requiring huge amounts of resources and outstripping the Earth's ability to recover.

A Word of Inspiration

For stand-up comic and television star Sarah Silverman, it was a very personal experience that changed her menu forever, and she shared it with others in her recent memoir, *The Bedwetter*:

> We lived on a farm, but it wasn't operational like our neighbors' farms, which produced stuff; we bought our meat and vegetables from them. When I was six years old, my dad took me there to see the turkeys. The farmer, Vic, told me to look at all the birds carefully and choose one that I liked. I saw a cute one with a silly walk and said, "Him!!" Before my pointing finger dropped back down to my side, Vic had grabbed the bird by the neck and slit his throat. Blood sprayed as the turkey's wings flapped back and forth in a futile attempt to unkill itself. Without realizing it, I had sentenced that turkey to death, and while maybe this sort of thing gave fat British monarchs a rush, to me it was horrifying. And though I'm probably projecting, I don't think it was in the turkey's top-five favorite moments, either.
>
> In hindsight, I'm sure my dad feels bad about our little excursion, but I see it as a gift. My father might not have realized or intended it, but that day he gave me the knowledge to make an informed decision for myself at a very early age: I would never eat turkey again. And once I figured out the connection between Happy Meals and cows, I would never eat beef again, either. Or any other meat.

Strange to think that your breakfast could save the Earth, prevent animal misery, or save human lives, isn't it? But it may well be just the way to do your part. Your coronary arteries don't care *why* you change your diet. But when you do, they breathe a sigh of relief.

Today's Quick Kitchen Tip: Local Produce

A vegan diet is kind to the Earth. And if you'd like to be especially kind, you might check out your local farmers' markets. You'll get the freshest produce, often picked just that morning.

Let me encourage you, too, to get involved with Community Supported Agriculture, or CSA. It is like magic: You just sign up, and a weekly box of vegetables and fruit is delivered for you, all local and fresh. You'll find more information at www.localharvest.org.

Day 20. Thinking About Our Loved Ones

Yesterday we looked at extra motivators that can help us stay on track. Today we'll look at one more. In fact, for many people it is the strongest motivator of all. Our food choices may be able to protect our loved ones.

Children's Health

Kids today face all manner of challenges. More than a third of US children are overweight. One in five has an abnormal cholesterol level. The Centers for Disease Control and Prevention predict that one in three children born since the year 2000 will develop diabetes at some point in his or her life.

These problems are not just physical. When children are out of shape, they take a beating emotionally, too. And it doesn't get better in adulthood as weight problems worsen and physical limitations become more and more serious.

The second kindest thing parents can do for their children is to show them how to follow a diet based on healthful vegetables, fruits, whole grains, and beans, throwing out the animal products and greasy foods. It is hands-down the healthiest diet for children of any age.

For starters, a plant-based diet helps prevent obesity. A study of 1,765 children and adolescents in Southern California showed that vegetarian children were slightly leaner than their meat-eating friends, and were about an inch taller. So far, so good. But their real advantage arrives as the years go by. Not only are children raised on plant-based diets more likely to stay slim, but they are also much less likely to develop heart disease, diabetes, and certain cancers than their nonvegetarian counterparts.

Don't think for a minute that children will shy away from healthful foods. My research team did a test in schools in South Florida. Broward County is the sixth largest school district in the United States, and demographically very diverse. One day, we gave schoolchildren a chance to taste bite-size samples of veggie burgers. The kids loved them. And the next day, veggie burgers were served in the lunch line. And they outsold the other offerings two to one! Later, we tried veggie chili, and beans and rice, and they were hugely successful, too. Today Broward County includes healthful vegan options on its regular school menu, giving children a huge advantage.

So what is the kindest thing parents can do? Follow a healthful diet *themselves*. When children have a solid example to follow, they are more likely to take it to heart.

Our Spouses and Partners

While we are thinking about the next generation, let's not forget the present one. Our girlfriends, boyfriends, wives, and husbands need help, just like children do. Some of our loved ones are eager to jump into health; others need some coaxing. And a few will hold their breath till they turn blue rather than eat a vegetable. But when we bring home healthy foods and cook them up, we're doing everyone a favor. Just as the previous generation finally accepted the fact that cigarette smoking really had to go, the current one is wrestling with food in exactly the same way. And the health vote is slowly winning the day.

A Doctor's Prescription

Benjamin Spock was one of the most influential doctors who ever lived. As a pediatrician who was also trained in psychoanalysis, he advocated for better parenting methods to help children to grow into healthy, well-adjusted adults.

When it came to nutrition, Dr. Spock encouraged a balanced diet of meat, dairy products, vegetables, and fruits. That is, until his own health began to fail. He changed his diet, throwing out meat, dairy products, eggs, and junk food, and rapidly recovered his health and strength. Then, in an updated edition of his best-selling book *Baby and Child Care*, Dr. Spock humbly pointed out that his dietary advice in previous editions had been shortsighted. Meat, dairy products, and eggs were not health foods. And children who were raised as vegetarians, he realized, would get real advantages that he had not appreciated.

In 1992, Dr. Spock and I held a press conference in Boston to alert parents to new research showing that dairy products could be linked to type 1 diabetes. The problem, it seemed, was that dairy proteins trigger the production of antibodies that can destroy the insulin-producing cells of the pancreas. Children were better off being breast-fed, and there was actually no need for cow's-milk products at any point in life.

At the press conference, Dr. Spock's wife, Mary Morgan, stepped up to the microphone to share a story about Ben. She told how Ben occasionally went out to buy very expensive cheese, which he prized. Looking in the refrigerator later, he would ask Mary, "What happened to the cheese I bought?" to which Mary would reply, "I threw it out, Ben. I love you too much to let you have anything that's not good for you." And Ben—a wise and kind man, if ever there was one—lived to be ninety-four.

Today's Quick Kitchen Tip: Giving Kids Choices

Most children are shy about new foods. They are reluctant to try a new vegetable, and they don't want foods to touch each other on the plate. So how can you introduce children to healthier fare?

First, avoid arm-wrestling with children about vegetables. They may balk at asparagus and broccoli; don't force the issue. Just serve carrots, corn, peas, green beans, and whatever other healthy foods they like. The rest will come when they are older.

Second, let them make choices. The key is to be sure that every choice is okay with you. So they can choose to have their sandwiches cut in squares or triangles, to have their dressing on the salad or on the side, and so on. You will want to make sure that any choice they make is a healthful one.

Day 21. Graduation Day!

Congratulations! It's graduation day! I hope you've enjoyed the Kickstart experience and that you've learned a lot about food and health that you can carry with you for life. And I hope you'll be able to share what you've learned with others.

So what's ahead? Having helped a great many people sort out their diets, I have noticed that, at this stage, the road forks into three possible paths.

1. The best way, obviously, is to keep going. You've gained momentum, you're trimming away weight, and you've left some not-so-healthy habits behind. Now you can see how far this approach will take you. You can maximize your gains and avoid backsliding into the food habits that caused your problems.

Many people are surprised as they decide to do just that. They had intended just to try it out, hopefully lose a few pounds, and then go back to their previous way of eating. But suddenly, about halfway through the Kickstart, food starts making sense. They see what has gotten them into trouble, and have found a much healthier path ahead. It is a bit like opening a new book or turning on a television program, intending to just see what it's about, and becoming enraptured.

One participant told me, "Having lost all this weight and feeling really great, I don't ever want to go back. I finally have power in my hands, and I'm not giving it up."

Three weeks is more than enough time to get started with a healthy diet and for your benefits to begin. But if you have a substantial amount of weight to lose or if you've been dealing with serious health issues, it will take more time for the results to fully come in. Through the Kickstart, you've succeeded in making a down payment on a whole new body. And now is the time to let that investment pay off for you.

You have shaken off your past. Imagine your future, reaching your goal weight and staying there, feeling really energetic and healthy. Imagine how you will feel and how you can look on your next birthday or on your next vacation.

A Kickstart participant who decided to continue after three weeks let me know how she was doing at the two-month mark:

"When I started, I was at 185. Today, I weigh 169.5 and am walking into a gym to join. This has been the easiest lifestyle change I have ever made. Life is full of tasty foods, my body feels better, and I'm headed home to my normal body weight of 132."

Another Kickstart participant from Arizona shared her experience after deciding to keep going once the program finished:

"In the first 4 months, I lost 37 lbs! I was amazed at how easy it was because I was not dieting and was eating full meals. Now my husband has joined the 21 days and in just 7 days lost 4.6 lbs. I'm proud of him and hopeful that he will lose a good enough amount that after the 21 days he will want to stick to it, because he looks and feels better. He is getting lots of support from friends and family and we are tracking it all."

Another Kickstart participant told us of her experience, having made the change and resolving to stick with it. A year later, she wrote: "I started a year ago, weighing 223. Today I weighed in at 146. Yay! I have 14 more pounds until I reach a healthy BMI." That's a drop of more than seventy-five pounds. Imagine how she feels, and what others are saying to her when they see her success.

And even now, as you plan to reach new goals, there is no need for a long-term commitment. There is no need to decide now what you will eat in the distant future. Instead, simply decide to continue a healthy diet for another week, three weeks, month, or whatever time frame works best for you. Step by step, you're getting to exactly where you want to be.

2. Some people go back to their old ways of eating. This invariably leads to return of any lost weight. But at least they know what a healthy diet is, and can come back to it in the future.

3. A common, but risky, path is to decide to continue, but in a modified program. The idea is to keep meat out of the diet, for example, but to bring back cheese. Or maybe do it vegan until dinnertime, or something similar.

This sort of compromise is tempting to many people, especially if you have had a love-hate relationship with one food or another. The problem, of course, is that foods are stronger than we are. A joyful reunion with a little cheese or other "favorite" nearly always has the unintended consequence of making your progress grind to a halt. Smokers who finally managed to quit come to recognize that they are better off not tempting fate; the same is even more true with foods, since food temptations are absolutely everywhere—much more than cigarettes.

The voice that is pushing you to bring back this or that unhealthy food is not actually *your* voice. That is the little Devil on your shoulder who is trying to lure you back. He is there when we try to break any sort of habit—smoking, drinking, all kinds of food habits, you name it. And he repeats the same lines every time: A little bit won't matter, you can handle it, et cetera, et cetera. There is something to be said for just ignoring that little Devil's entreaties. Sticking with your healthy routine will continue to pay you huge dividends. As time goes on, it will absolutely feel like second nature. And eventually, that little Devil might turn vegan himself. Who knows?

We developed this program very carefully, aiming to bring you the best of health and the greatest power over temptations and addictive behavior. So my suggestion is to keep taking advantage of it, but continuing a simple short-term focus that keeps you in the driver's seat.

What to Check, and When

In our first week, we discussed the changes to expect, but let me give you a quick recap:

Weight Loss. If you have a lot of weight to lose, let it come off gradually. I encourage people to aim for about a pound per week. A little faster or slower is fine. But do not try to starve it off by skipping meals and do not avoid carbohydrates; both of these steps are recipes for long-term weight gain. Some people are surprised that I suggest such gradual weight loss. But if you think of it, a pound a week is fifty-two pounds per year. And if it's a one-way street, you'll reach your goal and stay there.

By the way, in case you were wondering whether weight loss might continue until you just disappear, let me reassure you. Your new way of eating will help your weight descend toward your ideal weight, and as you arrive there, your weight loss will naturally plateau. Then, as long as you stick with healthful foods, they will help you stay in a healthy weight range. There is no need for one diet to lose the weight and a different one for maintenance.

Cholesterol. Your cholesterol has probably already fallen significantly over the last three weeks. But give yourself two to three months before testing your cholesterol (unless your health care provider wants to check it earlier). It takes about that long for the full effect of the diet change to manifest.

Blood Pressure. Three weeks is more than enough time to see changes. However, if you are working on a significant weight issue, your blood pressure will probably keep improving for as long as the weight loss continues.

Blood Sugar. If you have diabetes, your blood sugar can start improving within the first few days of your diet change. It should keep getting better week by week. And with continued weight loss, you will very likely continue to see improvements.

Aches and Pains. If you have rheumatoid arthritis or migraines, and if dairy products, eggs, or meat happen to be your trigger foods, relief should come in a matter of weeks of a diet change. However, even very small amounts of these foods can cause the problem to recur, so you will want to read food labels carefully. If you are dealing with menstrual cramps, relief should occur during the first menstrual cycle for which you've followed the diet the entire month (from one period to the next). However, for some people, it takes a few months to see the full effect.

See Your Health Care Provider

If you have diabetes, high blood pressure, high cholesterol, or any other health problem, be sure to track your progress with your doctor or other health care provider. Do not do what one of our research participants once did: He figured that his new diet should cure his diabetes and cholesterol problem, so he threw his medications away and relied on the diet alone. What he did not realize is that *things take time*. Even with the best diet, these problems are not cured overnight, and you may well need some medication into the future. So have that discussion with your health care provider, and keep him or her in the game with you.

One of the advantages of working with your health care provider is that he or she may be seeing the results of a healthy diet for the very first time. Many are stunned at the weight loss and health improvements that can occur, and they very often become strong advocates for good nutrition.

A Word of Inspiration

I recently gave a talk at the American Library Association convention. Just before I spoke, I happened to meet a man named John, who lived near Chicago. He was running a booth next to the stage, demonstrating photocopy equipment for libraries. He said that he had diabetes and a long-standing weight problem, and that he had learned about our approach about two months earlier. He decided to try it. And in two months' time he had lost twenty-eight pounds. He was amazed. His hemoglobin A1c (a diabetes indicator that is supposed to be below 7, and normally drops about a point with medications) had fallen from 8.5 to 6.4 in this same time period. His doctor felt this was all beyond the realm of possibility and scheduled a special follow-up session to see what is happening to him.

A month later, he sent me an update. His weight loss was now thirty-seven pounds, his hemoglobin A1c had fallen even farther— to 6.1—and his snoring had disappeared.

Don't get me wrong. His first three weeks were great. But things kept getting better and better. Every week brought him new success and helped him achieve things he had not thought possible.

A Doctor's Prescription

Throughout this book, we've heard from a great many doctors and researchers, and now that we're at the end of your 21-day adventure, I'd like you to be able to take them with you. Most are members of the Physicians Committee for Responsible Medicine, and you can join us. Whether you are a physician or a person who would like to support good medicine and ethical research, we have many programs to help you stay informed, pumped up, and on track.

At our website, www.pcrm.org, we have a huge range of resources for you, including books, DVDs, and a chance to keep in touch with others who are on the same path. We'll let you know about the latest scientific breakthroughs and will keep you posted about upcoming events.

In turn, I'll ask you to let us know how you are doing and, especially, to share what you've learned with others. So many people are looking for answers. I will be very grateful to you for helping us spread the word.

Part III

MENUS AND RECIPES

21 Days of Kickstart Menus

Here are 21 days' worth of menus, designed to show what a full breakfast, lunch, or dinner might look like. These are examples only. You may wish to have smaller meals, and you can pick and choose any recipes and any convenience foods that fit with the Kickstart guidelines. By all means do not feel that you need to cook fresh meals each day; there is a lot to be said for preparing a big batch to last a few days.

Day 1

Breakfast
Mango Lime Pancakes with maple syrup (page 241)
Fresh strawberries

Lunch
Blue Corn Chip Salad (page 261)
Sliced watermelon drizzled with lime juice

Dinner
Fettuccine with Grilled Asparagus, Peas, and Lemon (page 272)
Caldo Verde (page 256)
Pears in Balsamic Glaze (page 262)

Day 2

Breakfast

Costa Rican Rice and Beans (Gallo
   Pinto) (page 242)
Sliced pineapple and mango
Pumpernickel toast with orange jam

Lunch

BST (Bacon, Sprout, and Tomato
   Sandwich) (page 268)
Sweet Potato Fries (page 300)

Dinner

Rustic Tomato Soup (page 250)
Salad of mixed greens with
   Roasted Red Pepper Vinaigrette
   (page 260)
Slice of toasted sourdough bread

Day 3

Breakfast

Citrus and Sage Oatmeal
   (page 244)
Multigrain toast
Orange slices

Lunch

Balsamic Zucchini Sandwich
   (page 267)
Artichoke Heart and Tomato Salad
   (page 262)

Dinner

Red Beans and Rice with Collard
   Greens (page 283)
Bananas in Berries Artesia
   (page 302)

Day 4

Breakfast

Mango Spice Breakfast Smoothie
   (page 248)
Oatmeal with blueberries

Lunch

Hummus and Sun-Dried Tomato
   Wrap (page 264)
Low-fat baked tortilla chips
Fresh apple

Dinner

Quick Black Bean Chili (page 254)
Rice topped with Tomatillo Sauce
   (Salsa Verde) (page 294)
Warmed corn tortillas

Day 5

Breakfast

Breakfast Burrito with potatoes
and spinach (page 248)
Sliced cantaloupe

Lunch

Mixed greens with light balsamic
vinegar
Baked potato topped with
black beans and Basic Salsa
(page 297)

Dinner

Cuban Black Bean and Potato
Soup (page 255)
Toasted garlic bread
Arugula salad drizzled with
balsamic vinegar

Day 6

Breakfast

Pancakes with sliced strawberries
(page 241)
Caribbean Passion Breakfast
Smoothie (page 248)

Lunch

The Perfect Portobello Burger
(page 269)
Sweet Potato Fries (page 300)

Dinner

French Onion Sourdough Soup
(page 253)
Linguine with Seared Oyster
Mushrooms (page 271)
Baked Cardamom Pears
(page 303)

Day 7

Breakfast

Pancakes with maple syrup
(page 241)
Fresh raspberries

Lunch

Quinoa and Red Bean Salad
(page 261)
Hummus (page 299) and pita
bread

Dinner

Mixed greens with balsamic
vinegar
Penne al Forno (page 272)
Sautéed spinach with fresh lemon
juice

Day 8

Breakfast

Ginger Banana Breakfast Smoothie
(page 248)
Toast with jam

Lunch

Pita Pizza (page 279)
Mixed greens with Roasted Red
Pepper Vinaigrette (page 260)

Dinner

Curried Tomato Lentil Soup
(page 257)
Steamed asparagus, broccoli, and
cauliflower
Crusty whole-grain bread
Mali Chips (page 300)
Fresh strawberries

Day 9

Breakfast

Green Apple Oatmeal (page 244)
Lemon soy yogurt with
blueberries

Lunch

French Onion Sourdough Soup
(page 253)
Balsamic Zucchini Sandwich
(page 267)
Banana slices

Dinner

Garden salad
Black refried beans with salsa
Blue corn tortillas
Quinoa Verde (page 286)
Sliced melon

Day 10

Breakfast

Chickpeas
Cinnamon Raisin Oatmeal (page 244)
Veggie bacon strips

Lunch

Artichoke Heart and Tomato Salad (page 262)
Black Bean Chipotle Burger (page 268)
Fresh grapes

Dinner

Red Curry Chickpea and Sweet Potato Soup (page 259)
Brown rice
Spinach salad with cherry tomatoes

Day 11

Breakfast

Thai Red Curry Breakfast Scramble (page 245)
Sliced papaya and mango

Lunch

Insalata d'Arance (Salad of Orange and Fennel) (page 263)
Rustic Tomato Soup (page 250)
Toasted rye bread
Fresh pear

Dinner

Spicy Baked Beans with Kale (page 282)
Grilled corn on the cob
Baked sweet potato

Day 12

Breakfast

Basil Tomato Breakfast Scramble
(page 245)
Toasted whole-grain bread
Veggie sausage

Lunch

Black Bean Burrito (page 264)
Fresh orange

Dinner

Sicilian Lentil and Escarole Soup
(page 251)
Collard greens with toasted
almonds
All-fruit sorbet

Day 13

Breakfast

Potato and Spinach Breakfast
Scramble (page 245)
Sliced honeydew melon

Lunch

Portobello Fajitas (page 265)
Hummus (page 299) with pita
wedges

Dinner

Israeli Couscous with Carrots,
Peas, and Red Wine Vinegar
(page 274)
Seared Cauliflower with Garlic and
Tamari (page 288)
Fresh blueberries

Day 14

Breakfast

Breakfast Burrito (page 248)
Banana

Lunch

Tuscan Harvest Soup (Ribollita)
(page 252)
Pita bread
Apple

Dinner

Dan Dan Mian (page 273)
Side of quinoa
Mango Lime Sorbet (page 303)

Day 15

Breakfast

Peppery Raspberry Pancakes
(page 241)
Veggie bacon strips
Watermelon and Supergreens
Breakfast Smoothie (page 248)

Lunch

Pears in Balsamic Glaze (page
262)
Black Bean Chipotle Burger (page
268) on whole-grain bun

Dinner

Green salad with Creamy Chipotle
Dressing (page 260)
Israeli Couscous with Carrots,
Peas, and Red Wine Vinegar
(page 274)
Steamed kale with fresh-squeezed
lemon juice

Day 16

Breakfast

Green Glamour Breakfast
Smoothie (page 248)
Apricot Oatmeal (page 244)

Lunch

Red Curry Chickpea and Sweet
Potato Soup (page 259)
Whole-grain crackers or bread
Steamed Swiss chard

Dinner

Lentil soup
Fettuccine with Grilled Asparagus,
Peas, and Lemon (page 272)
Fresh blueberries

Day 17

Breakfast

Berries and Rosemary Oatmeal
(page 244)
Roasted, chopped sweet potatoes
drizzled with maple syrup

Lunch

Quinoa and Red Bean Salad (page
261)
Warmed corn tortillas
Fresh orange slices

Dinner

Jamaican Stir-Fry (page 276)
Bananas in Berries Artesia (page
302)

Day 18

Breakfast

Berry Blaster Breakfast Smoothie
(page 248)
Oatmeal (page 244) with sliced
banana

Lunch

Hakka Noodles (page 277)
Hummus (page 299) and fresh
veggies

Dinner

Caldo Verde (page 256)
Zucchini Pasta with Sun-Dried
Tomato Sauce (page 275)
Sliced pear

Day 19

Breakfast

Huevos Rancheros (page 247)
Veggie sausage
Pumpernickel bagel with black-
berry jam

Lunch

Quick Black Bean Chili (page 254)
Baby carrots and sliced
cucumbers

Dinner

Enfrijoladas (page 279)
Mixed greens with corn and
squash
Quinoa Verde (page 286)

Day 20

Breakfast

Fig and Mint Oatmeal (page 244)
Sliced melon

Lunch

Shredded Barbecue (page 284)
Mixed greens with Creamy
   Chipotle Dressing (page 260)

Dinner

Black Mushroom Cantonese Stir-
   Fry (page 278)
Pita bread

Day 21

Breakfast

Pancakes (page 241)
Veggie bacon
Fresh strawberries

Lunch

Sun-Dried Tomato Lentil Loaf
   (page 281)
Thinly sliced baked sweet
   potatoes

Dinner

Mixed green salad
Penne al Forno (page 272)
Masala Chai Apple Crisp (page
   304)

Recipes

Chef Jason Wyrick has inspired many people, including other chefs, to discover a world of healthful and delicious foods. As a youth, Jason was tall (six foot three), slim, and athletic. But a diet of meat, cheese, sodas, and junk food gradually caught up with him, as it does with so many people. He was still in his twenties as his weight climbed to more than three hundred pounds and he was diagnosed with diabetes.

That was his wake-up call. Jason realized he needed to make a change. He threw out the animal products, and gradually dropped more than a hundred pounds. All signs of diabetes disappeared, his joint pains went away, and his energy came roaring back. In fact, his stamina was better than in his high school basketball days. He found he could go through three straight hours of intense martial arts classes and barely be winded. He hiked the Grand Canyon rim-to-rim.

But the transition was not always easy. There were some temptations along the way, and Jason's soft spot was cheese. It had been a huge part of his routine, especially on Wednesdays.

"Wednesday was all-you-can-eat enchilada day at my favorite

Mexican restaurant," Jason recalled. "I loved it. But I started to notice that I didn't feel that great after eating a platter of cheese enchiladas. So I cut back to every other week. And again, I noticed how poorly I felt afterward. So I cut back to once a month. And one day, I ordered them, they came to my table, and I looked down at the platter and stared for well over a minute. The enchiladas had lost their appeal. I saw the harm they had been doing to me all those years. I pushed the platter away, paid the bill, and never looked back."

Jason decided to leave his career as director of marketing for a computer company to help others make the transition to health. For many years, Jason has shown others how to create delicious, healthful meals, and he shares his secrets in this collection of wonderful recipes.

A Note About the Recipes

Most of these recipes serve two and can easily be multiplied for a larger group or to make extra for later in the week. They can also be cut in half, if you are cooking for one. The recipes include a few extra tips:

Making It Simple cuts things down to basics, if you are looking to keep it super-quick.

The Gourmet Touch adds that extra something, if you would like to be more adventurous.

Core Concepts highlights techniques or ingredient combinations that are especially handy and easy to transfer to other recipes.

Companion Recipes will let you know which recipes or techniques go especially well with others.

Breakfasts

Pancakes

Serves 2 (makes 4 large pancakes)

The nutty scent of toasting whole wheat flour makes these pancakes really special.

⅔ cup whole wheat pastry flour
¼ teaspoon salt
2 teaspoons baking powder
⅔ cup almond milk or soy milk
Nonstick cooking spray (optional)

Instructions: Mix the flour, salt, and baking powder together in a metal bowl. Add the almond or soy milk to the dry ingredients and mix them until they are well combined. Put this mixture in a measuring cup. Using a nonstick pan (or a pan lightly sprayed with nonstick cooking spray) on medium heat, pour ⅓ cup pancake batter onto the middle of the pan. When the top side bubbles and is mostly firm, flip the pancake over. Keep this on the heat for another 1 to 1½ minutes. Repeat until you've used all the batter.

Per 2-pancake serving: 145 calories, 6 g protein,
31 g carbohydrate, 3 g sugar, 1 g total fat, 6% calories from fat,
10 g fiber, 340 mg sodium

Optional Ingredients

Here are six ways to add extra flavor to pancakes. When you use fresh ingredients like berries or nuts, stir them into the batter after the liquid and dry ingredients are combined. Be gentle when you stir them because the less the flour is disturbed, the softer your pancakes will be. If the list calls for dry ingredients, combine them with the flour, salt, and baking powder mix.

Blueberry: ⅓ cup fresh blueberries. It's important to use fresh berries because frozen berries bleed color into the batter, leaving you with purple pancakes.

Peppery Raspberry: ⅓ cup fresh raspberries, ¼ teaspoon black pepper.

Bright Cardamom: ⅛ teaspoon ground cardamom.

Chocolate Chili: ¼ cup nondairy cocoa powder, 3 tablespoons almond milk or soy milk, ¼ teaspoon chipotle powder.

Mango Lime: ¼ cup finely diced mango, 1 teaspoon lime juice.

Chai Spice: ¼ teaspoon freshly ground black pepper, ¼ teaspoon ground cloves, ¼ teaspoon ground cardamom, 1 teaspoon ground cinnamon, 2 teaspoons freshly grated ginger.

Costa Rican Rice and Beans (Gallo Pinto)
Serves 2

Rice and beans is a combination found all over the world, but it's not just for lunch and dinner. This Costa Rican dish, which translates into "Painted Rooster," is a breakfast staple. It is enhanced by a sofrito, another Latin cuisine classic made from onion, bell pepper, and garlic.

    ½ onion, diced
    1 red bell pepper, diced
    2 cloves garlic, minced
    ⅞ cup water
    ¼ teaspoon salt
    ½ cup rice
    ¾ cup cooked, rinsed black beans
    Hot sauce to taste

Instructions: Over medium heat, sauté the onion and bell pepper in a pot until the onion turns a light brown color. Add the garlic and sauté for 1 more minute. Add the water and salt and bring the water to a boil. Add the rice, bring the water back to a boil, cover the pot, and reduce the heat to low. Cook the rice for about 20 minutes. Remove from the heat, stir in the beans, and dress the Gallo Pinto with hot sauce.

Making It Simple: There are two easier versions of this recipe. One way is to forgo sautéing the onion, pepper, and garlic. Simply bring the water to a boil and add the diced onion, pepper, and garlic to the water along with the rice. The other way is to sauté the onion, pepper, and garlic and stir them into any leftover cooked rice that you have on hand.

The Gourmet Touch: The traditional hot sauce for this dish is called Salsa Lizano. If you're not in Costa Rica, you can find it online. It's very tangy and tastes more like black pepper than chili pepper. You can also serve Gallo Pinto topped with baked or sautéed slices of plantains dressed with lime juice, with or without Salsa Lizano.

Per serving: 226 calories, 9 g protein, 44 g carbohydrate, 4 g sugar, 2 g total fat, 6% calories from fat, 9 g fiber, 290 mg sodium

Garlic Hash Browns with Kale
Serves 2

Hash browns are a comfort food, and they don't have to be heavily fried to be good. The added garlic makes them irresistible.

2 Yukon Gold potatoes, shredded
¼ teaspoon salt
2–3 large kale leaves, shredded
6 cloves garlic, minced
Nonstick cooking spray
½ teaspoon freshly ground black pepper
Option: 2 cups shredded sweet potato

Instructions: Rinse the shredded potatoes and pat them dry. Mince the garlic. Spray a skillet with nonstick cooking spray. Over medium-high heat, sauté the potatoes with the salt until the potatoes are crisp. Once the potatoes are done, add the kale and garlic to the pan and continue sautéing everything for about 2 more minutes. Remove from the heat. Add the pepper.

Option: Substitute 2 cups shredded sweet potato for the shredded Yukon Gold potatoes.

Core Concept: You don't need very much oil to get these, or most other foods, crisp. You just need a whiff of cooking spray so the potatoes don't stick to the pan.

Per serving: 450 calories, 10 g protein, 102 g carbohydrate, 2 g sugar, 1 g total fat, 2% calories from fat, 7 g fiber, 366 mg sodium

Oatmeal

Serves 2

Oatmeal makes a perfect breakfast, especially when combined with fresh or dried fruit. Below are recipes for the most common types of oats along with some added flavorings. The liquid in the recipes can be water, almond milk, soy milk, rice milk, or even hazelnut milk. With all types of oats, make sure that they come off the heat as soon as the liquid is absorbed. Oats are sticky and burn easily to the bottom of the pan, making for tedious cleanup if you don't get them off the heat in time.

Rolled Oatmeal

Rolled oats are steamed and flattened, creating a flaky texture that easily absorbs cooking liquid.

   1 cup rolled oats
   2 cups liquid

Instructions: If you like your oatmeal creamy, just mix the oats with water (or other liquid), then bring to a boil and simmer for a few minutes. If you like it crunchier and less creamy, bring the liquid to a simmer first, over slightly less than medium heat. Then add the oats and stir. Keep the oats at a very low simmer, cooking them for about 15 minutes. Be sure to stir the oats occasionally, especially toward the end of the cooking process, so that they do not burn on the bottom of the pan. If you are going to add a flavoring, add it about 5 minutes before you are done cooking the oats.

   Per ½-cup (uncooked oats) serving: 303 calories, 13 g protein, 52 g carbohydrate, 0 g sugar, 3 g total fat, 9% calories from fat, 8 g fiber, 2 mg sodium

Steel-Cut Oatmeal

Steel-cut oats have been cut into small pieces that can be cooked in about 15 minutes. Their texture is more like rice than typical oatmeal.

   ½ cup steel-cut oats
   1½ cups liquid

Instructions: Bring the liquid to a boil. Add the oats, boiling them for 5 minutes. Remove from the heat, cover, and allow to sit for about 10 minutes. If you are going to add a flavoring, stir it into the oats just after they come off the heat, but before you cover them.

Oat Bran

These oats have added bran fiber. Because they are traditionally cut finely, they have a shorter cooking time—but thanks to the bran they may need a bit more flavoring. Oat bran creates porridge-like oatmeal.

Oatmeal Flavorings

Here are six ways to flavor oatmeal. Some are sweet, some are savory, and all are delicious! Add the ingredients about 5 minutes before the oatmeal is finished cooking unless stated otherwise.

Fig and Mint: ¼ cup pureed fresh figs, 1 tablespoon chopped fresh mint.

Berries and Rosemary: 4 sliced strawberries, ½ teaspoon chopped fresh rosemary leaves. Add the rosemary while the oatmeal is cooking, but leave the strawberries fresh.

Citrus and Sage: 6 whole kumquats, 1 teaspoon chopped fresh sage, ¼ teaspoon freshly ground black pepper.

Apricot: 4–6 chopped dried apricots, pinch of nutmeg.

Cinnamon Raisin: 3 tablespoons raisins, ¼ teaspoon cinnamon.

Green Apple: 1 green apple, diced. You can add the apple while the oatmeal is cooking or add it completely fresh.

Breakfast Scramble

Serves 2

Extra-firm tofu, when crumbled, has a scrambled egg texture and a bit of an egg-like flavor, without the heaviness.

8 ounces extra-firm tofu, crumbled
1 Yukon Gold potato, diced
¼ teaspoon salt
2 teaspoons ground turmeric

Instructions: Crumble the tofu in a mixing bowl with a whisk or by hand. Steam the potato for about 5 minutes. While it is steaming, heat a sauté pan up to medium heat. Add the tofu and salt, gently and slowly stirring it while it is in the pan, and cook it for about 3 to 4 minutes. Stir the turmeric and potato into the scramble, cooking for 1 more minute.

The Gourmet Touch: Give the scramble an even more egg-like taste by using Indian black salt (available at many Indian markets). By the way, you could use any sort of potato in this recipe, but Yukon Golds maintain their texture well and have a flavor advantage over common russets.

Companion Recipes: Tofu scrambles lend themselves to an endless number of recipes, as you'll see. If you like, you can make a big batch of the basic tofu scramble early in the week and then use it in several different recipes over the next few days.

Tip: Breakfast Scramble lasts about a week in the refrigerator. Note that many of the tofu scramble recipes call for only half a batch to serve two people, so one batch of the basic recipe goes a long way.

Core Concepts: Crumbled extra-firm tofu with a touch of turmeric and salt works very well in most recipes that call for scrambled eggs.

Per serving: 177 calories, 13 g protein, 17 g carbohydrate, 2 g sugar, 7 g total fat, 34% calories from fat, 2 g fiber, 315 mg sodium

Breakfast Scramble Variations

Here are a few ideas for spicing up your breakfast scramble.

Potato and Spinach Scramble: 1 extra potato, 2 cups spinach, black pepper to taste. Cook an extra diced potato. Add the spinach to the scramble as it is cooking and cook until the spinach reduces. Garnish with freshly ground black pepper.

Thai Red Curry Scramble: 1 tablespoon Thai red curry paste, juice of 1 lime. Over medium heat, toast the red curry paste for about 2 minutes; add the scramble and cook for 1 more minute. Dress the finished scramble with fresh lime juice.

Basil Tomato Scramble: 1 large chopped tomato, 8–10 sliced basil leaves, ½ teaspoon freshly ground black pepper, ¼ teaspoon crushed red pepper. Cook the scramble with the chopped tomato until the tomato has softened. Remove from the heat and garnish with fresh basil, freshly ground black pepper, and crushed red pepper.

Yellow Curry Scramble: 1½ teaspoons yellow curry powder (instead of the turmeric), ½ cup green peas, 3 tablespoons chopped fresh cilantro. Cook the scramble and add the curry powder and peas about 1 minute before the scramble is done. Garnish with chopped cilantro.

Huevos Rancheros

Serves 3–4

A good-quality salsa and tostada make all the difference in this Mexican treat. They'll take this recipe from good to spectacular!

Breakfast Scramble ingredients
½ teaspoon chili powder
½ cup salsa
3–4 tostadas
3 tablespoons chopped fresh cilantro
1 Roma tomato, diced

Instructions: Follow the directions for the Breakfast Scramble, adding the chili powder when you add the turmeric. After the scramble has fully cooked, stir in the salsa. Place equal portions of the scramble on each tostada, then top with the cilantro and tomato.

Leftovers: Warm the scramble over medium heat for about 3 minutes, adding the chili powder and salsa to the scramble about 1 minute after you start warming it. Cook for another 2 minutes and then top with the other ingredients.

Per serving: 153 calories, 8 g protein, 19 g carbohydrate, 1 g sugar, 5 g total fat, 24% calories from fat, 3 g fiber, 119 mg sodium

Breakfast Burrito
Serves 3

You can quickly cook up potatoes and greens to add to your scramble. A breakfast burrito travels surprisingly well if you are on the road or heading off to work.

Any of the Breakfast Scramble variations

3 whole wheat tortillas

¾ cup salsa

Options: 2 sliced roasted red peppers; 2 diced red potatoes (if your scramble doesn't already contain potatoes); 1 cup baby spinach leaves or chopped kale (if your scramble doesn't already contain spinach or kale); 4–5 sliced green olives

Instructions: Make your Breakfast Scramble of choice or warm up your leftovers. Fill about a third of each tortilla, starting from an edge. Top with salsa. Fold the tortilla, starting with the edge that has the scramble, and tuck the fold underneath the other side of the scramble. You should have the scramble completely covered. Fold in the top and bottom about an inch apiece, then finish rolling the tortilla.

Options: If you use diced potatoes, sauté them over medium heat in a very thin layer of water or veggie broth until they're almost ready to eat. Allow the liquid to evaporate, then stir the Breakfast Scramble together with the potatoes. If you use spinach or kale, gently wilt it over medium heat, or you can wilt it by cooking it with the tofu scramble or potatoes.

The Gourmet Touch: Add about 1 cup soy chorizo to your scramble when you cook it. This makes a flavorful, perhaps even addictive breakfast burrito.

Per serving: 357 calories, 13 g protein, 37 g carbohydrate, 2 g sugar, 6 g total fat, 15% calories from fat, 3 g fiber, 428 mg sodium

Breakfast Smoothie
Makes about 3 cups

1 very ripe banana (with plenty of brown speckles)

2 cups frozen fruit/berries (see the next page for suggested fruit and berry combinations)

1 cup nondairy milk (try almond milk or soy milk for the best flavor)

Instructions: Combine the ingredients in a blender. Start your blender on the lowest setting and slowly crank it up as the smoothie starts to puree. (If you were to start with the machine on high, you'd end up with smoothie splattered all over the top and would probably have to stop your blender several times to get the smoothie ingredients to rest back on the blades.) Once you're up to optimal speed, blend for about 2 minutes to get everything smooth.

Per 1½-cup serving: 190 calories, 2 g protein, 46 g carbohydrate, 35 g sugar, 2 g total fat, 9% calories from fat, 5 g fiber, 79 mg sodium

Here are eight smoothie variations, to be added to the banana and nondairy milk described above:

Mango Blueberry: 1½ cups mango chunks, ½ cup blueberries.

Ginger Banana: 1 extra banana, ½ cup ice, ¼ teaspoon cinnamon, ½-inch piece of ginger, thinly sliced.

Workout Smoothie: 1 extra banana, 2 tablespoons almond butter, ¼ cup blueberries.

Green Glamour: 1 cup sliced strawberries, ½ cup blueberries, ½ cup blackberries, 1 cup packed chopped kale leaves.

Caribbean Passion: ½ cup pineapple chunks, ½ cup mango chunks, 1 peeled orange, ⅛ teaspoon allspice, ¼ teaspoon cinnamon.

Berry Blaster: ½ cup blueberries, ½ cup sliced strawberries, ½ cup raspberries, 3–4 mint leaves.

Mango Spice: 1 extra banana, 1½ cups frozen mango, juice of 1 lime, ¼ serrano pepper.

Watermelon and Supergreens: 1½ cups watermelon chunks, 1 pitted white peach, 1 teaspoon spirulina powder.

Tips: Berries, mangoes, and other fruit can be used frozen, but work best if partially thawed. Of the various nondairy milks, soy milk gives the thickest consistency, while almond milk may have more flavor. Rice milk will be very thin.

Soups and Stews

Rustic Tomato Soup

Serves 2

The secret to this recipe is getting just the right amount of salt, which takes some experimenting. The proper amount of salt will unify all the flavors without overpowering the primary flavor of the dish. Once you've got that down, you can use this technique to make tomato soups that will have guests begging for your recipes!

½ yellow onion, diced
2 cloves garlic, minced
4 Roma tomatoes, chopped
1 teaspoon fresh thyme leaves
¼ teaspoon salt
¼ teaspoon freshly ground pepper
⅛ teaspoon ground cumin
1 cup water
½ cup short-grain rice
Options: 1 cup rinsed red beans; ¼ teaspoon crushed red pepper

Instructions: Sauté the onion over medium heat until it just starts to brown. Add the garlic, sautéing for another minute. Add the rest of the ingredients (including the optional crushed red pepper, if you're using it), except for the rice. Simmer these until the tomatoes are soft. As the tomatoes cook, smash them occasionally with the back of your spatula or stirring spoon until they have mostly turned into sauce. Add the rice. Cover the pot, reduce the heat to low, and cook the rice for 25 minutes. Add the optional beans, if you like, once the soup comes off the heat.

> *Making It Simple:* You can make this even quicker by simply simmering the onion and garlic with an 8-ounce can of crushed tomatoes straightaway, instead of developing the flavor of the onion and garlic first. You'll have a meal with only about 3 minutes of actual preparation time!

> *Tip:* This soup will keep for well over a week in the refrigerator, but it will thicken up into a rice stew after the first day. If you

want it to be more soup-like, add about ¼ cup water when you reheat it.

Per serving: 142 calories, 4 g protein, 30 g carbohydrate, 5 g sugar, 1 g total fat, 7% calories from fat, 4 g fiber, 292 mg sodium

Sicilian Lentil and Escarole Soup

Serves 2

The earthy flavor of this country soup comes from the light cooking of the escarole.

½ onion, diced
2 stalks celery, diced
1 small carrot, diced
3 cups low-sodium veggie broth
3 Roma tomatoes, chopped
1 cup chopped escarole
1 cup green lentils
2 cloves garlic, minced
1 red potato, chopped
2 tablespoons chopped parsley
½ teaspoon freshly ground black pepper
Toasted whole wheat bread
Options: Spinach, kale, or mustard greens instead of escarole

Instructions: Sauté the onion, celery, and carrot over medium heat until they are soft. Add the garlic and sauté for 2 more minutes. Add the veggie broth and bring it to a simmer. Add the tomatoes, escarole, and lentils. Allow the soup to come back to a simmer. Cover the pot. Reduce the heat to low. Cook the soup for 20 minutes. About 15 minutes into cooking the soup, quickly add the potato, stir, and re-cover the pot. After 5 more minutes, remove the soup from the heat. Immediately stir in the parsley and pepper. Plate each serving over a slice of toasted whole wheat bread. If you can't find escarole, use the optional greens, adding them when you would add the escarole.

Making It Simple: Instead of sautéing all the veggies, you can simply add them to the pot along with the veggie broth and bring the broth to a boil. Add the lentils, cover the pot, reduce the heat to low, and cook everything for 20 minutes.

Per serving: 564 calories, 31 g protein, 106 g carbohydrate, 12 g sugar, 3 g total fat, 4% calories from fat, 35 g fiber, 378 mg sodium

Tuscan Harvest Soup (Ribollita)
Serves 4

The real base of this soup is the onion, carrot, celery, garlic, and tomatoes. While the other ingredients all go together to make a great recipe, they're just suggestions. Add whatever other veggies you might have, and you'll have an ever-changing recipe to play with.

1 onion, chopped
1 large carrot, sliced
2 stalks celery, sliced
3 cloves garlic, minced
6–8 Roma tomatoes, chopped, or 1 15-ounce can crushed fire-roasted tomatoes
½ cup water
½ teaspoon salt
½ teaspoon freshly cracked black pepper
1 bay leaf
1 teaspoon fresh thyme leaves
1 cup chopped cabbage
1 potato, chopped
1 zucchini, chopped
1 cup cooked, rinsed red beans
1 cup cooked brown rice
Option: Sliced fresh basil leaves, for garnish

Instructions: Over medium heat, sauté the onion until it starts to brown. Add the carrot, celery, and garlic and continue sautéing for 2 more minutes. Add the chopped tomatoes, water, salt, pepper, bay leaf, and thyme. Simmer the soup until the tomatoes turn into a rough sauce. Add the cabbage and simmer the soup for about 3 minutes. Add the potato and simmer for about 2 minutes. Add the zucchini and simmer for 1 more minute. Remove the soup from the heat and immediately stir in the red beans and cooked rice. Garnish with the basil, if you like.

Making It Simple: This recipe has a long list of ingredients, but it really boils down to adding three different sets of veggies to a pot at different times, giving the first set a quick sauté and simmering the rest. If you'd like it simpler still, add the onion, carrot, celery, garlic, tomatoes, water, herbs, and spices all at the same time and bring them to a simmer. Add the cabbage, zucchini, and potato about 5 minutes before you're done cooking. And if you use a 15-ounce can of crushed fire-roasted tomatoes, you'll have instantly sauced tomatoes.

Core Concepts: A ratio of 2 parts onion, 1 part celery, and 1 part carrot forms the base of many Italian and French soups, creating a veggie stock right in the pot.

Per serving: 211 calories, 9 g protein, 44 g carbohydrate, 8 g sugar, 1 g total fat, 4% calories from fat, 9 g fiber, 162 mg sodium

French Onion Sourdough Soup

Serves 2

The key to a good French onion soup is getting the onions very browned and imparting substance via the wine and salt. Once you master the browning technique used in this recipe, you'll be able to caramelize onions for any recipe you could imagine: onions for pizza, chili, or fajitas, or for garnishing grilled sandwiches, and so on. You can also add extra bread to this recipe, allow it to completely dissolve in the soup, and have an incredible gravy at hand. Have fun with it!

2 yellow onions
¼ teaspoon salt
¼ cup red wine, divided
2¼ cups water, divided
1 teaspoon fresh thyme
½ teaspoon cracked black pepper
2 slices whole wheat sourdough bread

Instructions: Slice the onions into pieces roughly 2 inches long. Put a wok or pot on medium-high heat. Add the sliced onions and salt and sauté until the onions are heavily browned. Add in 2 tablespoons of the red wine and stir quickly. Once it completely evaporates, allow the onions to cook for another minute and then add in the remaining 2 tablespoons of red wine. Allow it to evaporate, allow the onions to sauté again, and repeat this twice more, using 2 tablespoons of water each time. Add the remaining 2 cups of water to the pan, along with the thyme, pepper, and bread; allow the soup to simmer for about 2 minutes. You should find that the bread starts to roughly dissolve and thicken the soup. Once that happens, it's ready to serve.

> *Making It Simple:* Go through the browning process with the onion just two times (you'll only be using the red wine to do this) and then add all the ingredients to the pan, simmering everything for about 5 minutes.

> *Tip:* The best way to slice an onion is to first slice it in half. Lay each section flat, and then slice it in half across its longest dimension. You now have four wide onion sections. Slice each of those into lots of thin onion pieces.

> *Core Concepts:* Try this browning technique in other dishes where you want a sweet, heavy onion flavor.

Per serving: 149 calories, 4 g protein, 28 g carbohydrate, 8 g sugar, 1 g total fat, 7% calories from fat, 3 g fiber, 453 mg sodium

Quick Black Bean Chili

Serves 2

Yes, you can make a big bowl of delicious chili in 15 minutes without compromising on taste! Black beans have a dark flavor that combines exquisitely with the caramelized onions, fire-roasted tomatoes, and the zing of the chili powder. It is ready in minutes and just keeps getting better as it sits. If anyone ever asks how it can be chili without meat, remind them that it's called chili, not carne! Then give them a spoonful and watch them beg for more.

1 yellow onion, diced
Water
2 cloves garlic, minced
16 ounces cooked, rinsed black beans
8 ounces crushed fire-roasted tomatoes
¼ cup chili powder

2 teaspoons ground cumin

1 teaspoon dried Mexican oregano (Greek oregano can be substituted, or you can use 2 teaspoons fresh of either type)

Options: 2–3 tablespoons chopped fresh cilantro leaves; squeeze of lime

Instructions: Over medium-high heat, sauté the onion until most of the pieces are significantly browned. Add a thin layer of water and quickly stir the onion. Let the onion sit and the water evaporate. Repeat this process two to four more times (the more you do it, the deeper the flavor of the onions grows). Reduce the heat to medium. Add the garlic and sauté for 1 minute. Add the black beans, fire-roasted tomatoes, chili powder, cumin, and oregano, mixing everything together. Simmer for at least 5 minutes. This recipe works best in a wok.

> *Options:* Add the lime juice and/or cilantro immediately after the chili comes off the heat and stir.

> *The Gourmet Touch:* Add the chili powder after the garlic has cooked for 1 minute. Allow the chili powder to cook for about 30 seconds, slowly stirring it. Quickly add the black beans with their liquid and then the rest of the spices. The flavor of chili powder is best developed if it can be exposed to direct heat for a short amount of time. However, it can become bitter quickly, which is why you have to make sure to get the black beans and liquid in the pot at the right time.

Per serving: 359 calories, 20 g protein, 67 g carbohydrate, 12 g sugar, 4 g total fat, 9% calories from fat, 23 g fiber, 657 mg sodium

Cuban Black Bean and Potato Soup

Serves 4

This soup may only serve two because everyone always goes back for seconds and sometimes thirds!

1 onion, diced

1 red bell pepper, chopped

1 green bell pepper, chopped

6 cloves garlic, sliced

6 cups cooked black beans
Water
1 tablespoon ground cumin
1 tablespoon chopped fresh oregano leaves
1 bay leaf
2 tablespoons white wine vinegar
½ teaspoon salt
3 potatoes, chopped
Diced red onion for garnish

Instructions: Sauté the onion, peppers, and garlic over medium heat until they are soft. Puree the onion, garlic, and peppers, creating what is called a sofrito. Add about half the beans and puree these with the sofrito plus enough water to create a semi-thick soup. Return this to the pot and add the remaining ingredients (except the potatoes and garnish). Bring the soup to a simmer. Add the potatoes and continue simmering until they're soft. Remove the bay leaf (or eat around it). Garnish with diced red onion.

> *Making It Simple:* Forgo pureeing the onion, garlic, and peppers and simply leave them intact in the pan. Next, add 1 16-ounce can vegetarian refried beans and 2 16-ounce cans black beans instead of pureeing the beans as called for in the standard recipe. Add enough water to create a semi-thick soup and proceed as normal.

> *The Gourmet Touch:* Use white balsamic vinegar instead of white wine vinegar.

> Per serving: 489 calories, 27 g protein, 65 g carbohydrate, 6 g sugar, 2 g total fat, 3% calories from fat, 27 g fiber, 431 mg sodium

Caldo Verde

Serves 2

Caldo Verde is a Portuguese extravaganza of pureed potatoes with simmered kale, spiked with garlic, and made hearty with a touch of spicy sausage.

4 cups water
½ yellow onion, chopped
4 medium-size potatoes, preferably Yukon Gold

1 sliced Italian veggie sausage link or 1 cup cooked, rinsed red
  beans
¼ teaspoon salt
¼ teaspoon black pepper
2 cloves garlic
1 bunch kale, sliced
Options: 1 cup soy chorizo instead of the veggie sausage or beans;
  ¼ teaspoon crushed red pepper

Instructions: Bring the water to a simmer. Add the onion, potatoes, salt,
pepper, garlic, and optional crushed red pepper, if desired. Simmer
these ingredients for 10 minutes, until the potatoes are soft. Blend the
ingredients with an immersion blender (or in a standard blender and
then return to the pot). Return the soup to a simmer. Add the sliced kale
and sausage or optional chorizo to the simmering soup, cooking it for
about 5 minutes. If you use the red beans instead of the veggie sausage, add them immediately after the soup comes off the heat.

> *The Gourmet Touch:* Chop the potatoes and roast them at 400
> degrees F until they are slightly browned, then proceed with mak-
> ing the soup. If you want to create a more intense flavor, smoke
> the veggie sausage over a wood-fired grill before chopping it and
> adding it to the soup.

Per serving (with red bean option): 457 calories, 26 g protein,
61 g carbohydrate, 8 g sugar, 2 g total fat, 3% calories from fat,
13 g fiber, 367 mg sodium

Curried Tomato Lentil Soup (Shorba Addis)
Serves 3

This recipe is based on an Ethiopian soup with a rich, deep curry flavor and complex textures. It's easy to make in a big batch for the week
ahead, but it's so good, don't expect it to last more than a couple of
days.

½ yellow onion, diced
1 small carrot, diced
1 teaspoon freshly grated ginger
3 cloves garlic, minced
1 tablespoon curry powder (berbere is preferable)

1 teaspoon fenugreek seeds
2½ cups vegetable broth
¼ cup tomato paste
¼ cup brown or green lentils
1 Yukon Gold potato, diced
¼ cup whole wheat orzo pasta

Instructions: Over medium-high heat, sauté the onion until it is brown. Reduce the heat to medium. Add the carrot, ginger, garlic, curry powder, and fenugreek, sautéing them for about 1 minute. Add the veggie broth and tomato paste, stirring until the tomato paste is thoroughly combined with the broth. Bring the soup to a simmer. Add the lentils and stir. Once the soup comes back to a simmer, cover the pot and reduce the heat to low. Cook the soup for 20 minutes. Add the potato and orzo; cook the soup, covered, for 5 more minutes.

> *Making It Simple:* Bring the veggie broth and tomato paste to a simmer, making sure the tomato paste is thoroughly combined with the broth. Add the onion, carrot, garlic, ginger, curry, fenugreek, and lentils and proceed with the above recipe as if you had just added the lentils.

> *The Gourmet Touch:* This is an Ethiopian soup, so its flavor is best created using berbere—an Ethiopian curry mix.

> *Core Concepts:* The key to this soup is timing when you add the ingredients. Lentils require time to cook, while diced potatoes and orzo pasta need only a few minutes; these are best added to a soup during the last few minutes of cooking.

Per serving: 359 calories, 16 g protein, 75 g carbohydrate, 14 g sugar, 1 g total fat, 4% calories from fat, 12 g fiber, 152 mg sodium

Red Curry Chickpea and Sweet Potato Soup
Serves 2

This very quick soup has heartiness from the sweet potato and chick-peas, as well as a mellow spinach flavor. It bursts with the myriad ingredients found in the Thai curry paste.

- 2 tablespoons Thai red curry paste
- 2 cups water
- 1 small sweet potato, chopped into small, bite-size pieces (about 1 cup's worth)
- 1 cup cooked, rinsed chickpeas
- 1 cup baby spinach leaves

Instructions: Place a dry soup pot over medium heat. Add the red curry paste and slowly stir it for about 2 minutes. Slowly stir in the water, making sure the curry paste thoroughly integrates with the water. Add the sweet potato and chickpeas. Simmer the soup for about 5 minutes, until the sweet potatoes are al dente. Add the spinach immediately after you remove the soup from the heat.

Per serving: 213 calories, 10 g protein, 39 g carbohydrate, 10 g sugar, 2 g total fat, 9% calories from fat, 9 g fiber, 598 mg sodium

Salads

Roasted Red Pepper Vinaigrette

Makes enough dressing for 1 large salad

Roasted red peppers are ideal for creating a creamy salad dressing without packing in the fat and calories.

1 large roasted red pepper
1 clove garlic
2 tablespoons balsamic vinegar
⅛ teaspoon salt
¼ teaspoon pepper
½ teaspoon fresh thyme leaves

Instructions: Blend the ingredients.

Companion Recipe: Blue Corn Chip Salad

Per serving: 63 calories, 2 g protein, 14 g carbohydrate, 11 g sugar, 0.5 g total fat, 9% calories from fat, 3 g fiber, 263 mg sodium

Creamy Chipotle Dressing

Makes enough for 2 large salads

This dressing is extra-creamy with a low, rumbling heat from the chipotle. It will lightly coat all the ingredients of your salad. Use sparingly.

¼ teaspoon coriander seeds
1 cup salsa
1 cup vegan mayonnaise (such as Nayonaise)
1 chipotle in adobo sauce, diced
¼ teaspoon pepper

Instructions: Blend the ingredients together, making sure the coriander seeds go into the blender first. Otherwise, they may not blend enough and you'll have crunchy seeds in your salad.

Per serving: 189 calories, 2 g protein, 44 g carbohydrate, 22 g sugar, 0.5 g total fat, 2% calories from fat, 3 g fiber, 584 mg sodium

Blue Corn Chip Salad

Serves 2

Blue corn chips are a feast for the eye and the taste buds.

- 4 cups baked blue corn chips (other colored corn chips can be substituted)
- 1 small head red-leaf lettuce, torn into bite-size pieces
- 16 ounces cooked, rinsed black beans
- 1 cup salsa
- 3 roasted red peppers, sliced into strips about 2" long by ½" thick
- 1 Roma tomato, diced
- *Option:* ¼ cup pepitas (green pumpkin seeds)

Instructions: Place the corn chips on the plates first, followed by the lettuce, then the beans, then the tomatoes, then the salsa, and top it off with the sliced roasted red peppers.

> *Option:* If you add pepitas, make them the final ingredients you place on the salad.

> *Core Concepts:* Baked corn chips make excellent croutons, a perfect substitute for the bready kind that are usually fried in and laden with oil.

Per serving: 239 calories, 10 g protein, 39 g carbohydrate, 16 g sugar, 2 g total fat, 9% calories from fat, 15 g fiber, 340 mg sodium

Quinoa and Red Bean Salad

Serves 2

The combination of Salsa Verde and apple cider vinegar really makes this salad, letting simple ingredients play the bass notes, with salsa's pop and sizzle over the top.

- ¾ cup Salsa Verde (page 294)
- 2 teaspoons apple cider vinegar
- 1 small tomato, diced
- 1 yellow squash, diced
- 4 green onions, sliced
- 2 cups sliced Napa cabbage
- ½ cup corn
- ½ cup cooked quinoa

½ cup cooked, rinsed red beans

Option: 1 teaspoon chopped fresh oregano leaves

Instructions: Combine the Salsa Verde with the apple cider vinegar. Toss all the salad ingredients together.

> Per serving: 250 calories, 11 g protein, 46 g carbohydrate, 90 g sugar, 3 g total fat, 9% calories from fat, 12 g fiber, 180 mg sodium

Pears in Balsamic Glaze

Serves 2

With just a few ingredients, this salad packs a smile just waiting to happen. You'll love the sweet, clean crispness of the Asian pears coupled with the acidity of the balsamic glaze, the spiciness of the radishes, and the robustness of the cashews.

6 tablespoons balsamic vinegar

2 pears, chopped (Asian pears work best)

4 cups arugula

2 radishes, thinly sliced

2 tablespoons chopped roasted cashews

Coarse sea salt

Instructions: Over medium heat, simmer the balsamic vinegar until it reduces by half, creating a glaze. Immediately spoon the glaze over the pears and toss them. Toss the arugula, radishes, and cashews together, then top with the balsamic pears and a very small sprinkle of coarse sea salt.

> *Core Concepts:* It's easy to make your own balsamic glaze, pumping up the flavor of dressings and sauces without adding fat to the dish.

> Per serving: 154 calories, 4 g protein, 38 g carbohydrate, 24 g sugar, 2 g total fat, 14% calories from fat, 7 g fiber, 137 mg sodium

Artichoke Heart and Tomato Salad

Serves 2

This recipe is inspired by a favorite Italian recipe, Roman-style stuffed artichokes. The original calls for artichokes stewed in white wine and lemon juice and stuffed with rice, tomatoes, herbs, and pine nuts. This version is a fresh, quick, and easy take on the Italian classic.

2 large tomatoes, chopped
2 tablespoons chopped flat-leaf parsley
3 tablespoon chopped fresh mint
¼ teaspoon coarse sea salt or 1 tablespoon capers
1 cup artichoke hearts
Pine nuts or slivered almonds, for garnish

Instructions: Toss everything together.

Per serving: 89 calories, 15 g protein, 8 g carbohydrate, 6 g sugar, 2 g total fat, 18% calories from fat, 7 g fiber, 343 mg sodium

Insalata d'Arance (Salad of Orange and Fennel)
Serves 2

This Sicilian salad illustrates how complexity in texture and flavor can be derived from just a few ingredients. The crunch and licorice from the fennel, the delectably sweet oranges, and the salty olives make each bite a lush explosion of flavor.

3 oranges
½ cup sliced fennel
⅛ teaspoon salt
¼ teaspoon freshly ground black pepper
2 tablespoons chopped flat-leaf parsley
2 tablespoons chopped fresh basil

Options: 10 or so sliced green olives or 1 tablespoon capers; ⅛ red onion, sliced

Instructions: Peel the oranges, getting as much of the pith off the inside as you can. Separate the oranges into their sections, then slice the sections into bite-size pieces. Mix the oranges and fennel with the salt and pepper. Mix the parsley and basil into the salad.

Options: Mix in either of the optional ingredients when you add the basil and parsley to the salad.

Per serving: 102 calories, 2 g protein, 25 g carbohydrate, 19 g sugar, 0.3 g total fat, 3% calories from fat, 5 g fiber, 115 mg sodium

Hummus and Sun-Dried Tomato Wrap

Serves 1

With no cooking and minimal preparation, you have a delicious meal in minutes.

¼ cup Hummus
1 whole wheat tortilla
6–8 sun-dried tomatoes
½ cup sprouts
⅛ teaspoon freshly ground black pepper
Options: Hot sauce to taste; ¼ cup shredded zucchini or carrot

Instructions: See the hummus recipe on page 299, or choose a commercial brand. Spread the Hummus over half of the tortilla. About 2 inches in from one of the edges, make a line of sun-dried tomatoes, repeating with the sprouts, and topping with the black pepper. Roll the tortilla to make your wrap.

> *Options:* Pour hot sauce over the sprouts. Then shred some zucchini and carrot with the large slats of a cheese grater and place them between the sun-dried tomato and sprout layers for a great texture.

Per serving: 424 calories, 18 g protein, 84 g carbohydrate, 8 g sugar, 3 g total fat, 6% calories from fat, 13 g fiber, 613 mg sodium

Black Bean Burrito with Cilantro Lime Rice

Serves 2

In just a few minutes, leftover rice, black beans, peppers, and onions can be turned into a sensational, rustic meal. Just cook up the peppers and onions, add some lime juice and cilantro to the rice, and you're ready to go.

1 cup cooked rice
2 tablespoons chopped fresh cilantro
Squeeze of lime
½ green bell pepper, sliced

¼ yellow onion, sliced

1 clove garlic, minced

1 tablespoon chopped fresh oregano

1 cup black beans, drained but not rinsed

Salsa Verde to taste (page 294)

2 whole wheat tortillas

Instructions: Mix the rice with the cilantro and lime juice. Over medium-high heat, sauté the pepper and onion until the onion is browned. Add the garlic and oregano and sauté for 1 more minute. Place all the ingredients in the tortilla.

> *Using Leftovers and Making It Super-Fast:* If you have some leftover rice on hand, you'll cut the preparation time to almost nothing. If you want to cut the time down even further, you can leave the green bell pepper raw, use only half the onion called for in the recipe, and omit the garlic. Chop the oregano or simply tear the leaves and give them a quick press to get some extra flavor out of them. Doing it this way means you don't even have to cook any of the ingredients.

Per serving: 530 calories, 20 g protein, 98 g carbohydrate, 7.5 g sugar, 1 g total fat, 9% calories from fat, 15 g fiber, 717 mg sodium

Portobello Fajitas

Serves 2

Portobellos are thick and juicy, with lots of flavor, making them a satisfying alternative to meat. If you cook them separately from the other veggies in this recipe, you can even sear them on high heat and make them a bit crispy!

½ onion, thinly sliced

Splash of water (about 3 tablespoons)

2 large portobello caps, thickly sliced

2 cloves garlic, minced

½ teaspoon ground cumin

1 teaspoon chili powder

1 large roasted red pepper, sliced

3 tablespoons chopped fresh cilantro
Corn or whole wheat flour tortillas
Salsa or lime wedges

Instructions: Over medium-high heat, sauté the onion until it turns a rich, dark, brown color. Add a splash of water and quickly stir. The liquid will evaporate in just a few seconds. Reduce the heat to medium. Add the portobellos and garlic and sauté until the mushrooms glisten and lose their raw, whitish look. Add the cumin and chili powder; sauté for 15 to 30 more seconds. Remove the pan from the heat. Immediately add the roasted red peppers and cilantro. Serve with tortillas as well as salsa or lime wedges.

Making It Simple: Once the onion is browned, reduce the heat to medium. Add the splash of water and then all the other ingredients (except for the tortillas and toppings). Make sure that a very thin layer (about ⅛ inch) of water stays in the pan while everything cooks. As soon as the mushrooms are done, the fajitas are ready to serve.

The Gourmet Touch: Turn the heat to high once the onions just start to brown. Add the portobellos and sear them until you see some of the outer bits start to crisp. Turn the heat down to medium and proceed with the above recipe. Use a nut-brown ale instead of water. Alternatively, you can grill the portobellos over mesquite wood and add them at the very end of the recipe.

Core Concepts: Portobellos are best when they're cooked enough to be softened or cooked at a high enough heat to sear, but not cooked so long that they become overly soft.

Per serving: 286 calories, 10 g protein, 60 g carbohydrate, 5 g sugar, 3 g total fat, 10% calories from fat, 5 g fiber, 668 mg sodium

Balsamic Zucchini Sandwich

Serves 2

This quick sandwich combines the flavors of fresh zucchini sautéed in balsamic vinegar with the creaminess of roasted red pepper and cannellini bean spread.

2 zucchini, cut lengthwise into ½''-thick strips
4 cloves garlic, sliced
1 tablespoon balsamic vinegar
1 cup rinsed white kidney beans (cannellini beans)
1 large roasted red pepper
2 whole wheat sandwich rolls (mini baguettes or bolillo rolls)
6–8 fresh basil leaves
½ teaspoon freshly cracked black pepper

Instructions: Over medium-high heat, sauté the zucchini strips for about 1 minute (do not overcrowd the pan). Reduce the heat to medium. Add the garlic and balsamic vinegar and stir immediately. Sauté this for about 30 seconds and remove from the heat. Puree the white beans and roasted red pepper. Toast the buns. Spread the pureed beans on the bottom bun, then add the basil, then the zucchini, and finish off with a garnish of black pepper.

Making It Simple: Instead of making the roasted red pepper and white bean spread, simply use a commercial roasted red pepper hummus.

The Gourmet Touch: Instead of sautéing the zucchini slices, toss them in the balsamic vinegar and then grill them over mesquite wood.

Per serving: 380 calories, 19 g protein, 76 g carbohydrate, 11 g sugar, 2 g total fat, 5% calories from fat, 14 g fiber, 465 mg sodium

BST (Bacon, Sprout, and Tomato Sandwich)

Serves 2

This sandwich, a variation on the traditional BLT, draws its flavors from smoked bacon-flavored nutty tempeh and juicy tomatoes.

    1 package tempeh "bacon" (about 8 strips)
    1 large tomato, sliced thinly
    1 cup sprouts
    ¼ cup vegan mayo (such as Nayonaise)
    4 slices whole wheat bread

Instructions: Warm the tempeh bacon over medium heat in a dry sauté pan for about 2 minutes per side. Tear the tempeh bacon slices in half and set them aside. Place the tomato slices, then the tempeh bacon slices, and then the sprouts between slices of mayonnaised bread and press the sandwiches together.

> *Making It Simple:* Technically, the tempeh is already cooked before it gets packaged, so you can forgo cooking it in the pan. The flavor won't be as deep, but it saves you a few minutes.

> *The Gourmet Touch:* Smoke the tempeh with hickory chips for about an hour before adding it to the sandwich. You can make a huge batch of tempeh like this and then store it in the refrigerator for a couple of weeks, using it in various recipes.

Per serving: 320 calories, 20 g protein, 46 g carbohydrate, 10 g sugar, 6 g total fat, 8% calories from fat, 9 g fiber, 884 mg sodium

Black Bean Chipotle Burger

Serves 4

This tasty burger combines simple ingredients and spices with the tangy tamarind flavor of steak sauce.

    ¼ red onion, minced
    1 cup black beans
    1 chipotle pepper in adobo, minced
    2 tablespoons minced fresh cilantro
    1 teaspoon ground cumin
    ¾ teaspoon freshly ground black pepper

6 cloves roasted garlic
2 tablespoons A1 Steak Sauce
½ cup cooked oats
1½ cups bread crumbs
Nonstick cooking spray, for sautéing

Instructions: Sauté the red onion over medium-high heat until it just starts to turn brown. Mash the beans, chipotle, onion, cilantro, cumin, black pepper, garlic, and steak sauce together until you have a rough paste (there should still be some texture to the beans, but the mixture should mostly be smashed). Add the oats. Stir the bread crumbs into the black bean mix and let it sit for about 5 minutes. Press everything together and add more bread crumbs, if necessary, until you have a tight dough. Lightly oil your hands so the dough doesn't stick when you form it into patties. Create palm-size patties. Spray a skillet with nonstick cooking spray. Sauté the burgers over medium-high heat until slightly browned on both sides.

Per serving: 265 calories, 10 g protein, 45 g carbohydrate, 3 g sugar, 5 g total fat, 16% calories from fat, 6 g fiber, 332 mg sodium

The Perfect Portobello Burger

Serves 2

This burger has it all: heartiness and dark, full portobello flavor, pungency from the garlic, smokiness from the paprika, sweet tanginess from the balsamic vinegar, and a rich lushness from the roasted red pepper.

Water
3 cloves garlic, sliced along the length
¼ teaspoon salt
½ teaspoon smoked paprika (common paprika can be substituted if smoked is not available)
2 large portobello mushrooms, de-stemmed (it's not necessary to remove the gills)
2 whole wheat buns
Malt vinegar (balsamic can be substituted)
1 roasted red pepper, cut in half

2 pieces romaine lettuce, about the size of a portobello
Option: ¼ yellow onion, thinly sliced

Instructions: Add about ¼ inch of water to a sauté pan and bring it to just above medium heat. Add the garlic, salt, and smoked paprika to the water and stir. Add the portobello caps. Cook this until the portobello is no longer raw on either side. Replenish the water as necessary so that the portobello and garlic are not left to cook in a dry pan. Once the portobello is cooked, allow the water to evaporate from the pan. Immediately remove it from the heat and stir the portobellos around so that they pick up the residual salt and smoked paprika on the bottom of the pan. Remove everything from the pan as soon as possible and set the portobellos and garlic aside.

Sprinkle or quickly dip the bottom buns in the malt vinegar. Add the portobellos, roasted red pepper halves, and lettuce to the buns and serve.

Options: Over medium-high heat, sauté the sliced onion until it is golden brown and very soft. If it starts to stick, add a very thin layer of water to the pan and repeat until the onion has fully cooked and is thoroughly browned. Add the onion to the burger once the portobellos are done. You can also toast the buns either in the oven directly on the rack at 350 degrees F for 2 to 3 minutes or in a dry pan over medium heat for about 2 minutes.

Making It Simple: This recipe is actually surprisingly simple as is. It looks like it has a lot of steps, but it really consists of only a few simple parts. The first part is simmering portobello caps and garlic slices in spiced water. The next part consists of slicing two roasted red peppers. The last part is simply putting ingredients on and between the buns.

Per serving: 149 calories, 7 g protein, 28 g carbohydrate, 9 g sugar, 3 g total fat, 16% calories from fat, 18 g fiber, 421 mg sodium

Main Dishes

Linguine with Seared Oyster Mushrooms
Serves 2

Crispy, caramelized oyster mushrooms contrast with the slightly sweet tomato sauce to make this dish explode with flavor.

2 cups oyster mushrooms
Water
6 ounces whole wheat vegan linguine
16 ounces crushed fire-roasted tomatoes
1 tablespoon capers
Juice of 1 lemon
Option: ½ teaspoon crushed red pepper
4 large basil leaves

Instructions: Chop the oyster mushrooms into very large pieces. Over high heat, sear them until they partially brown. Set them aside. Bring enough water to a boil to cook the pasta. Boil the pasta until it is just barely done. Drain. While the pasta is boiling, add the crushed fire-roasted tomatoes, capers, lemon juice, and optional crushed red pepper to a pot. Simmer this for about 5 minutes. Roll the basil leaves together and slice the roll along the width into thin strips. Plate the pasta, then pour the sauce over it and top with the fresh basil. Finish the dish off by topping each serving with the seared oyster mushrooms.

The Gourmet Touch: Use half the oyster mushrooms, preparing them as above. In a separate pan, simmer ½ cup chanterelle mushrooms in white wine until they are soft. Remove the chanterelles from the white wine and mix them with the seared oyster mushrooms, topping the finished dish with them.

Tip: Crisping oyster mushrooms works best in an iron skillet.

Per serving: 385 calories, 17 g protein, 80 g carbohydrate, 1 g sugar, 2 g total fat, 5% calories from fat, 7 g fiber, 693 mg sodium

Fettuccine with Grilled Asparagus, Peas, and Lemon
Serves 2

Asparagus and peas, with the lightness of lemons and parsley, create a beautiful springtime dish, perfect for lunch or dinner.

6–8 stalks asparagus

2 cloves garlic, minced

Juice of 1 lemon, about 2 tablespoons

Pinch of coarse sea salt

Water

6 ounces fettuccine

2 tablespoons minced parsley

1 cup peas

Instructions: Toss the asparagus in the garlic, lemon juice, and salt. Grill the asparagus until it just starts to develop a few blackened spots. The asparagus should still have some crispness to it. Cut the asparagus into 2-inch pieces. Bring the water to a boil. Boil the pasta until it is al dente. Toss the cooked pasta with the asparagus, parsley, and peas.

Per serving: 375 calories, 11 g protein, 77 g carbohydrate, 6 g sugar, 0.3 g total fat, 0.7% calories from fat, 9 g fiber, 209 mg sodium

Penne al Forno
Serves 4

While you don't need to bake this dish, it finishes off nicely in the oven, helping everything set and giving the sauce a slightly caramelized taste.

8–10 basil leaves

2 carrots, sliced

2 stalks celery, sliced

2 zucchini, sliced

½ yellow onion, chopped

Water

16 ounces brown rice penne pasta

2 roasted red peppers, chopped

3 Roma tomatoes, chopped

6–8 green olives stuffed with garlic, sliced, or ¼ cup pitted whole
kalamata olives

2 cups Basic Tomato Sauce (page 289)

Option: 2 cups cooked, rinsed cannellini beans

Instructions: Roll the basil leaves tightly and slice them into ribbons.
Over medium heat, sauté the carrots, celery, zucchini, and onion for
about 3 to 5 minutes (this will ensure they are soft enough by the time
they are done baking and will help all the flavors meld). Bring the water
to a boil. Add the brown rice pasta and stir. Cook the pasta until it is
slightly underdone (it will finish cooking in the oven). Immediately mix
all the ingredients together in a deep baking dish. Cover the dish. Bake
the pasta at 350 degrees F for 10 to 12 minutes. If you want to add the
beans, stir them into the pasta just after it comes out of the oven.

Making It Simple: Slice all the veggies and forgo sautéing them. Just
throw it all in a baking dish and bake it for about 15 to 20 minutes.

Tip: Cook the pasta after you are done preparing the veggies so that
it does not sit for a long time.

Per serving: 554 calories, 13 g protein, 109 g carbohydrate, 18 g sugar,
0.8 g total fat, 1% calories from fat, 13 g fiber, 428 mg sodium

Dan Dan Mian (Szechuan-Style Street Peddler's Noodles)
Serves 2

This is a fast, filling dish that shows the boldness of Szechuan cooking.
Every ingredient stands out, from the pickled greens and chili vinegar
soy sauce, to the soft, succulent noodles.

Water

8 ounces dan dan noodles or soba (buckwheat) noodles

4 green onions, sliced

¼ cup pickled mustard greens or pickled cabbage (see the next
page for a cheat on the pickled veggies)

1½ teaspoons soy sauce

2 teaspoons rice wine vinegar

1 teaspoon chili paste

1 teaspoon toasted sesame seeds

Instructions: Bring a pot of water to a boil. Add the noodles and cook them until they are slightly soft. Drain the water and set the noodles to the side. Over medium-high heat, add the green onion and pickled greens to a wok. Cook these for about 1 minute. Remove them from the wok. Add the soy sauce, vinegar, chili paste, and noodles to the wok and cook them for about 30 seconds. Plate each serving and garnish them with the cooked green onions, pickled greens, and sesame seeds.

> *Pickled Green Cheat:* Pickled greens should be available at most Asian markets, but you can make a quick version by sautéing sliced cabbage or mustard greens in rice wine vinegar and a pinch of salt until the veggies are soft. You'll need about ½ cup of fresh greens to start, and you should end with about ¼ cup once they cook.

> *Making It Simple:* Cook the noodles. Mix the soy sauce, rice wine vinegar, and chili paste together and pour over the noodles. Top each serving with uncooked green onions, pickled greens, and sesame seeds.

> *The Gourmet Touch:* Use black rice vinegar and add 2 teaspoons of Szechuan peppercorns to the wok when you sauté the pickled greens and green onion. You can also add ½ cup chopped seitan to the recipe. Chop the seitan and marinate it in a mixture of chili paste and rice wine vinegar for at least 2 hours, then sauté it for about 1 minute. Serve on top of the noodles.

> *Tip:* Good-quality soba noodles are made entirely of buckwheat, making a great gluten-free version of this dish.

> Per serving: 428 calories, 18 g protein, 87 g carbohydrate, 3 g sugar, 3 g total fat, 6% calories from fat, 5 g fiber, 315 mg sodium

Israeli Couscous with Carrots, Peas, and Red Wine Vinegar
Serves 2

Large Israeli-style couscous is creamy, holding all the different flavors and balancing out the bite of the onion and vinegar.

> 1¼ cups veggie stock
> 1 cup Israeli couscous

1 carrot, diced
1 stalk celery, diced
½ red bell pepper, diced
¼ red onion, diced, or 3 tablespoons diced shallot
3 tablespoons chopped parsley
2 tablespoons chopped fresh mint
¼ cup peas
¼ teaspoon ground cinnamon
3 tablespoons red wine vinegar

Instructions: Bring the stock to a boil. Add the Israeli couscous and remove it from the heat. Stir the couscous until it absorbs all the stock and set it aside. Toss all the ingredients together and chill.

Per serving: 439 calories, 14 g protein, 90 g carbohydrate, 4 g sugar, 1 g total fat, 2% calories from fat, 1 g fiber, 273 mg sodium

Zucchini Pasta with Sun-Dried Tomato Sauce
Serves 2

Simple and fresh, this dish is perfect for a summer day.

2 zucchini
Sun-Dried Tomato Sauce (page 293)
A few fresh basil leaves
2 teaspoons pine nuts

Instructions: Prepare the Sun-Dried Tomato Sauce. Shave the zucchini lengthwise with a vegetable peeler. Do not discard the peel. It's part of the zucchini pasta! Rotate the zucchini slightly after each shave to keep the zucchini strips as even as possible. When you get to the point where you are shaving the seedy part of the zucchini, just set it aside and move on to the next zucchini. Top the shaved zucchini pasta with the sauce. Roll a few basil leaves together and slice them thinly. Garnish the pasta with the sliced basil and pine nuts.

Per serving: 154 calories, 8 g protein, 29 g carbohydrate, 17 g sugar, 3 g total fat, 16% calories from fat, 8 g fiber, 71 mg sodium

Jamaican Stir-Fry

Serves 2

Tropical flavors pop out of this dish. Spiciness from the habanero and ginger, sweetness from the plantains and bell pepper, and the heady aroma of allspice give you something new to discover in each bite.

1 red bell pepper, sliced

½ red onion, sliced

1 plantain, sliced

3 cloves garlic, minced

1 teaspoon grated fresh ginger

½ habanero, minced (use a jalapeño or serrano for much less heat)

1 teaspoon curry powder

½ teaspoon allspice

½ teaspoon fresh thyme

Pinch salt

2 tablespoons almond milk

1½ cups cooked long-grain rice

Instructions: Over medium-high heat, sauté the bell pepper and onion until they start to soften. Add the plantain. Once it starts to brown, reduce the heat to medium. Add the garlic, ginger, minced pepper, curry powder, allspice, thyme, and salt; sauté for about 30 seconds. Remove from the heat and immediately stir in the almond milk, which will create a light curry that just sticks to the veggies. Serve over the cooked rice.

> *Making It Simple:* Add the bell pepper, red onion, plantain, garlic, ginger, and pepper and cook it all at the same time over medium heat until soft. Add the spices and continue with the above recipe.

> *Tip:* Look for plantains that are not quite ripe, with just a few brown spots on the peel. They are more starchy than sweet—that is, more like a potato than a banana—and that will make a great stir-fry.

Per serving: 328 calories, 6 g protein, 78 g carbohydrate, 17 g sugar, 2 g total fat, 5% calories from fat, 6 g fiber, 165 mg sodium

Hakka Noodles

Serves 2

Hakka noodles are a fun example of fusion cuisine. Combining Chinese and Indian ingredients, done stir-fry style, these noodles are quick, pungent, and loaded with flavor.

Water

8 ounces fettuccine-size rice noodles

¼ cup low-sodium ketchup

¼ cup low-sodium soy sauce

1 tablespoon apple cider vinegar

½ teaspoon crushed red pepper

1 small head cauliflower, cut into bite-size florets

2 carrots, sliced into 2" sticks

½ cup thinly sliced cabbage

6 green onions, sliced

2 cloves garlic, minced

1 teaspoon grated fresh ginger

½ cup fresh green beans, cut into 2" pieces

3 tablespoons chopped fresh cilantro

Instructions: Boil the water. Cook the noodles until they are soft, about 2 minutes. Drain the water and give the noodles a quick rinse. Combine the ketchup, soy sauce, vinegar, and crushed red pepper. Heat a wok up to high. Sauté the cauliflower until it starts to brown. Add the carrots and sauté for 30 seconds. Reduce the heat to medium-high. Add the cabbage, green onions, garlic, ginger, and green beans; cook for 1 minute. Add the noodles and sauce and stir quickly. Cook for 1 more minute. Remove from the heat and garnish with cilantro.

Making It Simple: Once you cook the noodles, turn the wok to medium-high heat and add all the veggies at once. Sauté for 2 minutes. Reduce the heat to medium and add the noodles, sauce, ginger, garlic, and cilantro; simmer for 3 more minutes.

Per serving: 346 calories, 9 g protein, 74 g carbohydrate, 27 g sugar, 0.6 g total fat, 2% calories from fat, 8 g fiber, 860 mg sodium

Black Mushroom Cantonese Stir-Fry

Serves 2

Black (also called shiitake) mushrooms are delicious and healthful. If you love mushrooms, you'll adore this dish.

½ cup water
2 teaspoons cornstarch
3 small, hot, dried red chili peppers
½ yellow onion, sliced thinly
3 cloves garlic, minced
8 fresh shiitake mushrooms, sliced
½ cup bamboo shoots
½ cup sugar snap peas
2 tablespoons low-sodium soy sauce
2 cups cooked rice
2 tablespoons coarsely chopped almonds, for garnish

Instructions: Mix together the water and cornstarch. Heat a wok to high. Add the dried red peppers and sauté them for 10 seconds. Add the onion and garlic and sauté for 30 seconds or until the onion just softens. Add the shiitakes and sauté for 30 more seconds. Add in the bamboo shoots, sugar snap peas, and soy sauce. Add the water-cornstarch mix and reduce the heat to a simmer. Simmer this for 5 minutes. Serve each portion over rice and garnish the top with a small amount of the chopped almonds.

Making It Simple: Sauté the mushrooms, onion, bamboo shoots, sugar snap peas, garlic, and peppers all at the same time over medium-high heat. After 2 minutes, add the sauce and corn-starch mixture.

Tip: If you're not used to working with dried hot peppers, pay very close attention to them. As you heat them, they release spicy capsaicin into the air, and you'll find yourself starting to cough! To prevent that, simply add them when you add the sauce.

Core Concepts: Cornstarch makes a great thickener for most East Asian–style sauces. The trick is to combine liquid with cornstarch and then add it back to the stir-fry.

Per serving: 309 calories, 11 g protein, 66 g carbohydrate, 9 g sugar, 3 g total fat, 9% calories from fat, 8 g fiber, 547 mg sodium

Pita Pizza

Serves 1

This recipe is fast, with a savory flavor from the hummus, which makes an excellent alternative to cheese. It's even good sans baking!

¼ cup Hummus (page 299)

1 whole wheat pita

¼ teaspoon cracked black pepper

Baked Toppings: Fresh thyme, sliced green olives, whole roasted garlic, sun-dried tomatoes, sliced roasted red peppers, sliced cippolini onions

Fresh Toppings: Sliced basil, sliced Roma tomatoes, Peppadew peppers

Instructions: Spread the hummus over the pita, except for at the edge. Sprinkle with cracked black pepper. Add the baked toppings (these toppings are not baked before they go on the pizza; the name just refers to toppings that get baked on top of the pizza). Bake the pita pizza at 350 degrees F for 7 to 8 minutes. Then spread any of the fresh toppings on the pizza after it comes out of the oven.

Per serving: 93 calories, 4 g protein, 14 g carbohydrate, 0 g sugar, 3 g total fat, 26% calories from fat, 4 g fiber, 148 mg sodium

Enfrijoladas

Serves 2

Enfrijoladas are similar to Sonoran enchiladas, but they're smothered with a bean sauce instead of a chili sauce, hence the translation "in bean sauce." They are so filling, you may be hard-pressed to finish one!

4 corn tortillas

½ yellow onion, diced

Water

2 cloves garlic, minced

2 cups cooked black beans, with liquid

¼ teaspoon salt

2 teaspoons chopped fresh oregano

Options: ¼ teaspoon anise seed; 1 chipotle in adobo sauce; 2 teaspoons smoked paprika or chili powder

1 Roma tomato, diced

Instructions: Over medium heat, toast the tortillas in a dry pan for about 30 seconds per side, then set them aside. Over medium-high heat, sauté the onion in a dry pan until it turns dark brown. Add a very thin layer of water to the pan, no more than ⅛ inch. Stir immediately. Reduce the heat to medium. Add the garlic, sautéing it for 1 minute. Add the beans and liquid, salt, oregano, and any or all of the optional ingredients you desire. Simmer this for about 5 minutes, adding more water as the liquid cooks out. Puree the beans and simmered ingredients, adding enough water to make a semi-thick sauce. Place a tortilla on a plate and cover it with a quarter of the bean sauce. Place another tortilla on top of this and cover it with another quarter of the bean sauce. Repeat this for a second plate. Add diced tomato to garnish each serving.

> *The Gourmet Touch:* The anise seed is actually a substitute for mango leaves, which can be difficult to find. However, if you do find them, toast them for about 10 seconds and then add them to the bean sauce, using them as you would a bay leaf.

Per serving: 354 calories, 19 g protein, 67 g carbohydrate, 4 g sugar, 3 g total fat, 6% calories from fat, 20 g fiber, 335 mg sodium

Grilled Portobello Steaks

Serves 2

This is a great recipe when you're having an outdoor barbecue. Portobellos quickly pull in the smoky flavor from the grill and mingle it with the intense balsamic marinade.

- ½ cup Mushroom Gravy (preferably using the dried wild mushroom option) (page 290)
- 2 large portobello mushrooms, stems removed
- 4 cloves garlic, crushed
- 10–12 sage leaves, crushed
- ¼ cup balsamic vinegar or red wine
- 1 teaspoon cracked pepper
- 1 teaspoon fresh thyme
- ¼ teaspoon coarse sea salt

Instructions: Make ½ cup of the Mushroom Gravy recipe. Add the portobellos, garlic, sage, balsamic vinegar, pepper, thyme, and salt to a shallow bowl. Marinate the portobellos for about 2 hours, then remove them from the marinade. Sprinkle the sea salt on each portobello. Grill the portobellos over medium heat on a wood-fire grill, drizzling them with leftover marinade to keep them hydrated. They should take about 5 to 10 minutes per side. Once they are done grilling, warm the Mushroom Gravy back up and top them with the gravy, or simply serve the portobellos on their own.

> *Making It Simple:* Instead of marinating and grilling the mushrooms, simply bake them in the marinade in a covered baking dish on 375 degrees F for 25 minutes, then sprinkle them with the sea salt once they are out of the baking dish.

> *The Gourmet Touch:* Wrap the grilled portobello steaks in several sheets of phyllo dough, spritz the dough with water, and bake the phyllo-wrapped mushrooms at 400 degrees F for 10 minutes.

Per serving: 138 calories, 10 g protein, 37 g carbohydrate, 11 g sugar, 0.8 g total fat, 5% calories from fat, 5 g fiber, 446 mg sodium

Sun-Dried Tomato Lentil Loaf

Serves 4

This is an upscale version of a lentil loaf, a delicious alternative to meat loaf. The sun-dried tomatoes add a tangy, caramelized flavor.

    1 onion, chopped
    3 cloves garlic, chopped
    1½ cups water
    1 teaspoon paprika
    ½ teaspoon freshly ground pepper
    1 teaspoon fresh thyme
    ¾ cup green lentils
    ½ cup sun-dried tomatoes
    1 tablespoon balsamic vinegar
    ½ teaspoon salt
    Oil for the loaf pan

Instructions: Over medium heat, sauté the onion until lightly browned. Add the garlic and sauté for 2 more minutes. Add the water, paprika, pepper, and thyme and bring the water to a boil. Add the lentils and stir. Bring the water back to a boil, cover the pot, reduce the heat to low, and cook the lentils for 20 to 25 minutes. Puree the lentils with the sun-dried tomatoes, balsamic vinegar, and salt until the mixture is coarsely ground. Lightly oil a small loaf pan. Press the lentil-and-tomato mix into the loaf pan and cover it with foil. Bake at 325 degrees F for 30 to 40 minutes. Uncover the lentil loaf once it comes out of the oven. Allow the lentil loaf and pan to cool enough to safely handle. Using a knife or thin spatula, separate the edge of the lentil loaf from the pan. Place a plate over the loaf pan and quickly turn it over. Tap on the pan to help the loaf separate from the pan. Gently remove the pan. Slice the lentil loaf.

Fun Options: Instead of baking this, you can serve it as a pâté. Lightly oil a ramekin (a small cylindrical serving dish) and then press the lentil loaf into the ramekin. Next, do the knife-and-plate trick from the above recipe to get the pâté on the serving plate. With the addition of oats or bread crumbs, you can also turn this into a Sun-Dried Tomato Lentil Burger. Just add enough oats or bread crumbs to create a tight dough, form it into patties, and bake or sauté them.

The Gourmet Touch: To make a delicious pâté, add 2 cups roasted and smoked cremini mushrooms, plus ¼ cup smoked almonds. Cook the lentils with 2 tablespoons berbere, an Ethiopian curry spice mix.

Per serving: 164 calories, 11 g protein, 30 g carbohydrate, 5 g sugar, 0.6 g total fat, 3% calories from fat, 17 g fiber, 451 mg sodium

Spicy Baked Beans with Kale

Serves 2

This Southern recipe features beans and greens in a sauce so flavorful, it might be habit forming.

½ onion, diced
2 cloves garlic, minced
1 chipotle, diced

1 bunch kale, chopped
½ teaspoon cracked black pepper
½ teaspoon ground cumin
1 teaspoon fresh thyme
2 cups low-sodium baked beans
2 teaspoons maple syrup

Instructions: Over medium-high heat, sauté the onion until it browns. Reduce the heat to medium. Add the garlic, chipotle, kale, pepper, and cumin, sautéing until the kale is soft. Add the thyme, beans, and maple syrup, sautéing for 1 more minute. Bake at 350 degrees F for 20 minutes.

Making It Simple: Once you've got the ingredients cut, simply put everything into a baking dish and bake at 350 degrees F for 30 minutes. You'll need the extra baking time to develop the flavor of the onions, but this cuts down on the labor by about 5 minutes.

The Gourmet Touch: Add the juice of 1 small orange and use 10 cloves roasted garlic instead of 3 cloves fresh garlic.

Per serving: 359 calories, 17 g protein, 79 g carbohydrate, 29 g sugar, 0.9 g total fat, 2% calories from fat, 13 g fiber, 480 mg sodium

Red Beans and Rice with Collard Greens

Serves 2

A New Orleans staple, this recipe takes advantage of the great nutrition and wonderful texture of collard greens. This recipe should always be served over rice, not tossed with it.

½ onion, diced
1 green bell pepper, diced
2 stalks celery, sliced thinly
3 cloves garlic, minced
1 bay leaf
2 cups cooked red beans with at least 2 tablespoons liquid
½ teaspoon cracked black pepper
1 teaspoon fresh thyme leaves
¼ teaspoon salt
Water

2 cups sliced collard greens
Cooked brown rice
Hot sauce for garnish

Instructions: Over medium heat, sauté the onion, bell pepper, and celery until the onion is lightly caramelized. Add the garlic and sauté for 1 more minute. Add the bay leaf, red beans with liquid, pepper, thyme, and salt. Add water to create enough sauce to look like a stew (about ¼ cup). Simmer the sauce for at least 10 minutes, though the longer you let it simmer, the better it gets. Replace the water as it evaporates. Smash the beans until the sauce thickens, but don't worry about getting every bean smashed. The sauce should have a lot of texture. While the sauce is simmering, steam the collard greens. Combine the collard greens with the finished bean sauce. Serve over rice and top with hot sauce.

The Gourmet Touch: Slowly smoke 2 veggie Italian sausages, then slice them into thin rounds. Add these to the simmering bean sauce, about 5 minutes before it is done. This will give the dish a smoky, spicy flavor.

Per serving: 493 calories, 21 g protein, 97 g carbohydrate, 5 g sugar, 3 g total fat, 6% calories from fat, 21 g fiber, 295 mg sodium

Shredded Barbecue

Serves 4

This recipe works best when you can smoke the seitan before shredding it. By letting the seitan sit in the Barbecue Sauce for at least an hour, it achieves a tender, pulled texture.

1 batch Barbecue Sauce (page 296)
3 cups baked shredded seitan made with the following mix:
    2 cups vital wheat gluten
    1 tablespoon onion powder
    1 teaspoon garlic powder
    1 teaspoon smoked paprika
    1 teaspoon freshly ground black pepper
    ½ teaspoon dried oregano
    1½ cups water

¼ cup low-sodium tamari
2 tablespoons vegetarian "oyster" sauce
2 tablespoons tahini

Instructions: Make the Barbecue Sauce according to the instructions. Use the baked method for the seitan. Start by assembling the dry mix of wheat gluten powder, spices, and herbs. Combine the water, tamari, "oyster" sauce, and tahini. Add this to the dry mix, knead everything together, and bake the seitan. Once it cools, shred the seitan in a food processor. Add this to the Barbecue Sauce and simmer it over low heat for at least 15 minutes. It does even better in a slow cooker overnight. Serve this as is or on toasted whole wheat buns.

Per serving: 243 calories, 28 g protein, 40 g carbohydrate, 21 g sugar, 2 g total fat, 7% calories from fat, 6 g fiber, 723 mg sodium

Sides

Toasted Brown Rice

Makes 3 cups

This simple method produces a delicious, light, and fluffy brown rice. You'll find conventional methods for cooking brown rice in appendix 2.

1 cup short-grain brown rice
3 cups water

Instructions: Place the rice into a saucepan and rinse briefly with water, then drain away the water completely. You are now left with damp rice in a pan. Put pan on high heat and stir the rice until it's dry, about 1 to 2 minutes. Add the water. Bring to a boil, then simmer until the rice is thoroughly cooked but retains just a hint of crunchiness—about 40 minutes. Drain off the extra water (do not cook it until all the water is absorbed).

Top this rice with soy sauce, sesame seeds, or the topping of your choice. It will be the best brown rice you've ever tasted.

Per ½-cup serving: 115 calories, 3 g protein, 24 g carbohydrate, 0.4 g sugar, 0.9 g fat, 7% calories from fat, 3 g fiber, 5 mg sodium

Quinoa Verde

Serves 2

The great thing about this recipe is that it can be used as a side, as a main dish, or even as a bed for something like Grilled Portobello Steaks.

2 cups Tomatillo Sauce (page 294)
¾ cup water
1 cup quinoa
Option: ¼ cup pepitas

Instructions: Make one batch of the Tomatillo Sauce (about 2 cups' worth), then add ¾ cup water to it. If the sauce turns out particularly thick, add another ½ cup water. Bring the liquid to a simmer. Add the quinoa. Bring the liquid back to a simmer. Cover the pot, reduce the heat to low, and cook the quinoa for 15 to 17 minutes.

Option: Once the quinoa is done, top each serving with a smattering of pepitas.

Making It Simple: Use 1 15-ounce jar salsa verde instead of making the Tomatillo Sauce from scratch.

The Gourmet Touch: For a fire-roasted version, about 5 minutes before the quinoa is done cooking, add in about 2 tablespoons of crushed, dried ancho peppers.

Per serving: 389 calories, 14 g protein, 68 g carbohydrate, 6 g sugar, 7 g total fat, 16% calories from fat, 11 g fiber, 294 mg sodium

Crispy Sage Mashed Sweet Potatoes
Serves 2

Sweet potatoes, particularly white sweet potatoes, have a special lushness, making them creamy when mashed. The sage offsets the sweetness of the potatoes.

1 small sweet potato, baked
¼ teaspoon salt
½ teaspoon cracked black pepper
6–8 sage leaves, chopped

Instructions: Wrap the sweet potato in foil. Bake it at 450 degrees F for 45 minutes. Mash the sweet potato with the salt and black pepper. In a small pan over medium heat, toast the sage leaves until they start to get crispy. Sprinkle the sage over the mashed sweet potatoes.

Options: If you would rather not turn on your oven, you can simply steam or boil the sweet potato until it is soft.

Core Concepts: Crispy sage makes a great topping for pastas, enchiladas, and any other dish with a deep flavor. Use sparingly.

Per serving: 112 calories, 2 g protein, 26 g carbohydrate, 5 g sugar, 0.1 g total fat, 0.8% calories from fat, 4 g fiber, 342 mg sodium

Seared Cauliflower with Garlic and Tamari
Serves 1–2

This is a simple side dish that can be eaten as a snack or even served on its own if you make a big enough batch. The tamari caramelizes onto the cauliflower, giving it a wonderful robustness.

1 head cauliflower, cut into florets

2 tablespoons tamari

Water

3 cloves garlic, minced

2 tablespoons minced parsley

Instructions: Over medium-high heat, sauté the cauliflower, slowly stirring it until it just browns. Then add the tamari. When the tamari starts to stick to the pan, add 3 to 4 tablespoons of water and the garlic; allow the sauce to reduce until it just coats the cauliflower. Remove the cauliflower from the heat and immediately toss it with the parsley.

Options: Toss the cauliflower with the garlic, parsley, and tamari (no water) and bake it in a covered baking dish at 375 degrees F for 15 minutes.

Core Concepts: Soy sauce and tamari reduce and then caramelize onto your veggies in a few seconds, intensifying the flavors.

Per serving: 144 calories, 11 g protein, 31 g carbohydrate, 14 g sugar, 0.6 g total fat, 4% calories from fat, 14 g fiber, 173 mg sodium

Sauces

Basic Tomato Sauce

Makes about 1½ cups

Roma tomatoes are the tomatoes par excellence for sauces. They are inexpensive, and you'll taste their depth of flavor and robustness in the finished dish.

- ½ yellow onion, diced
- 2 cloves garlic, minced
- 4 medium tomatoes (preferably large Romas), chopped
- ¼ cup water
- ⅛ teaspoon salt
- ¼ teaspoon freshly ground pepper
- 1 teaspoon chopped fresh thyme or oregano or ½ teaspoon chopped fresh rosemary
- *Options:* ¼ teaspoon ground cumin; 3 tablespoons chopped fresh basil or cilantro

Instructions: Over medium heat, sauté the onion until it turns a rich brown color. Add the garlic and sauté for 1 more minute. Add the tomatoes and then the water and stir. Add the salt, pepper, and thyme/ oregano/rosemary. Simmer the tomatoes until they turn into a sauce (only 3 or 4 minutes for a very fresh tomato sauce, and about 7 to 10 minutes for a smooth, heavily cooked sauce). Press on the tomatoes every 30 seconds or so as they cook to help them release their juices. Add extra water as needed to achieve the desired consistency.

> *Options:* If you use cumin, add it along with the salt and pepper. If you are using fresh basil, stir it into the sauce immediately after it comes off the heat. Only cook the sauce for 3 to 4 minutes and as soon as it comes off the heat, stir in the fresh cilantro.

> *Making It Simple:* Instead of chopping and cooking down the tomatoes, stir in 12 ounces of crushed fire-roasted tomatoes and simmer the sauce until it's warm.

Companion Recipes: Rustic Tomato Soup, baked pasta

Per 1½-cup serving: 74 calories, 2.7 g protein, 15 g carbohydrate, 8.8 g sugar, 0.5 g total fat, 6% calories from fat, 4 g fiber, 330 mg sodium

Mushroom Gravy

Makes about 1¾ cups

Mushrooms are one of those polarizing ingredients. You either love them, or you're crazy! This sauce is excellent for smothering over veggie burgers or serving over a portobello steak.

½ yellow onion, diced

2 cups sliced cremini mushrooms (white button mushrooms can be substituted)

⅛ teaspoon salt

¼ teaspoon freshly ground pepper

2 cloves garlic, minced

½ teaspoon fresh thyme or oregano

1½ tablespoons whole wheat flour (whole wheat pastry flour works best)

Water (at least ½ cup)

Instructions: Over medium-high heat, sauté the onion until it just turns brown. Add the mushrooms and continue sautéing these ingredients until the mushrooms brown and release some of their water. Reduce the heat to medium. Add the salt, pepper, garlic, and thyme or oregano, sautéing for another minute. Add the whole wheat flour and gently stir the ingredients for about 1 minute. Slowly add the water, about ¼ cup at a time. Stir and make sure the flour incorporates with the water before adding the next batch. Continue doing this until you get a consistency that looks just slightly thinner than you want for the finished gravy. The gravy will thicken when it comes off the heat, so if you cook it to what looks like the right consistency, it will become thicker than desired once it's off the burner. For a smooth gravy, add about 2 tablespoons more water and puree the gravy once it is done cooking.

> *Making It Simple:* Add the onions, mushrooms, garlic, salt, pepper, and thyme or oregano to the pan all at the same time. Over medium heat, sauté everything until the onions and mushrooms soften. Put everything in a blender, along with the flour and ½ cup water; puree the mix. Return it to the pan and simmer it for about 3 minutes.

> *The Gourmet Touch:* If you want to use dried wild mushrooms—which will be very tasty, but more expensive than the cremini

mushrooms—rehydrate them in hot water and save the water. Add them to the pan at the same point you would add the cremini mushrooms, but you only need to sauté them for about 1 minute. Continue on with the recipe as written, but use the water in which the mushrooms soaked when you add water to the pan to create the gravy.

Companion Recipes: Crispy Sage Mashed Sweet Potatoes, any veggie burger, any pasta

Per 1¾-cup serving: 104 calories, 6 g protein, 18 g carbohydrate, 5 g sugar, 0.6 g total fat, 5% calories from fat, 2 g fiber, 283 mg sodium

Chili Sauce

Makes about ½ cup

Some chili sauces use tomatoes as the base, but this one showcases the flavors of the chilies, imparting a glorious sizzle to your meals!

3 tablespoons chili powder (mild or hot, according to your preferences)

1 teaspoon ground cumin

¾ teaspoon dried oregano (preferably Mexican)

Salt to taste

4–6 tablespoons water

Options: 2 teaspoons whole wheat flour or corn flour + 2 tablespoons water

Instructions: Combine the chili powder, cumin, oregano, and, if desired, salt, and set them aside. Bring a sauté pan up to medium heat. Add the chili powder mix and toast the powder, slowly stirring it with a spatula, until you smell the chili aroma coming off the pan (this generally takes about a minute and a half). Wait another 15 seconds or so and then slowly stir the water into the chili powder, adjusting the amount depending on how thick you want your sauce. Be careful not to overtoast the chili powder. If you are using the optional flour, combine the flour with the chili powder mix before adding it to the pan. This stretches the chili sauce out because you'll need to add some extra water, giving the entire sauce more bulk. It also makes it more viscous, helping it cling to other ingredients.

Making It Simple: If toasting chili powder frays your nerves, fear not! You can add the chili powder to the warm pan and immediately start stirring the water in. You won't have the extra flavor gained from toasting the powder, but you won't have to worry about burning it, either.

The Gourmet Touch: This is a great way to make your own chili powder. Remove the stems from 3 ancho peppers, 1 guajillo pepper, and 1 dried chipotle pepper. Snip them open along the length with scissors and shake out the seeds (do not rinse the peppers!). Place them in a blender or spice grinder and grind them until they turn into powder.

Per ¼-cup serving: 48 calories, 3 g protein, 6 g carbohydrate, 1 g sugar, 2 g total fat, 37% calories from fat, 4 g fiber, 108 mg sodium

Roasted Red Pepper Sauce

Makes about 1 cup

This sauce is sweet, thick, and versatile. It makes a great simmering sauce, can be used as a topping, and works well on the grill.

    2 cloves garlic
    4 large roasted red peppers
    ½ cup water
    ¼ teaspoon ground cumin
    ⅛ teaspoon salt
    Options: Juice of 1 lime; ¼ cup caramelized onions (you can use either or both)

Instructions: Puree all the ingredients together until smooth. Over medium heat, cook the sauce for about 10 minutes. The ingredients near the exposed edges of the pan will start to caramelize, so occasionally stir them back into the sauce.

Options: If you are using lime, add it just after the sauce comes off the heat, again keeping the fresh flavors intact. If you are using caramelized onions, puree them with all the other ingredients. This will give the sauce extra sweetness and create more depth.

Making It Simple: Reduce the amount of garlic to 1 clove (since you're not cooking the sauce with this method, 2 cloves of garlic would be, let's just say, painful), puree the sauce, and you're done. You can use it as is or warm it over medium heat in a saucepan.

The Gourmet Touch: Smash 6 cloves roasted garlic into a paste and add that to the simmering sauce. If you roast your own red peppers, leave the skins on and only pulse the peppers in a blender or small food processor a few times. This will give the sauce a rough texture and will also show off the blackened parts of the skin, creating an appetizing visual. Make sure the garlic is minced before you add it to the blender, since it won't be thoroughly pureed with this method. Finally, you can add a dash of ancho pepper flakes or chipotle flakes to the sauce for some heat and extra texture.

Companion Recipes: Any veggie burger, Linguine with Seared Oyster Mushrooms

Per 1-cup serving: 155 calories, 5 g protein, 31 g carbohydrate, 20 g sugar, 1 g total fat, 8% calories from fat, 10 g fiber, 325 mg sodium

Sun-Dried Tomato Sauce

Makes about 1 cup

"Here I am!" the sauce shouts. With concentrated flavors from the sun-dried tomatoes and balsamic vinegar, and a very hearty texture, this sauce refuses to be ignored.

1 medium tomato, chopped
½ clove garlic
½ cup sun-dried tomatoes (not the ones packed in oil)
1 tablespoon balsamic vinegar
1 teaspoon fresh thyme
¼ teaspoon freshly ground black pepper
Water as needed

Instructions: Add the tomato and garlic to the blender first, then add the rest of the ingredients. The tomato and garlic are easier to puree when they start near the blades. This creates a sauce at the bottom of the blender, which will then catch the sun-dried tomatoes and make them easier to puree. The amount of water added will depend on how thick or thin you want the sauce. You may also need a bit more water if your blender is not especially powerful. Always start with just 1 tablespoon or so. You can add water as needed, but you can't take it out once it's in the sauce.

Making It Simple: Don't worry about trying to guess the amount of water and just go with ¼ cup. It will produce a thick sauce, and the amount of water is generally enough to get most blenders to properly puree the sauce.

Companion Recipe: Zucchini Pasta with Sun-Dried Tomato Sauce

Per 1-cup serving: 91 calories, 4 g protein, 18 g carbohydrate, 12 g sugar, 0.9 g total fat, 4% calories from fat, 4 g fiber, 39 mg sodium

Tomatillo Sauce (Salsa Verde)

Makes about 2 cups

Tomatillos start out tart, but once they're stewed or roasted, the natural sugar in the fruit develops, striking a nice balance in the sauce. You can use this as a dipping salsa instead of a cooking salsa if you omit most of the water in the recipe!

1 yellow onion, diced
3 cloves garlic, minced
8 large tomatillos, papery husks removed and cut in half
½ cup water
⅛ teaspoon salt
½ teaspoon ground cumin
3 tablespoons chopped fresh cilantro
Option: Juice of 2 limes

Instructions: Over medium-high heat, sauté the onion until it is lightly browned. Reduce the heat to medium. Add the garlic and sauté for 1 more minute. Add the tomatillos, water, salt, and cumin. Simmer until the tomatillos have turned into a rough sauce. Remove from the heat and add the cilantro and optional lime juice.

Making It Simple: Add all the ingredients to the pot at once and simmer until the tomatillos have softened and turned into a sauce. You won't get the caramelized onion flavor, but you'll be done with the sauce in about 5 minutes plus however long it takes you to cut the ingredients.

The Gourmet Touch: Leave the tomatillos in their husks and add all the ingredients to a baking dish, including the water. Cover the dish and roast the ingredients at 400 degrees F for about 20 minutes. Puree them in a blender or mash them with a potato masher for a rougher texture.

Companion Recipe: Quinoa Verde

Per 1-cup serving: 76 calories, 2 g protein, 14 g carbohydrate, 6 g sugar, 2 g total fat, 18% calories from fat, 5 g fiber, 109 mg sodium

Bean Sauce

Makes about 1¾ cups

This sauce is the base for great, classic recipes like Red Beans and Rice and Enfrijoladas; it has a rich flavor and satisfying appeal. It is so delicious, you may decide to call it salsa de frijoles or puree de legumes. That is, until someone asks you if you mean bean sauce.

½ yellow onion, diced

2 cloves garlic, minced

1 teaspoon fresh thyme or chopped fresh sage, or 1 tablespoon roughly chopped oregano

2 cups cooked, rinsed black beans or kidney beans

¼ cup water

Salt to taste

Options: 1 large stalk celery, sliced; 1 carrot, diced, or 1 green bell pepper, diced

Instructions: Over medium-high heat, sauté the onion until it starts to brown. Reduce the heat to medium. Add the garlic and herbs and sauté for 1 more minute. Add the beans, water, and salt. Simmer the beans in the liquid for about 5 minutes, then, while they are still in the pan, mash them with either a large stirring spoon or a potato masher. Do not worry about getting everything perfectly smooth. In fact, you'll probably end up smashing only half the beans. This sauce is meant to be very thick.

Options: The base of many sauces is celery, carrot, and bell pepper, and you can make a great bean sauce with the addition of those ingredients. Simply add celery and carrot about 1 minute after you start cooking the onion. For a New Orleans flair, use green bell pepper instead of carrot.

Making It Simple: Use canned beans with all the liquid from the can.

The Gourmet Touch: Use a smoked salt or add 2 teaspoons smoked paprika to the pan about 10 seconds before you add the liquid and beans.

Companion Recipes: Red Beans and Rice with Collard Greens, Enfrijoladas

Per recipe: 523 calories, 40 g protein, 87 g carbohydrate, 2 g sugar, 2 g total fat, 3% calories from fat, 31 g fiber, 94 mg sodium

Barbecue Sauce

Makes about 2½ cups

Making your own barbecue sauce is easy and allows you to skip commercial sauces and all their less-than-healthful ingredients.

½ yellow onion, chopped

2 cloves garlic, sliced

2 cups crushed fire-roasted tomatoes

¼ cup prepared yellow mustard

2 tablespoons molasses

2 tablespoons agave nectar or maple syrup

Juice of 1 lemon

2 teaspoons soy sauce

½ teaspoon ground allspice

½ teaspoon crushed red pepper

2 tablespoons chopped parsley

Options: 1 tablespoon peanut butter; ½ teaspoon Liquid Smoke

Instructions: Over medium heat, sauté the onion until it softens. Add the garlic and sauté for 1 more minute. Add the rest of the ingredients, simmering them for about 5 minutes, then puree.

Options: The optional ingredients should be added when the bulk of the ingredients are added to the barbecue sauce.

Making It Simple: Simply add all the ingredients to a blender before cooking anything and puree them. Then pour the sauce into a pot and simmer for at least 5 minutes, but preferably simmer it over a very low heat for at least 30 minutes.

The Gourmet Touch: If you can get your hands on berbere, an Ethiopian curry powder, add about 1 tablespoon to the sauce. The flavor is powerful and rich and complements ingredients like sweet potatoes and portobello mushrooms.

Companion Recipe: Shredded Barbecue

Per ½-cup serving: 100 calories, 3 g protein, 35 g carbohydrate, 13 g sugar, 0.5 g total fat, 4% calories from fat, 3 g fiber, 413 mg sodium

Basic Salsa

Makes about 1½ cups

Salsas that are crushed instead of pureed tend to be superior. Crushing pushes the flavor out of the ingredients into the saucy part of the salsa without homogenizing it, creating a more complex taste.

¼ red onion, diced

3 Roma tomatoes, diced and crushed

1 jalapeño, stem and seeds removed, minced (use serrano or habanero peppers if you want a hotter salsa)

1 clove garlic, minced

⅛ teaspoon coarse sea salt

¼ teaspoon ground cumin

2 tablespoons chopped fresh cilantro

Juice of 1 lime

Options: ½ cup corn; ½ cup cooked, rinsed black beans; 1 minced chipotle in adobo sauce

Instructions: Place all the ingredients in a bowl in which you can crush them until the tomatoes are mostly pulped (a potato masher works just fine for crushing them, and a Mexican molcajete, a sort of mortar and pestle, works wonders). Give everything a quick stir to make sure all

the ingredients are evenly distributed. Allow the salsa to sit for at least
10 minutes for the flavors to meld.

> *Options:* Stir any or all of the optional ingredients into the salsa *after*
> the main ingredients have been crushed.

> *Making It Simple:* Instead of crushing the ingredients, pulse them
> three or four times in a food processor.

> *The Gourmet Touch:* Before cutting the tomatoes and jalapeño,
> place them in a dry pan over medium heat (a cast-iron skillet
> works best) and pan-roast them. You will see the tomatoes and
> jalapeño soften and then develop some spots of charring. Rotate
> the tomatoes and peppers until at least a quarter of their surface
> area has blackened. Remove the stem and seeds from the pep-
> per. Give the tomatoes and pepper a quick chop, then crush
> them with the other ingredients.

Per 1½-cup serving: 57 calories, 2 g protein, 11 g carbohydrate,
6 g sugar, 0.5 g total fat, 8% calories from fat, 3 g fiber, 324 mg sodium

Spreads, Dips, and Snacks

Hummus

Serves 4–6

Hummus is a flavorful Middle Eastern bean dip made from chickpeas, lemon juice, and garlic. Usually served as a dip paired with pita bread or with cauliflower or other fresh vegetables, it can also be used as a flavor powerhouse spread for sandwiches, wraps, and burgers.

- 1 clove garlic, smashed
- Juice of 1 lemon
- 2 cups cooked, rinsed chickpeas
- 1 tablespoon tahini
- ½ teaspoon salt
- Water

Instructions: Add the ingredients to a blender or food processor in order, with just enough water to achieve your desired texture, whether thick or only slightly viscous (about 2–4 tablespoons of water).

Per ½-cup serving: 234 calories, 10 g protein, 44 g carbohydrate, 0.2 g sugar, 3 g total fat, 12% calories from fat, 10 g fiber, 236 mg sodium

Tofu Ricotta

Recipe by Riva Gebel

Makes 8 servings

This vegan version of ricotta is tasty and light, perfect for stuffed shells or lasagna.

- ½ cup chopped parsley
- 1 clove garlic
- 1 pound lite firm silken tofu
- ½ teaspoon dried oregano
- 1 teaspoon dried basil
- ½ teaspoon onion powder
- ¼ teaspoon dried thyme
- ½ teaspoon ground nutmeg

½ teaspoon salt
¼ teaspoon black pepper

Instructions: In a food processor, finely chop the parsley and garlic, then add the tofu and remaining ingredients and process until smooth and creamy.

Per serving (one-eighth of recipe): 27 calories, 4 g protein, 2 g carbohydrate, 0.4 g sugar, 0.6 g total fat, 19% calories from fat, 0.4 g fiber, 198 mg sodium

Mali Chips

Serves 4

This recipe shows you the beautiful colors of Mali: red, green, and yellow. Zucchini, sliced into rounds, makes a low-fat alternative to fried corn chips.

4 zucchini
½ cup Basic Salsa (page 297)

Instructions: Slice the zucchini into ¼-inch-thick rounds and set them aside (these are the "chips" for the salsa). You can serve the guacamole and salsa separately or you can stir them together.

Tip: If your zucchini is small, you can slice it along the diagonal to make bigger "chips."

Per serving: 80 calories, 5 g protein, 17 g carbohydrate, 9 g sugar, 0.8 g total fat, 9% calories from fat, 5 g fiber, 324 mg sodium

Sweet Potato Fries

Serves 2–3

Even without deep-frying, the flavor of these fries is wonderful. Use orange sweet potatoes with the Cajun seasoning option.

2 cups sliced sweet potatoes (french-fry-size pieces)
Nonstick cooking spray
¼ teaspoon coarse salt
3 cloves garlic, minced
1 tablespoon diced parsley

Spice Mix 1: ½ teaspoon cracked pepper, 1 teaspoon fresh thyme, ¼ teaspoon smoked paprika, pinch of ground cumin, pinch of cayenne pepper, pinch of allspice

Spice Mix 2: 2 teaspoons Cajun seasoning

Instructions: Spray the sweet potato slices with nonstick cooking spray and then toss them in the salt, garlic, parsley, and either of the spice mixes. Bake the fries at 375 degrees F for 30 to 40 minutes, and then finish them under the broiler for 5 minutes. You can serve this with a small side of maple syrup as an optional dipping sauce.

Per serving: 173 calories, 3 g protein, 40 g carbohydrate, 8 g sugar, 0.2 g total fat, 1% calories from fat, 6 g fiber, 370 mg sodium

Desserts

Bananas in Berries Artesia

Serves 4

Bananas are just one option for this delectable New Orleans berry-and-wine sauce. It also goes very well with other fruit and makes a great topping for waffles and pancakes.

½ cup strawberries
1 teaspoon vanilla extract or 1 vanilla bean
½ cup blackberries
½ cup raspberries
1 cup grape juice
1 cup apple juice
2 tablespoons maple syrup
1 bay leaf
2 tablespoons arrowroot or cornstarch
4 bananas
Option: Slivered almonds, for garnish

Instructions: Remove the stems from the strawberries and slice the berries. Split open the vanilla bean lengthwise and scrape out the seeds. Add all the berries, vanilla bean and pod (or vanilla extract), grape juice, apple juice, maple syrup, and bay leaf to a pot. Bring this to a simmer and simmer it for about 5 minutes. Place the arrowroot or cornstarch in a small mixing bowl. Take 3 to 4 tablespoons of the liquid, add it to the bowl, and stir until well combined. Add this to the pot and allow the sauce to simmer for another 2 to 3 minutes. Remove it from the heat. Remove the bay leaf and vanilla pod. Peel the bananas and slice them in half along the length. Pour the sauce over the bananas. Garnish with the optional slivered almonds, if you like.

> *Tips:* Make sure to add the liquid to the arrowroot or cornstarch and not the other way around. This keeps the mixture from clumping. In-season berries will work the best with this sauce, since you'll get the most sweetness out of them.

Per serving: 237 calories, 2 g protein, 61 g carbohydrate, 44 g sugar, 0.7 g total fat, 3% calories from fat, 5 g fiber, 2 mg sodium

Baked Cardamom Pears

Serves 2

Pears don't need a lot of help to make a delicious dessert. With just a few raisins to provide contrasting sweetness and cardamom to give the pears an intense, aromatic quality, this dish is a potent crowd pleaser.

1 pear, halved and cored
2 tablespoons raisins
½ teaspoon cardamom
2 small sprigs mint

Instructions: Cut the pear in half and remove the core, creating a small pocket. Place the raisins in the pocket. Place the pear halves in a baking dish, sprinkling cardamom over the fleshy part. Cover the baking dish. Bake the pears at 350 degrees F for 20 to 25 minutes. Place a fresh sprig of mint (just a cutting with two to four leaves) on each pear and serve.

Per serving: 103 calories, 1 g protein, 27 g carbohydrate, 19 g sugar, 0.2 g total fat, 2% calories from fat, 4 g fiber, 3 mg sodium

Mango Lime Sorbet

Serves 6

This dessert is a silky smooth sorbet inspired by the lush flavors of Thailand.

2 cups pureed partially frozen mango
½ cup agave nectar
Juice of 2 limes

Instructions: This recipe works best if the mango is frozen, and then allowed to thaw for about 15 minutes. Once it has partially thawed, puree the mango along with the agave nectar and lime juice. Pour the puree into a shallow glass or metal bowl and then place it in the freezer. After 30 minutes, stir the puree, then repeat every 15 minutes thereafter until you are ready to serve.

Making It Simple: Use store-bought frozen mango to avoid peeling and de-seeding several fresh mangoes.

Core Concepts: The freezing process accentuates tartness and reduces the sweet flavor. That means the puree should be slightly

less tart and slightly sweeter than you expect the final product
to be.

Per serving: 139 calories, 0.5 g protein, 35 g carbohydrate, 33 g sugar,
0.2 g total fat, 1% calories from fat, 2 g fiber, 2 mg sodium

Masala Chai Apple Crisp

Serves 6

Chai spices are the perfect accompaniment to this quintessential American dessert.

- ½ teaspoon ground cardamom (preferably from green cardamom pods)
- ½ teaspoon ground cloves
- ½ teaspoon freshly ground black pepper
- ½ teaspoon grated nutmeg
- 1 teaspoon ground cinnamon
- 2 tablespoons turbinado sugar
- 4 apples, cored and sliced thinly (2 Pink Ladies and 2 Granny Smiths, preferably)
- 1 tablespoon apple cider vinegar
- 1 cup apple jelly
- 1 tablespoon grated fresh ginger
- 1½ cups dried oats

Instructions: Combine all the spices and the sugar together. Place the apple slices in a mixing bowl and toss them with the spices and sugar. Allow this to sit for about 30 minutes. At this point, the apples will have released some liquid. Drain the juice from the bottom of the mixing bowl into a small saucepan. Over medium heat, reduce the juice until it is about half the original volume. Mix this with the apple cider vinegar, apple jelly, and grated ginger. Place the apples in a baking dish and spread the apple jelly mixture over them. Top with the dried oats. Bake this at 350 degrees F for 20 minutes.

The Gourmet Touch: Toast each spice individually, whole, for about 1 minute over medium-low heat, then grind each spice into a powder.

Core Concepts: Dried ingredients like sugar and salt pull out liquid from fruits and veggies through a process called maceration. When making a pie or crisp, this is important because it reduces the amount of liquid released by the fruit during baking, keeping the texture of the dessert tight instead of watery.

Per serving: 278 calories, 4 g protein, 70 g carbohydrate, 49 g sugar, 0.8 g total fat, 3% calories from fat, 5 g fiber, 1 mg sodium

Wacky Chocolate Cake
Recipe from Alka Chandna
Makes 9 3"×3" pieces

Here is a delightful version of legendary Wacky Cake, which is said to have its origins in World War II rationing, when milk and eggs were hard to come by. At the time, the cake was lower in fat and cholesterol, not by choice but by necessity. Today, those characteristics are virtues.

1½ cups unbleached pastry flour

¾ cup sugar

½ teaspoon salt

1½ teaspoons baking soda

3 tablespoons cocoa powder

2 teaspoons vanilla extract

5 teaspoons unsweetened applesauce

1 tablespoon vinegar

1 cup cold water

Instructions: Preheat the oven to 350 degrees F. Combine the flour, sugar, salt, baking soda, and cocoa powder in a bowl; stir with a fork until mixed. In a separate bowl, whisk the vanilla, applesauce, vinegar, and water. Pour the mixed wet ingredients into the dry ingredients. Stir with a fork until well mixed. Pour into a 9"×9" baking dish and bake for 30 minutes, until a toothpick inserted in the center comes out clean.

Per serving (one-ninth of recipe): 171 calories, 2 g protein, 36 g carbohydrate, 18 g sugar, 2 g total fat, 10% calories from fat, 1 g fiber, 343 mg sodium

Ingredients That May Be New to You

Agave Syrup

Agave syrup (or "nectar") is a mild honey-like sweetener that comes from the same cactus used to make tequila. It has a semi-thick consistency and will melt in cold liquids. Although it's a sugar, it's so potent and flavorful, you only need to use about two-thirds the amount of agave as you would need of another sweetener. You will find it in all health food stores and many regular groceries.

Berbere

This Ethiopian curry powder, made from hot peppers, cumin, coriander, and aromatic spices, has a full-bodied, aromatic flavor reminiscent of an Indian-style red curry, but with more emphasis on the chilies. You will find it online and at specialty food stores (such as World Market).

Ener-G Egg Replacer

This is a powdered mix that, when whipped with water, acts as an egg-like binder for batter or dough. It is available at all health food stores.

Hummus

This Middle Eastern puree of chickpeas, tahini (sesame "butter"), and various flavorings is a popular sandwich filling and dip. It is available at most grocery stores. But making your own is quick and easy, and cuts the fat content dramatically. See the recipe on page 299.

Jicama

Jicama is a large, bulbous root with a tan papery skin and a clean white center that tastes like an unripe pear or apple. It goes well in salads and can be turned into fresh chips and sticks. Often, it is dressed with chili powder and lime juice.

Mayonnaise, Vegan-Style

Health food stores carry mayonnaise-like products that omit the egg and its cholesterol. Common brands are Nayonaise and Vegenaise.

Nutritional Yeast

Nutritional yeast adds a cheesy flavor to foods without fat or calories. Sprinkle it into spaghetti sauce, soups, or casseroles, or onto vegetables. You'll find it in the supplement aisle of health food stores. Note that it's not the same as brewer's yeast or baker's yeast, both of which are bitter.

Pepitas

These squash seeds (typically green pumpkin seeds) are commonly used in Mexican cuisine as a garnish or to thicken sauces. They can be lightly roasted in a dry pan or spritzed with water and dressed with spices for extra flavor.

Plantains

Plantains are related to bananas, but tend to be larger and firmer. They can be grilled, sautéed, baked, added to curries, and even used as the main component of a dish. When shopping for plantains, very little browning indicates a hard, starchy plantain that is ideal for the grill. A few black splotches mean it is similar to a semi-ripe banana. A mostly black peel indicates it is soft and sweet, and ideal for dessert dishes.

To ripen plantains, store them in a dark place in a paper bag. To open a plantain, cut through the skin along the inner curve of its length, then pop the peel back.

Seitan

Also known as wheat gluten, seitan (pronounced *SAY-tan*) is concentrated wheat protein, and is used to simulate the taste and texture of meat. Originally created by Chinese Buddhist monks many centuries ago, it can be grilled, cooked with a sauce, shredded, ground, sautéed, added to soups and stews, sliced for sandwiches and tacos, and used in burgers.

Soy Sauce, Low-Sodium

Typical soy sauces are unfortunately high in sodium. Reduced-sodium brands are moderately lower in sodium content, although by no means salt-free.

Tahini

Tahini is made from ground sesame seeds and has a texture similar to peanut butter. It is used in hummus and Middle Eastern sauces. It is high in fat, so you will want to use it sparingly. It is available in most supermarkets and all health food stores.

Tamari

Tamari is a richly flavored, smooth soy sauce that, unlike most other soy sauce, contains little or no wheat. It is available in all supermarkets.

Tempeh

Tempeh (pronounced *TEHM-pay*) is made of fermented, cultured soybeans. Its texture makes it excellent for a thick, hearty burger, and it can also be sliced into strips like bacon or minced like ground beef. It is usually marinated, giving it a wide range of savory flavors. You will find it in all health food stores, next to the tofu. You will also find it sliced and flavored, for example, as tempeh bacon.

Textured Vegetable Protein

TVP is a soy protein that has been used for decades as an extender for ground beef. Somewhere along the line, cooks realized that they could skip the beef entirely and just use TVP. It is free of animal fat and cholesterol, and works very well in spaghetti sauce, chili, tacos, pizza toppings, sloppy joes, and anywhere else you might use ground beef. It is sold at health food stores in boxes and in bulk, and is quickly reconstituted with water.

Thai Curry Paste

Thai curry pastes are a mixture of fresh ingredients like shallots, chilies, garlic, galangal (a woody cousin of ginger), and lemongrass, along with aromatic spices, all pounded into a paste. You'll find several varieties at Asian markets. Although most contain shrimp paste and fish sauce, the Thai Kitchen brand is free of both, as are some others at Asian markets.

Tofu

Extremely popular throughout East Asia and becoming more and more popular everywhere else, tofu substitutes for everything from scrambled eggs and meats to yogurt and pudding. It is also a primary ingredient in its own right, apart from its ability to masquerade as other foods.

Most grocery stores stock it in the refrigerator case or the produce aisle in water-packed boxes. You'll also find it in convenient shelf-stable boxes that keep for months at room temperature. After you open the package, rinse the tofu and keep it refrigerated.

Tofu is sold in many varieties, some of which are reduced in fat. Firm and soft tofu are commonly used for stir-fries and soups. Silken tofu is often used when the tofu will be blended (such as in puddings).

Straight out of the package, it has a neutral flavor, very much like egg white, but it easily takes on the flavors with which it is cooked. You'll find it marinated and baked, ready to be cut up and added to wraps, stir-fries, salads, or stews. Organic, non-GMO brands are available.

Tomatillos

Crisp, sour, and slightly sweet, tomatillos are like a cross between a green apple and a small tomato with a bit of lime thrown in. They are a key ingredient in Mexican green sauces. Fresh, they make crisp, tart additions to salads and soups. Roasted, they lose much of their sourness and develop a sweeter taste.

Tomatillos look like small green tomatoes covered in a light green paper. They should have a tight feel and not be separated from the paper. There is an invisible sticky film between the paper and flesh of the tomatillo, which is easily removed by peeling under running water.

Tomatoes, Fire-Roasted

These delicious tomatoes are roasted over an open flame and then canned. They have a long shelf life.

Several different cuts are sold, but the crushed fire-roasted tomatoes are easiest to use. Organic versions are both superior in flavor and cheaper than non-organic versions. Look for the Muir Glen brand.

Tomatoes, Sun-Dried

Originally, sun-dried tomatoes were created by slicing leftover tomatoes from a harvest and leaving them on a roof or porch to dry. Today most are simply dried in massive dehydrators that shrink and partially caramelize the tomato. They make excellent garnishes and can also be blended into very potent sauces.

They are sold in small packages in the produce section or near the bulk bin section of supermarkets. Avoid the oil-packed versions sold in jars.

Whole Wheat Pastry Flour

Whole wheat pastry flour is not just for pastries, despite its name. Its fine texture makes it ideal not only as a thickener, but also for making tortillas and other flat breads. You will find it at health food stores and specialty markets.

A Primer of Basic Cooking Techniques

The Kickstart program is so simple. You don't need time or cooking talent to make it work. But many people who get to know the power of foods want to learn more tricks to use in the kitchen. For them, we have prepared this simple primer. It will guide you through the basics of selecting and using common ingredients and show you the cooking techniques that make meals quick and delicious.

Choosing and Preparing Healthy Greens

Greens are nutritional powerhouses. And they are also just plain delicious. Here are the basics for selecting and preparing them.

Selecting Greens. The smaller the leaves, the more tender they will be. Make sure that the stem looks fresh and the plant is springy. As you are choosing herbs, don't hesitate to experiment. It is fine to substitute one green for another in a recipe. Baby greens have a different flavor from mature greens, and cooked greens have a different flavor from fresh.

Storage. To keep your greens fresh, wrap them in a dry towel and store them in the refrigerator. The dry towel absorbs excess moisture and staves off the oxidation that can turn them brown.

Washing. Prewashed greens and frozen greens are already clean when you buy them. But typical fresh greens from the produce department need to be washed. If the leaves are easy to separate, you can wash the whole leaves. Otherwise, you may need to chop them first and then wash them in a basin.

Spinach is especially eager to hold on to a bit of grit. The easiest way to wash it is to fill your sink or a large mixing bowl with water. Remove the leaves from the stems with a few chops and place them in the basin. Swish the greens in the water, then allow them to rest for one or two minutes. Remove the greens from the top of the water. Drain the dirty water and repeat this process one or two more times. Then pat them dry with a towel or put them in a salad spinner.

Cutting. If you are serving fresh greens (in a salad, say), use a sharp knife and slice through the leaves, rather than chopping straight down at them. A dull knife and an ax-like chop can bruise the leaves. If you are cooking tougher greens (such as kale or collards), cutting them up in advance will make them easier to eat. To slice large leafy greens, remove the leaves from any hard stems, if necessary. Roll the leaves into a giant cigar shape and cut through the diameter of the "cigar." The tighter you roll them, the easier they will be to slice.

Cooking. Steaming is a great way to preserve flavor, without adding fat or anything else. You can also cook greens in a sauté pan, either dry or with just a very thin layer of liquid. Simmer them until they are soft. If you like, you can add other ingredients, such as sliced garlic, along with the greens. The longer you cook them, the milder they will be.

If you are adding greens to a soup or stew, you can add them directly to the pot. A tougher green, like collards, will need fifteen to twenty minutes in a simmering soup to properly soften. Spinach, on the other hand, is so flimsy that it can be added immediately after the soup comes off the heat.

The Brassicas

The Brassica family includes a broad range of staples, from broccoli and cauliflower to cabbage and Brussels sprouts. Here are the leafy members of the family:

Collard Greens. Look for springy leaves with a deep green color and with no sign of yellowing. To remove the stems, stack the leaves as best you can and then rip each side along the stem. The stems are generally too tough to eat, though you can add them to a homemade veggie stock.

Kale. Make sure the leaves have a lot of spring, and avoid dull-looking or brownish leaves. To strip the leaves from the stems, simply grasp the entire leaf in your left hand, and pull the stem with your right hand. Off it comes!

Raw kale is bitter, but makes a nice accent green for red leaf lettuce. Steamed kale is mild, and is delicious topped with flavored vinegars, Bragg Liquid Aminos, or a squirt of lemon juice.

Mustard Greens have a light, yellowish green color and curly leaves. The seeds of this plant are the source of prepared mustard, and like those seeds, the leaves can be spicy. Mustard greens can be eaten raw or lightly simmered for a couple of minutes. Try a fresh leaf before using it to gauge the spice level of the greens you have at hand.

Turnip Greens. Look for smaller turnip leaves, because they gradually turn more bitter as they grow. Turnip greens will have a slightly sweet flavor and can be eaten raw or lightly cooked for two to three minutes. Turnip leaves keep freshest when they are still attached to the turnip.

Arugula. It is surprising that this soft leaf is in the same family as collards and kale, since it is more likely to end up in a salad than steamed or sautéed. With an earthy, peppery taste, it also works on pizza or pasta dishes.

The Asters

Chard. This versatile plant comes in a variety of colors, from red to white to a variegated rainbow color. Check the stems and leaf edges for freshness. Chard works well in fresh salads. When cooked, its bitterness fades and it becomes soft and delicious.

Escarole is a type of endive with very broad leaves that loosely expand from the stem and turn jagged toward the top. It has an earthy taste and can be used fresh or added to soups. The mildest leaves are those closer to the center of the plant.

Frisée. Related to escarole, frisée is also referred to as chicory. It has curly, almost tentacle-like leaves. The lighter-colored leaves are less bitter.

Beet Greens are the leafy parts of the common beet, a close relative of chard. They are soft and sweet with striking red stems. Beet greens can be used in salads, soups, or stews. They can also be added to stir-fries, though they should be cooked for no more than a couple of minutes. Like turnip greens, beet greens store best when they are still attached to the beet.

The Amaranths

Spinach is one of the most common and familiar greens. At the store, look for green stems with a pinkish bottom. In the kitchen, its soft leaves cook down quickly, so take care not to overcook it. Its rich flavor pairs well with heavy spices and chilies.

Romaine is a hearty lettuce, with crisp leaves and a thick rib along each leaf. If it has started to brown around the stems, it is quickly on its way out. Its mild flavor and slightly longer shelf life make it a popular salad green. Occasionally, it is grilled for a few seconds before being added to salads.

Red-Leaf Lettuce and Green-Leaf Lettuce. These soft leaves make for a very light salad. They can be used interchangeably, the only difference being their color. At the market, check to be sure these fragile leaves have been kept moist and that they have a fluffy springiness to them.

Butter-Leaf Lettuce. Also known as butter-head, Bibb, or Boston lettuce, butter-leaf has broad, cup-shaped, loose leaves that are semi-soft and resistant to bruising. They're ideal for lettuce wraps. Butter-leaf can sometimes be found at markets with the roots and some of the soil still attached, greatly preserving its freshness.

Iceberg Lettuce. While iceberg's nutritional content is less robust than that of heartier varieties, it still has its place in healthy diets. Served as a wedge with a light dressing, it can be absolutely trendy.

Choosing and Preparing Grains

Whole grains retain their bran and germ, and have advantages over grains that have lost them in the refining process. So brown rice is preferable to white rice, and whole wheat bread is preferable to white bread. This is not to say refined grains should be banished. As mentioned in chapter 2, white pasta has a surprisingly low glycemic index, despite having lost its fiber in processing. Here are some tips for selecting and preparing popular grains.

Rice

Beyond the differences between refined and unrefined varieties, there is one other distinction that makes a difference in the kitchen, and that is "stickiness." Nonsticky varieties work well when the rice is going to act as a bed for vegetables, beans, and sauces. The sticky versions, which tend to be the shorter grains, are rich in *amylopectin*, a type of starch that is the botanical equivalent of Velcro, and so they stick to your fingers, your chopsticks, and other rice grains. This makes them great for sushi.

Preparing Rice

In the recipe section, we presented a simple toasting method for preparing delicious brown rice. If you haven't tried it, by all means do. Here are more traditional methods for preparing rice:

Boiling. This common method calls for about 1¾ parts water to 1 part rice. Bring the water to a boil, add the rice, stir, and cover the pot. Reduce the heat to low and cook for twenty minutes. While this method is easy, it produces a pressed, unrefined texture that works better for some varieties than others, as we'll see below.

Boiling and Baking Rice. This method produces a much fluffier rice. You'll need four to five parts water, a squeeze of lemon, and one part rice. Bring the water and lemon juice to a boil, add the rice, stir, and boil it for about eight minutes. Drain the rice, then place it in a baking dish along with any desired spices and herbs, cover, and bake at 325 degrees F for twenty minutes. Because there is so much water in the pot, the grains of rice will rumble around in the water instead of getting pressed together. The lemon juice also helps keep the grains separate. This method is ideal for cooking spices into the rice or for simply creating fluffy rice.

Steaming. This traditional method allows the grains to stick together without being as compressed as they are by the boiling method. Start by placing rice in water and swishing the rice around, letting the water turn cloudy. Drain the water and rinse the rice again, repeating this process until the water stays clear. Then let the rice stand in water for about two hours. Drain and give it one last quick rinse.

Next, you'll need 1½ parts water to 1 part rice, and either a rice basket or a heavy pot with a lid. If you have a rice basket (usually a wicker basket sold at Asian markets), place the rice in the basket, and put the basket over a steaming pot of water. Steam the rice for about twenty minutes.

If you don't have a rice basket, but you do have a heavy pot, add the rice and liquid to the pot and bring it to a boil. Cover and reduce the heat to low. Cook for fifteen minutes, then remove from the heat and allow it to stand for ten minutes.

If you prefer, an electric rice cooker will perform the steaming method for you.

Slow Simmering. If you have risotto or paella on your mind, this is the technique to use. Spread the rice out in a wide pot or pan and add just enough water that it comes up through the grains. Bring it to a simmer over medium heat. Just before the water completely evaporates, ladle in enough water to just come through the grains again. Repeat this process until the rice is almost al dente and then let the water cook down one last time. If you're making paella, allow the rice to keep cooking to the point where it crisps on the bottom of the pan.

Cooking Rice Directly into Soups. If you are cooking rice directly into a soup, increase the cooking time by five minutes for a slightly thick soup (such as tomato soup) and ten minutes for a thick soup (say, potato soup). If the soup is very brothy, you won't need to add any extra liquid until it starts to thicken. If you're preparing a thick soup, you'll need to add the full 1¾ parts water for every 1 part rice.

Explore the Many Varieties

Here are some of the common types of rice, presented to inspire you to try a few of them. For any of the recipes in this book, brown short- or long-grain rice will work perfectly fine.

Jasmine. This wonderfully aromatic long-grain Thai variety is usually steamed.

Basmati. This flavorful long-grain Indian rice stays fluffy when cooked. It is typically steamed. Curiously enough, cooking causes it to expand along its length, but very little in its diameter.

Arborio, Carnaroli, and Vialone Nano. These are the classic medium-grain sticky varieties used for risotto. Use the slow-simmering method.

Bomba and Calasparra Rice. These Spanish short-grain varieties are used for paella. The grains expand to about three times their original size, but remain distinct and separated. Use the slow-simmering method.

Sushi Rice is a very sticky, short- or medium-grain rice. Outside Japan, sushi rice is typically Calrose rice, which is also used for rice bowls. Inside Japan, you'll often find Akita Komachi rice and Koshihikari rice used for sushi. These varieties are best cooked by steaming.

By the way, if you hear of sticky rice being referred to as "glutinous" rice, that just means it's sticky (glue-like); it does not contain gluten (notice the different spelling). So if you're avoiding gluten, you'll be fine with rice.

Parboiled rice has been partially boiled and then dried, gelatinizing the starch in the rice. The bran is then removed. This method keeps the grains separated. Use the boiling method.

Black Japonica. This California blend of black sticky rice and medium-grain brown rice has a nutty flavor. It is best cooked by boiling.

Red. This rust-colored rice is usually only partially hulled, so it retains many of its nutrients. It has a nutty flavor and is typically steamed or boiled.

Japonica is a large category, signifying a short-grain, sticky rice.

Indica is another blanket category, with a long, nonsticky grain that expands lengthwise when cooked.

Wild Rice. Despite its name, wild rice is only a distant relative of actual rice. It is very flavorful, and because of its high fiber and protein content, it takes about forty minutes to cook (it is typically boiled). Soaking overnight allows you to reduce the cook time to twenty minutes. Cook by boiling or steaming.

Barley

Barley is a hearty cereal grain with an earthy, nutty flavor. It is high in protein, with a low glycemic index. Hulled barley has had its outermost layer removed. The more common pearl barley has been steamed and then its bran has been scrubbed off, making it softer and quicker to cook, although it still retains a fair amount of its fiber.

Here is a basic recipe for cooking barley:

2 parts liquid (water or vegetable stock)
1 part barley
Pinch of salt (about ½ teaspoon per cup of uncooked barley)

Instructions: Bring the liquid to a boil. Add the barley and salt, stir, and cover. Reduce the heat to low, and cook for 20 to 22 minutes. For added flavor, you can toast the barley in a dry pan over medium heat for 5 minutes before adding it to the cooking liquid. If you are adding any spices or herbs to the barley, add them when you add the salt. If you are adding vegetables (such as carrots or mushrooms), they'll do best if you sauté them before the cooking liquid is added to the pot.

Quinoa

An ancient and wonderful South American crop, quinoa (pronounced *KEEN-wah*) is protein-rich and easy to prepare. Here is a simple boiling method:

Makes about 2½ cups

1¾ cups water
1 cup quinoa

Instructions: Bring the water to a boil. Add the quinoa, stir, and bring the water back to a boil. Cover and reduce the heat to low. Cook for about 15 minutes. For a softer quinoa, increase the cooking time by about 5 minutes.

You can also use a steamer, so long as it has fairly small holes. Don't worry if some of the quinoa falls through into the water. Most of it will expand and stick together soon enough, keeping the bulk of it from falling through. Steam for 20 minutes, fluffing with a fork at the 10- and 15-minute marks.

Buckwheat

Despite its name, buckwheat is not related to wheat. But, like wheat, it can be turned into flour for pancakes or crêpes, and can be turned into noodles. Raw buckwheat can be found in cereals, and hulled buckwheat can be cooked and used like barley. It is gluten-free.

To cook buckwheat, bring two parts water to a boil. Add one part buckwheat. Cover the pot, reduce the heat to low, and cook for ten to fifteen minutes (the longer time is for a larger batch). Avoid overcooking.

Oats

Oats are best known for their role in breakfast cereals. They are a high-fiber, high-protein grain that helps regulate blood sugar and reduces cholesterol levels. Details on cooking oats are found in the Breakfasts section.

Pasta

Pasta is a key ingredient throughout the Mediterranean, North America, and East Asia. With so many styles to choose from, you could have a pasta dish every day of the year and still not exhaust your options. The major types of pasta used in this book include whole wheat pasta, rice pasta, and buckwheat pasta. White pasta is much more common in stores and is perfectly acceptable to use, if you prefer it. Surprisingly enough, it has a very low glycemic index, just as other pastas do. Since it lacks the fiber you'll find in other pastas, you will want to make up for that with legumes and vegetables in the toppings.

Two quick tips for any kind of pasta:

Do not add oil to the cooking water. Some people use oil to keep the pasta from sticking, but properly cooked pasta will not stick, and oil interferes with water absorption.

Pasta should usually be cooked al dente. Literally "to the tooth" in Italian, it means that the pasta still has a bit of texture, as opposed to being soft and overcooked.

Whole Wheat Pasta

This is a traditional Italian-style pasta made with whole wheat flour and is the easiest to work with. The cooking time depends on the size of the pasta, because whatever the time, the pasta should be cooked until it just becomes al dente (see below). To keep the pasta from cooking past this point, add a glass of cold water to the pot and then drain the water. Do not rinse the pasta. Either toss it with a sauce as soon as possible or add the pasta to a simmering sauce and allow the sauce to simmer for another minute or two.

When cooking whole wheat pasta, you need about four cups of water per quarter pound of pasta. The water should come to a rapid boil before the pasta is added. Once it is added, it should be slowly stirred for the first two minutes and then stirred once every minute or so after that. After the first couple of minutes, turn the heat down so the starchy water isn't splattering out of the pot. To test when whole wheat pasta is done, take a piece from the boiling water and cut or break it. If the middle still looks whitish, or rather tan, the pasta is not yet done.

When working with fresh whole wheat pasta, the cooking time is very short regardless of the size of the pasta, about two or three minutes. Some of the pasta will float as it finishes cooking. It is even more important to toss this pasta immediately with sauce than it is with the dried pasta. When shopping for whole wheat pasta, look for varieties without eggs.

Long Thin Pasta. Spaghetti, capellini, angelhair (capelli d'angelo), and vermicelli cook in about six or seven minutes.

Long Thick Pasta. Fettuccine, long fusilli, and tagliatelle cook in about ten to eleven minutes.

Short Thick Pasta. Penne rigate, rigatoni, and ziti need about eight or nine minutes to cook.

Rice Pasta

Asian-style rice pasta usually comes in long strips and can be super-thin or wide and flat. It goes well in soups, in stir-fries, and in spring rolls and cooks very quickly. In fact, you can easily cook it by just pouring boiling water over the pasta (enough to cover by about two inches) and letting the pasta soak for two to eight minutes, depending on the size. Smaller noodles need less time. Check it every thirty seconds or so once you start getting close to finishing the soaking process. As soon as the pasta is soft, but not mushy, drain it and rinse it. Rice pasta quickly becomes mushy if it is overly soaked. If you are adding the rice pasta to a soup, you can also cook it directly in the soup. It will cook about twice as fast as the soaking method and requires more attention, but the benefit is that the rice pasta will absorb the flavor of the broth. If you use this method, the soup should be served right away. If that is not possible, keep the soaked pasta and soup separate until just before serving.

Asian rice pasta is usually made with white rice flour. There are also Italian styles of rice pasta that are made from brown rice flour. They are between the white rice pasta and wheat pasta in texture, so they require cooking, rather than soaking in hot water, usually about four to six minutes, depending on the size. Bring four cups of water to a boil for every quarter pound of pasta. Add the pasta after the water is strongly boiling and stir it for about two minutes. Reduce the heat to a simmer and stir the pasta every minute or so. Because rice pasta can be very sticky and lose its structure under pressure, it needs to be either rinsed in cold water right after cooking or immediately tossed in a sauce. Leaving hot brown rice pasta to sit will result in a gelatinous mush. Unlike whole wheat pasta, it doesn't store well when part of a leftover dish.

Buckwheat Pasta

Buckwheat pasta is commonly used in Japanese and Chinese cuisine. Despite its name, it is not a wheat; nor does it contain gluten, although some buckwheat noodles do have wheat flour mixed into them (check labels, if you are avoiding gluten). The most common buckwheat noodles, soba noodles, have a dark brown color and a slightly sweet taste and come in long, thick strands.

To cook, bring six cups of water to a strong boil for every three and a half ounces of noodles. Add the noodles and slowly stir for about two minutes. Turn the heat down to a simmer for six more minutes. Drain and rinse. If you are working with fresh (not dried) buckwheat noodles, they cook in about two minutes, and some of them will start to float. Drain and rinse these as well.

Gnocchi

These small potato and wheat dumplings cook within just three or four minutes. Fresh gnocchi cook in one to two minutes and float as soon as they are done. When that happens, rinse them immediately with cold water or toss them in a sauce. By the way, if you'd like to impress your friends, *gnocchi* is plural; the singular is *gnoccho*.

Couscous

Couscous is a tiny pasta made from a semolina flour, which in turn is made from crushed durum wheat. It should not be cooked in boiling water; cooking is actually much easier than that. For every cup of couscous, you will need 1¼ cups of water. Bring the water to a boil, then remove it from the heat and allow it to sit for ten seconds. Pour the water over the couscous and immediately fluff the couscous with a fork. Continue fluffing it every fifteen seconds or so until all the water has been absorbed.

An even better method is to use a steamer. Just combine one cup of couscous with half a cup of water until the couscous absorbs the water, and then steam the couscous for fifteen minutes. You can use almost any steamer—even a standard bamboo steaming basket if you like—as long as its holes are no larger than a quarter inch. The couscous will have expanded enough during the preliminary soaking that there will be no danger of its falling through.

Israeli couscous is larger, very creamy, and can even be worked like a risotto. It is usually sold packaged, rather than in bulk, at health food stores. To cook, bring 1¼ to 1½ cups of water per cup of dried couscous to a simmer, then add the couscous. Keep stirring, and remove it from the heat when it becomes al dente. Drain any excess water. You can also toast the couscous in a dry pan over medium heat before cooking to give it a nutty flavor.

Orzo

Orzo is a small, barley-shaped pasta made from hard semolina flour. It cooks rapidly and expands to about double its size. Orzo should be cooked like other pasta, but only needs five or six minutes because of its small size. If cooked too long, or left in liquid too long, orzo becomes mushy.

Once the Pasta Is Finished

Italian-style pasta is served with very little sauce, so a small amount of water should be left with the cooked pasta as the sauce is added. American-style pasta is topped with so much sauce that there is no need for added water. Asian-style pasta is usually added to a soup just before serving, or sautéed with other veggies. If you sauté the pasta, make sure there is a small amount of liquid in the pan to prevent sticking. A minute in the pan is about all it will need.

Choosing and Preparing Legumes

Legumes (beans, peas, and lentils) are rich in protein, fiber, iron, calcium, and a host of other nutrients, with a wonderfully low glycemic index. They are versatile and easy to cook.

For convenience, most people choose canned beans. Because salt is often added during processing, you may wish to rinse them after opening or select no-salt-added brands.

It is also easy to cook beans from scratch. Check out the selection of dry beans at the supermarket, and especially in bulk bins and at Mexican, Asian, and Indian markets. Store them in a dry, cool place.

Cooking. Soaking overnight (or for at least six hours) reduces the cooking time and increases digestibility. After soaking, drain and rinse the beans, and discard the soaking water. Then, using fresh water—at least twice as much water as soaked beans—bring the water to a boil and simmer until very soft. If you like, you can add chopped onion, garlic, bay leaf, chili peppers, and so forth, discarding them once the beans are cooked. Do not salt the water; it toughens the beans and prolongs the cooking time.

Different beans have different cooking times, as you'll see on the next page. If you use the baking soda option, the time is reduced by about one-third. Extend the cooking time slightly for a larger batch. If you prefer to extend the soaking or cooking times for better digestibility, softer beans, or any other reason, by all means do. There is virtually no limit to how long you can soak or cook them.

Cooking Times for Beans

Black Beans: 45 minutes–1 hour
Chickpeas: 1½–2 hours
Cannellini Beans: 1½ hours
Kidney Beans: 1½ hours
Pinto Beans: 1½ hours
Red Beans: 1¼–1½ hours

A pressure cooker trims the cooking time dramatically. Just soak the beans for a couple of hours, then place the beans and water (your pressure cooker will determine the appropriate amount of water) in the cooker and put it on high heat with the lid on. Once it comes up to temperature, reduce the heat to low. Small beans (such as black beans) only need to cook for six to eight minutes, while larger beans need ten to fifteen minutes.

Lentils

Named for their lens shape, lentils are one of the oldest domesticated crops. Red lentils have a beautiful color and, because they tend to fall apart in cooking, they can be used to thicken soups. Green lentils are more substantial and turn a deep brown color when cooked. Green lentils work best when you want the individual lentils to retain their texture or you plan to puree them to form a pâté or veggie loaf.

Unlike beans, lentils do not need to be soaked. To cook, add two parts water to one part lentils. Bring to a boil in a covered pot and cook over low heat for fifteen to twenty minutes for red lentils, and about twenty minutes for green lentils.

Split Peas

Split peas are firmer than lentils and do well if soaked for three or four hours, but you can also cook them without presoaking. To cook green or yellow split peas, use at least two parts water to one part split peas. Cook over low heat in a covered pan for twenty to twenty-five minutes.

Basic Cooking Techniques

Sautéing

Sautéing is a way to soften ingredients and begin to caramelize them. It brings out wonderful flavors. There are a couple of keys to getting it right.

First, temperature. Sautéing is typically done at a medium to medium-high heat. Medium heat will soften your ingredients and give them a more delicate, mellow flavor, while medium-high heat will be a bit rough on the veggies and give them a more caramelized, robust taste. Some of the more volatile ingredients can cook at this higher temperature, but it's so easy to burn them that it's usually just best to reduce the heat when you are about to add them to the pan.

Second, timing. If you have multiple ingredients with different cooking times, add them in sequence, not all at the same time. Otherwise, by the time the longer-cooking ingredients are finished, the shorter-cooking ones will have burned.

Third, a dry pan. Add your long-cooking ingredients, like onions, with no liquid at all. Only if they start to stick or burn should you add a small layer of liquid to the pan, about an eighth of an inch. Some ingredients, especially starchy ones like potatoes, will start to stick pretty quickly, and you will need to add some sort of liquid. With iron, enamel, and nonstick skillets, veggies will be slower to stick. On stainless steel or straight aluminum, they will stick quickly.

Don't crowd the pan. There should be enough space to allow the liquid released from the veggies to evaporate. Otherwise, the veggies simply stew. You may need to work in batches or work with two or more pans at once if you are making quite a lot of food.

Once your ingredients are properly sautéed, you can add a sauce to the pan. This can be a splash of a sweet sauce like balsamic vinegar, which will quickly glaze on the veggies, or it might be something like a fire-roasted tomato sauce. The veggies, if not stewed overly long in the sauce, will keep their texture and caramelization, and the sauce will pick up some extra flavor from the sautéed bits on the pan.

Searing

Contrary to popular wisdom, searing does not actually lock in flavor. What it does is quickly form a caramelized outer layer and, in some cases, tighten the texture of an ingredient. It's also an excellent technique for creating heavily caramelized, crisped ingredients (you'll see it used in the Linguine with Seared Oyster Mushrooms recipe, for example).

Searing should be done at high heat either in a sauté pan or directly on the grill. If it is done in a sauté pan, make sure not to crowd the pan—it's the exposure to the direct surface heat of the pan that causes the ingredients to sear. This works particularly well in an iron skillet or in a nonstick pan.

Stewing

Stewed veggies are easy to make. All you need·is a slow cooker (Crock-Pot) or a pot placed over a low heat. There should be enough liquid to come at least a quarter of the way up the layer of veggies; you may wish to submerge them for a particularly saucy stew.

Some or all of the veggies can be sautéed first to develop caramelization, or simply added to the stew pot.

Plan on a stew taking at least forty-five minutes, with some taking up to several hours. Water can be used to stew food, but tomato sauce, veggie stock, and many other liquids make great stewing sauces. If you want a thick stewing sauce, mix about 1½ tablespoons of flour with ¼ cup of the stewing liquid for every total cup of stewing liquid used; blend this into the stewing sauce. It will create a thick sauce that sticks to the veggies. Keep the heat low—just enough so that the liquid occasionally bubbles.

Grilling

Before You Begin. Before you begin grilling, clean the grill. Leftover particles will burn and create bitterness in your food.

Minimizing Oil. Food tends to stick to a grill more than a pan, so most cooks use oil as a barrier between the food and the grill rack. If you do this, go easy. For an entire bunch of asparagus, one teaspoon of oil is more than enough. For a portobello mushroom, you'll only need about half a teaspoon.

Instead of drizzling oil over a food, measure out the oil, place the ingredients in a wide, shallow mixing bowl, and toss the ingredients with the oil. If you have a large ingredient, like the portobello or perhaps a block of tempeh, brush the oil onto it. Absorbent ingredients, such as eggplant, will suck up oil, so you may want to marinate them first. This saturates them with a liquid, keeping the oil on the outside.

Here's a great fat-free flavor trick: Wrap your ingredients in a large foil packet and pierce with a fork to allow the smoke from the grill to penetrate—it's like a hybrid of grilling and roasting. If your ingredients are starchy or prone to stick, you will need a light sauce in the packet to keep the foil from sticking to the food.

The Perfect Grilling Temperature. If your grill is too cool, the veggies won't cook. If it's too hot, they will burn. The ideal is a medium to medium-high heat.

Steaming

Steaming is a gentle way to cook ingredients and keep their structure intact. There are many types of steamers to choose from, but bamboo steamers are the most versatile. They are ideal for large cuts of veggies, and you can even steam soaked rice in a bamboo steamer. You will find them in a wide variety of sizes, many with multiple layers. If you plan on steaming grains, like quinoa, go for a wicker steaming basket. Its finer mesh holds the smaller grains better. You'll find them at Asian markets and some larger cooking stores.

To use the steamer, fill a wok or large, deep pan about halfway with water and simply place the filled steamer on the wok. Once the water is boiling, reduce it to medium-low or low heat. Small or thinly cut veggies steam in about five minutes. Midsize cuts, one to two inches across, need about ten minutes. Thicker items, like tamales, may take fifteen or twenty minutes to steam.

If you like, you can place spices and herbs in the steaming water.

Don't overpack your steamer. Just place one layer of food in each tier of the basket.

Marinades

A marinade adds wonderful flavors. An acidic marinade (such as vinegar or lime or lemon juice) cuts into vegetables and carries flavors along with it. Salty marinades (say, soy sauce) work well for porous foods like mushrooms, tofu, and seitan. For a really special marinade, try combining ingredients, for example:

- Soy sauce, chili paste, and rice wine vinegar
- Lime juice, orange juice, and salt
- Tamari, sage, rosemary, and roasted garlic

If you like, add some chilies. And don't worry. The sweetness in a marinade balances out both saltiness and spiciness. Also, vegetables only take on a fraction of their flavor, especially if you marinate for less than an hour, as opposed to a more thorough six-hour marinade. If you create your own marinade, make it strong so it can do the job right.

Oven Roasting

There is nothing like oven-roasted vegetables. To keep them moist, cover the baking dish or wrap the vegetables in foil. You might also roast the veggies with a layer of broth at the bottom of the dish. This keeps the portion of the veggies sitting in the broth completely hydrated and steams the portions not sitting in the broth. Both techniques will keep the veggies hydrated.

Hollow vegetables, like acorn and butternut squash or chilies, naturally trap steam as they roast. If you need to cut them open for some reason prior to roasting, either flip those veggies cut-side down onto the baking sheet or dish, or place a small amount of liquid in the pocket.

Large, hard vegetables (including potatoes, sweet potatoes, and hard squash) should be roasted at temperatures between 425 and 500 degrees F; they generally take less than an hour, sometimes much less. Other veggies roast at 375 to 425 degrees F and generally take less than forty minutes.

However, you can lower the cooking temperature by about 75 degrees F to create two different effects, dependent on whether or not you use broth. The first way, without broth, will slowly and more evenly caramelize an ingredient while it roasts, at the cost of significantly increased cooking time, which is often doubled or tripled. The second is to roast a vegetable in a deep broth (one that covers at least half the ingredient) to allow the broth to slowly work its way into the veggie. If you have broth left over, save it. It makes an excellent veggie stock!

Pan Roasting

Pan roasting is a wonderful technique for creating roasted, slightly charred and caramelized vegetables without turning on your oven or firing up your grill. All you need is a heavy pan, preferably an iron skillet. Put the pan on medium or slightly above medium heat. Add the ingredients and rotate them as they blacken.

This technique works great for smaller items. Try the following:

- Garlic. Separate the cloves from the bulbs, but leave the "paper" on. The paper will blacken where it's touching the pan, but that's okay. The garlic inside is not burning; the paper is protecting it.
- Tomatoes, whole or sliced into large pieces.
- Onions. Cut them into thick disks, about half an inch to one inch thick.
- Peppers. Leave them whole. The charring skin will partially separate from the soft fleshy part.
- Carrots. Leave them whole.
- Fennel, squash, and citrus should be sliced thickly.

Wait until you see browning on the items before flipping them over, and expect the process to take about ten minutes.

Caramelizing Onions and Other Veggies

Vegetables, particularly onions, have natural sugars in them that develop a rich, caramel flavor when exposed to the direct surface heat of a pot or pan.

To caramelize an onion, the pan should be at medium or medium-high heat. Over high heat, you run the risk of the onion searing and its natural sugar burning, making it very bitter. Add your cut onions to the dry pan and allow them to turn yellow and develop brown spots. Be patient and just leave them alone until they brown to a level with which you are happy. Then give them a stir. As the onions cook, they'll release liquid that will help the pan stay slightly moist. If they start to stick or get crispy, add about an eighth of an inch of water or other liquid and give them a quick stir.

Do not add liquid to the pan when you first start cooking the onions. This simply increases the cooking time and often simmers the onions instead of caramelizing them.

This technique also works well with other high-sugar veggies, like carrots.

Deglazing

This is the follow-up to caramelization. Deglazing basically means to de-sugar the pot or pan. Once your ingredients have caramelized, they'll leave some sugar on the bottom of the pan and also on the outside of the veggies. By adding a thin layer of liquid to the pan, the caramelization is lifted and disseminated throughout the liquid, creating a rich caramel sauce. This will then flavor whatever else you add to the pan. Make sure that you give everything a quick stir once the liquid is added or you won't properly pick up the caramelization from the pan.

You can also allow the liquid to evaporate. If you do this, the caramel sauce will recoat the vegetables, but will do so in an even manner; because the veggies will have simmered for a few seconds, they'll soften even more. The more times you repeat this, the browner the veggies will be and the softer they will be. This is the trick used to create those nice fajita-style onions, which should go through the adding liquid/evaporation process two to four times.

References

Introduction

1. Barnard ND, Scialli AR, Turner-McGrievy G, Lanou AJ, Glass J. The effects of a low-fat, plant-based dietary intervention on body weight, metabolism, and insulin sensitivity. *Am J Med* 2005;118:991–7.

2. Turner-McGrievy GM, Barnard ND, Scialli AR. A two-year randomized weight loss trial comparing a vegan diet to a more moderate low-fat diet. *Obesity* 2007;15:2276–81.

Chapter 1. Power on Your Plate

1. Ferdowsian HR, Barnard ND, Hoover VJ, Katcher HI, Levin SM, Green AA, Cohen JL. A multi-component intervention reduces body weight and cardiovascular risk at a GEICO corporate site. *Am J Health Promotion* 2010;24:384–7.

2. Levin SM, Ferdowsian HR, Hoover VJ, Green AA, Barnard ND. A worksite programme significantly alters nutrient intakes. *Public Health Nutr* 2010 Jan 15:1–7. [Epub ahead of print.]

3. Katcher HI, Ferdowsian HR, Hoover VJ, Cohen JL, Barnard ND. A worksite vegan nutrition program is well-accepted and improves health-related quality of life and work productivity. *Ann Nutr Metab* 2010;56:245–52.

4. Ornish D, Brown SE, Scherwitz LW, et al. Can lifestyle changes reverse coronary heart disease? The Lifestyle Heart Trial. *Lancet* 1990;336:129–33.

5. Ornish D, Scherwitz LW, Billings JH, et al. Intensive lifestyle changes for reversal of coronary heart disease. *JAMA* 1998;280:2001–7.

6. Esselstyn CB, Jr. Updating a 12-year experience with arrest and reversal therapy for coronary heart disease (an overdue requiem for palliative cardiology). *Am J Cardiol* 1999;84:339–41, A338.

7. Jenkins DJ, Kendall CW, Marchie A, et al. Effects of a dietary portfolio of cholesterol-lowering foods vs lovastatin on serum lipids and C-reactive protein. *JAMA* 2003;290:502–10.

8. Rouse IL, Beilin LJ. Editorial review: vegetarian diet and blood pressure. *J Hypertension* 1984;2:231–40.

9. Chlebowski RT, Blackburn GL, Thomson CA, et al. Dietary fat reduction and breast cancer outcome: interim efficacy results from the Women's Intervention Nutrition Study. *J Natl Cancer Inst* 2006;98:1767–76.

10. Pierce JP, Stefanick ML, Flatt SW, et al. Greater survival after breast cancer in physically active women with high vegetable-fruit intake regardless of obesity. *J Clin Oncol* 2007;25:2345–51.

11. Ornish D, Weidner G, Fair WR, et al. Intensive lifestyle changes may affect the progression of prostate cancer. *J Urol* 2005;174:1065–70.

12. Carter JP, Saxe GP, Newbold V, Peres CE, Campeau RJ, Bernal-Green L. Hypothesis: dietary management may improve survival from nutritionally linked cancers based on analysis of representative cases. *J Am Coll Nutr* 1993;12:209–26.

13. Saxe GA, Hebert JR, Carmody JF, et al. Can diet in conjunction with stress reduction affect the rate of increase in prostate specific antigen after biochemical recurrence of prostate cancer? *J Urol* 2001;266:2202–7.

14. Swinburn BA, Sacks G, Lo SK, et al. Estimating the changes in energy flux that characterize the rise in obesity prevalence. *Am J Clin Nutr* 2009;89:1723–8.

15. Barnard ND. Trends in food availability, 1909–2007. *Am J Clin Nutr* 2010;91 Suppl:1530S–6S.

Chapter 2. Foods That Tame the Appetite Demons

1. Drewnowski A, Krahn DD, Demitrack MA, Nairn K, Gosnell BA. Taste responses and preferences for sweet high-fat foods: evidence for opioid involvement. *Physiol Behav* 1992;51:371–9.

Chapter 3. Understanding the Calorie-Burning Secret

1. Sparks LM, Xie H, Koza RA, et al. A high-fat diet coordinately downregulates genes required for mitochondrial oxidative phosphorylation in skeletal muscle. *Diabetes* 2005;54:1926–33.

2. Greco AV, Mingrone G, Giancaterini A, et al. Insulin resistance in morbid obesity: reversal with intramyocellular fat depletion. *Diabetes* 2002; 51:144–51.

Chapter 4. Cardioprotection: Health for Every Part of You

1. Hooper L, Thompson RL, Harrison RA, et al. Risks and benefits of omega 3 fats for mortality, cardiovascular disease, and cancer: systemic review. *BMJ* 2006;332:752–60.

2. Hunninghake DB, Stein EA, Dujovne CA, et al. The efficacy of intensive dietary therapy alone or combined with lovastatin in outpatients with hypercholesterolemia. *N Engl J Med* 1993;328:1213–9.

3. Ornish D, Brown SE, Scherwitz LW, et al. Can lifestyle changes reverse coronary heart disease? The Lifestyle Heart Trial. *Lancet* 1990;336:129–33.

4. Jenkins DJ, Kendall CW, Marchie A, et al. Direct comparison of a dietary portfolio of cholesterol-lowering foods with a statin in hypercholesterolemic participants. *Am J Clin Nutr* 2005;81:380–7.

5. Anderson JW, Smith BM, Washnock CS. Cardiovascular and renal benefits of dry bean and soybean intake. *Am J Clin Nutr* 1999;70 Suppl 3:464S–74S.

6. Messina M, Messina V. *The Simple Soybean and Your Health*. Garden City Park, NY: Avery Publishing Group, 1994.

7. Barnett TD, Barnard ND, Radak TL. Development of symptomatic cardiovascular disease after self-reported adherence to the Atkins Diet. *J Am Diet Assoc* 2009;109:1263–5.

8. Ornish D, Scherwitz LW, Billings JH, et al. Intensive lifestyle changes for reversal of coronary heart disease. *JAMA* 1998;280:2001–7.

9. Berkow SE, Barnard ND. Blood pressure regulation and vegetarian diets. *Nutr Rev* 2005;63:1–8.

10. Rouse IL, Beilin LJ. Editorial review: vegetarian diet and blood pressure. *J Hypertension* 1984;2:231–40.

11. Barnard ND, Cohen J, Jenkins DJ, Turner-McGrievy G, Gloede L, Jaster B, Seidl K, Green AA, Talpers S. A low-fat, vegan diet improves glycemic control and cardiovascular risk factors in a randomized clinical trial in individuals with type 2 diabetes. *Diabetes Care* 2006;29:1777–83.

12. Turner-McGrievy GM, Barnard ND, Cohen J, Jenkins DJA, Gloede L, Green AA. Changes in nutrient intake and dietary quality among participants with type 2 diabetes following a low-fat vegan diet or a conventional diabetes diet for 22 weeks. *J Am Diet Assoc* 2008;108:1636–45.

13. Barnard ND, Noble EP, Ritchie T, Cohen J, Jenkins DJA, Turner-McGrievy G, Gloede L, Ferdowsian H. D2 Dopamine receptor Taq1A polymorphism, body weight, and dietary intake in type 2 diabetes. *Nutrition* 2009;25:58–65.

14. Barnard ND, Gloede L, Cohen J, Jenkins DJA, Turner-McGrievy G, Green AA, Ferdowsian H. A low-fat vegan diet elicits greater macronutrient changes, but is comparable in adherence and acceptability, compared with a more conventional diabetes diet among individuals with type 2 diabetes. *J Am Diet Assoc* 2009;109:263–72.

15. Barnard ND, Cohen J, Jenkins DJ, Turner-McGrievy G, Gloede L, Green A, Ferdowsian H. A low-fat vegan diet and a conventional diabetes diet in the treatment of type 2 diabetes: a randomized, controlled, 74-week clinical trial. *Am J Clin Nutr* 2009;89 Suppl:1588S–96S.

16. Fraser GE. Ten years of life: is it a matter of choice? *Arch Intern Med* 2001;161:1645–52.

Chapter 5. A Healthy Menu

1. Anderson JW, Major AW. Pulses and lipaemia, short- and long-term effect: potential in the prevention of cardiovascular disease. *Br J Nutr* 2002;88 Suppl 3:S263–71.

2. Papanikolaou Y, Fulgoni VL. Bean consumption is associated with greater nutrient intake, reduced systolic blood pressure, lower body weight, and a smaller waist circumference in adults: results from the National Health and Nutrition Examination Survey 1999–2002. *J Am Coll Nutr* 2008;27:569–76.

3. Westman EC, Yancy WS, Edman JS, Tomlin KF, Perkins CE. Effect of a 6-month adherence to a very low carbohydrate diet program. *Am J Med* 2002;113:30–6.

4. Knight EL, Stampfer MJ, Hankinson SE, Spiegelman D, Curhan GC. The impact of protein intake on renal function decline in women with normal renal function or mild renal insufficiency. *Ann Int Med* 2003;138:460–7.

5. Giovannucci E, Rimm EB, Wolk A, Ascherio A, Stampfer MJ, Colditz GA, Willett WC. Calcium and fructose intake in relation to risk of prostate cancer. *Cancer Res* 1998;58:442–7.

6. Chan JM, Stampfer MJ, Ma J, Gann PH, Gaziano JM, Giovannucci E. Dairy products, calcium, and prostate cancer risk in the Physicians' Health Study. *Am J Clin Nutr* 2001;74:549–54.

7. Turner-McGrievy GM, Barnard ND, Scialli AR, Lanou AJ. Effects of a low-fat, vegan diet and a Step II diet on macro- and micronutrient intakes in overweight, postmenopausal women. *Nutrition* 2004;20:738–46.

8. Turner-McGrievy GM, Barnard ND, Cohen J, Jenkins DJA, Gloede L, Green AA. Changes in nutrient intake and dietary quality among participants with type 2 diabetes following a low-fat vegan diet or a conventional diabetes diet for 22 weeks. *J Am Diet Assoc* 2008;108:1636–45.

9. Lanou A, Barnard ND, Berkow S. Calcium, dairy products, and bone health in children and young adults: a re-evaluation of the evidence. *Pediatrics* 2005;115:736–43.

10. Feskanich D, Willett WC, Colditz GA. Calcium, vitamin D, milk consumption, and hip fractures: a prospective study among postmenopausal women. *Am J Clin Nutr* 2003;77:504–11.

Chapter 7. Let's Go!

1. Wu AH, Yu MC, Tseng CC, Pike MC. Epidemiology of soy exposures and breast cancer risk. *Br J Cancer* 2008;98:9–14.

2. Shu XO, Zheng Y, Cai H, et al. Soy food intake and breast cancer survival. *JAMA* 2009;302:2437–43.

3. Yan L, Spitznagel EL. Soy consumption and prostate cancer risk in men: a revisit of a meta-analysis. *Am J Clin Nutr* 2009;89:1155–63.

4. Miller M, Beach V, Sorkin JD, et al. Comparative effects of three popular diets on lipids, endothelial function, and C-reactive protein during weight maintenance. *J Am Diet Assoc* 2009;109:713–7.

5. Nicholls SJ, Lundman P, Harmer JA, et al. Consumption of saturated fat impairs the anti-inflammatory properties of high-density lipoproteins and endothelial function. *J Am Coll Cardiol* 2006;48:715–20.

Chapter 8. Getting in Gear

1. Yeomans MR, Wright P, Macleod HA, Critchley JAJH. Effects of nalmefene on feeding in humans. *Psychopharmacology* 1990;100:426–32.

2. Silberman A, Banthia R, Estay IS, et al. The effectiveness and efficacy of an intensive cardiac rehabilitation program in 24 sites. *Am J Heath Promot* 2010;24:260–6.

3. World Cancer Research Fund/American Institute for Cancer Research. *Food, Nutrition, Physical Activity, and the Prevention of Cancer: A Global Perspective*. Washington, DC, 2007.

4. Chlebowski RT, Blackburn GL, Thomson CA, et al. Dietary fat reduction and breast cancer outcome: interim efficacy results from the Women's Intervention Nutrition Study. *J Natl Cancer Inst* 2006;98:1767–76.

5. Pierce JP, Stefanick ML, Flatt SW, et al. Greater survival after breast cancer in physically active women with high vegetable-fruit intake regardless of obesity. *J Clin Oncol* 2007;25:2345–51.

6. Ornish D, Weidner G, Fair WR, et al. Intensive lifestyle changes may affect the progression of prostate cancer. *J Urol* 2005;174:1065–70.

7. Frattoroli J, Weidner G, Dnistrian AM, et al. Clinical events in prostate cancer lifestyle trial: results from two years of follow-up. *Urology* 2008;72:1319–23.

Chapter 9. Going to the Max

1. Barnard ND, Scialli AR, Hurlock D, Bertron P. Diet and sex-hormone binding globulin, dysmenorrhea, and premenstrual symptoms. *Obstet Gynecol* 2000;95:245–50.

Index

About the Author

Neal D. Barnard, MD

Neal D. Barnard, MD, leads research studies to improve the health of people with diabetes, obesity, and other serious health problems, and spearheads efforts to improve nutrition in schools and in the workplace. He is an adjunct associate professor of medicine at George Washington University in Washington, DC. His groundbreaking research funded by the National Institutes of Health showed that nutrition can be more powerful than oral medicines for treating diabetes.

He received his MD degree at the George Washington University School of Medicine in Washington, DC, and completed his residency at the same institution. He practiced at St. Vincent's Hospital in New York before returning to Washington to found the Physicians Committee for Responsible Medicine (PCRM) in 1985. PCRM is a nationwide group of physicians and lay supporters that promotes preventive medicine and addresses controversies in modern medicine. He later initiated the Cancer Project, providing nutrition information for cancer prevention and survival, and the Washington Center for Clinical Research, a center for nutrition-related studies.

Dr. Barnard's research has been cited by the American Diabetes

Association and the American Dietetic Association in official policy statements on healthful diets. His articles have appeared in *Diabetes Care*, the *American Journal of Clinical Nutrition*, the *American Journal of Medicine*, *Pediatrics*, the *Journal of the American Dietetic Association*, *Scientific American*, the *American Journal of Cardiology*, *Obstetrics & Gynecology*, *Lancet Oncology*, *Preventive Medicine*, and many other scientific and medical journals. He is a frequent lecturer at scientific societies and a peer reviewer for many medical journals.

Jason Wyrick

Jason Wyrick is the executive chef and publisher of the magazine *The Vegan Culinary Experience*. In 2001, Chef Jason reversed his diabetes by switching to a low-fat, vegan diet. He has been featured in the *New York Times* and has catered for companies such as Google, the Frank Lloyd Wright Foundation, and Farm Sanctuary, and has been a guest instructor in the *Le Cordon Bleu* program at Scottsdale Culinary Institute.